CONSUMING CHILDREN

CONSUMING CHILDREN
education–entertainment–advertising

Jane Kenway and Elizabeth Bullen

OPEN UNIVERSITY PRESS
Buckingham • Philadelphia

Open University Press
Celtic Court
22 Ballmoor
Buckingham
MK18 1XW

email: enquiries@openup.co.uk
world wide web: www.openup.co.uk

and
325 Chestnut Street
Philadelphia, PA 19106, USA

First Published 2001

A catalogue record of this book is available from the British Library

ISBN   0 335 20299 3 (pb)   0 335 20300 0 (hb)

Library of Congress Cataloging-in-Publication Data
Kenway, Jane.
  Consuming children: education–entertainment–advertising / Jane Kenway
  and Elizabeth Bullen.
    p. cm.
  Includes bibliographical references and index.
  ISBN 0-335-20300-0 – ISBN 0-335-20299-3 (pb)
    1. Education–Marketing.   2. Commercialism in schools.
I. Bullen, Elizabeth, 1957–   II. Title.
LB2847 .K46 2001
370′.68′8–dc21

                                                                00-068749

Typeset in 10/12pt Meridien by Graphicraft Limited, Hong Kong
Printed in Great Britain by Biddles Limited, Guildford and King's Lynn

Jane dedicates this book to her father and friend
Patrick William Fox (July 7, 1919 – September 19, 2000)

Jane and Elizabeth also dedicate this book to their
daughters, Vashti, Rachel and Sophie

Contents

◐ Acknowledgements

We wish to express our gratitude to the Australian Research Council, Deakin University and the University of South Australia which funded much of the research upon which this book is based and provided us with the institutional bases within which to write. Many of the ideas which inform this book arose from research projects conducted during the 1990s at Deakin University with Lindsay Fitzclarence and Chris Bigum, and we sincerely thank both for their bracing intellectual company over many years. Indeed, a very early and much shorter incarnation of this book, Part 1 (Kenway *et al.* 1997), of *Changing Education: New Times, New Kids* written with Lindsay and Chris, forms its basis. It was this version which prompted Open University Press to offer a contract. We particularly thank Lindsay for his contribution to the many papers and conversations that provide the backbone of this book. Janine Collier, Karen Tregenza and Carol-Anne Croker worked as research assistants at various stages of these projects and we also thank them for their valuable input. Many principals, teachers, students and business people shared their ideas and time with us. Joan Fox provided valuable copy-editing. We express our sincere appreciation to them all. Finally, our families have inspired and supported us always and for that we are very grateful.

Introduction

The young often worry and baffle their parents, their teachers and, of course, politicians and policy makers – indeed any group of people that is responsible for their care. In his book *Generations* (1997), the Australian social commentator Hugh Mackay observes that young people have become the 'worry targets' (p. 82) of the 'baby boomer' generation whose parenting is plagued by anxieties. Boomer parents express a range of concerns to do with their kids. They fear for their children's safety because children are home alone more, and because of the apparent rise of predators peddling drugs and inflicting abuse. And they worry that their children may not gain adequate paid employment. They struggle to be 'responsible parents' and feel that their children need more protection, help and hope than they are able to give. At the same time, they are taken aback and mystified by children's behaviour. Indeed, Mackay suggests that many are 'appalled' at their 'assertiveness, materialism or sheer rudeness' (p. 123) and 'unnerved' by their 'swaggering overconfidence' (pp. 124–5).

Teachers, usually also baby boomers, are likewise often bothered and frustrated by the children in their care. 'It is *so* hard to be a teacher these days,' says one teacher. 'Kids are *so* different.' They are often considered more troublesome than students of former decades. They are more easily bored, restless and hard to control. They are also less attentive and respectful, and far less interested in their schoolwork. Many seem to come grudgingly to school. They are apathetic and disengaged when in class, 'turn on' mainly with their peers and seem to get their pleasures, find their identities and, indeed, live the 'important' parts of their lives elsewhere – out of class, out of school. Further, they are seen to subscribe to the sort of materialistic and hedonistic values that schools claim neither to accept nor promote (Fitzclarence, under review).

It is often the case that when parents and teachers try to explain the behaviour of 'young people today', they look to 'the media' – in particular, commercial TV, computer games, popular youth culture and advertising directed at the young. Moreover, 'the media' is blamed for kids' short attention spans, is seen to render them passive, to undermine their capacity to play independently, to entertain themselves and also to threaten their creativity. In addition, it is seen to corrupt their morals by favourably disposing them towards violence, individualism, hedonism and materialism (O'Regan 2000). In this view, the media discloses too much and exposes young people too early to the unpalatable and the forbidden.

Thus, teachers complain that they have to 'compete with' the media as a source of knowledge and values and, indeed, for kids' attention. Further, they say that even at school, kids expect to be entertained. They want curriculum materials to be as flashy, and curriculum activities to be as much fun, as media texts. They want teachers to be as engaging as TV personalities, but, at the same time, not to be 'cool try-hards'. Also, they adopt a 'dial-a-pizza' approach to school knowledge. They expect to have it delivered to them by compliant teachers and to get what they want from it with a minimum of fuss and effort (Fitzclarence, under review).

As a function of such views, many adults seem to fear that kids' absorption in and by 'the media' has resulted in the 'end of childhood' (Postman 1994) and, implicitly, the end of parents' and teachers' power and authority over children. As one teacher puts it, 'Kids don't automatically respect teachers. We always have to prove ourselves to them.' Many adults also fear that it results in young people learning about life out of order or sequence.

To the extent that the 'end of childhood–out of order' discourse is informed by a social construction perspective, we agree with it. The child is indeed a historical and social construction. This century has certainly seen sweeping changes in conceptions of childhood, and in child-rearing practices, family life and children's culture. The 'nature' of being young, the relationships of the young to adults, to the family and to other social institutions such as the school, have changed considerably across time and place. Although there are many factors that currently influence generational identities and relations, those that stand out, we agree again, are consumer culture and media culture. Indeed, this book rests entirely on the proposition that an adequate understanding of contemporary generational identities and relations must recognize the powerful role of consumer–media culture. However, we do not subscribe to many other implications of this discourse.

It is our view that the 'end of childhood–out of order' discourse is rooted in developmental notions of childhood and generation that cannot be sustained today. Developmentalism implies that the move-ment from childhood to adulthood involves a linear progression from the simple to the complex and from the irrational to the rational. Fur-ther, the 'end of childhood–out of order' discourse invokes a nostalgic version of the history of childhood. It implies that once there was a golden age of childhood in which individual adults were in control and children were under control. It also implies that this golden age can and should be recovered in some way. Further, the discourse is informed by a dystopian view of the present that fails on a number of counts. First, it suggests that there is a version of childhood to which we should assent, and that due to their lack of 'fit' the kids of today are deficient. Sec-ond, it can be read to suggest that traditional/hierarchical relationships between children and adults are preferable to any other. Third, it does not engage today's young people in the terms or on the grounds upon which they grow and seek to become somebody. In short, it is a form of denial.

In this book, we seek to avoid such misunderstandings. As the chapters unfold it will become clear that such views are too simple and, thus, are unhelpful. It will also become evident that the changes under scrutiny are not simply a matter for either regret or, indeed, celebration. One's position on this depends very much on one's standpoint of course, but this is bigger than the issue of standpoint. A key argument of this book is that we are entering another stage in the construction of the young as the demarcations between education, entertainment and advertising collapse and as the lines between the generations both blur and harden.

Our purpose here is to consider childhood, adulthood and intergen-erational relations in both historical (Chapter 2) and current contexts (Chapters 3 to 5). We discuss the evolving contexts of consumer culture, media culture and education culture, pointing to the uneven conver-gence of entertainment, advertising and education. In so doing, we con-sider the implications of the emergent hybrid forms for young people, parents and teachers and for the relationships among and between them. We also consider the power and pleasure dynamics that drench these emergent hybrid forms.

The articulations and disarticulations involved are tangled and per-plexing. Coming to grips with them means unravelling and reinterpreting much that is taken for granted about children and adults, power and powerlessness, pleasure and pain, and the differences between certain institutional cultures. It also involves recourse to some disciplinary and theoretical promiscuity on our part, for we found that no one field or framework is sufficient to the task of explaining what is happening. Although through this book we seek to contribute to the sociology and cultural studies of education, we have drawn on sociology, cultural studies, media studies, children's and youth studies, policy studies and studies of pedagogy. In theoretical terms we range widely, as we show in Chapter 1. Overall, in adopting a social and cultural constructionist view of young people, this book stands apart from those bodies of theory and research that render young people's historical, geographical and cultural locations largely irrelevant. Equally, it is disassociated from those forms of policy and practice that understand students as passive objects or render them invisible. It is also far removed from those who persist with a notion common in education policy circles that although times have changed, kids have not.

Generally, this book is concerned with young people and the cultural and institutional forms designed 'for' them – for instance, children's TV, advertisements and schools. More specifically, it is concerned with young people and their cultures in 'developed' English-speaking countries, although those whose voices emerge live in Australia. Our focus is largely on quite recent developments in young people's worlds, on the implications of their current commodity/image saturated lives for the ways they build their identities and relationships. We acknowledge that this is a partial focus, and that there is much else that could legitimately be included. We also recognize that history, culture and identity involve the interplay of competing tendencies – the dominant, residual, oppositional and emergent (Williams 1982: 204–5). In the chapters to follow, we identify and focus on emergent and intensifying trends in young people's life worlds. It is our view that these have the impetus to eventually supersede the institutional forms that now precede them. But to focus thus is not to deny the existence of other tendencies.

Educational sociology is often preoccupied with dominant cultural forms and their entrenched and enduring power relationships. This is both necessary and laudable. It reminds us that although things change, much also stays the same and that much of what stays the same includes patterns of inequality and injustice. No one should overlook this, least of all educators. However, it is also important to identify residual, oppositional and emergent tendencies in education and to consider their implications for those that are dominant. They may well reinforce, destabilize or, indeed, supersede them. Whether they do, how, why and with what effects are matters for inquiry.

Clearly, we are particularly concerned with the power relationships associated with age. Our interest is in the ways that these ebb and flow across time and space and in the ways that pleasure and power are implicated. But we also touch on enduring social inequalities associated with gender, race and social class – more specifically, the matrices of power that emerge as age, gender, race and social class intersect. Here we seek to do two things. First, we identify some of the ways that these power matrices are implicated in the changing commodified cultural formations under scrutiny. Second, we consider whether emergent hybrid forms in the life world of children reinforce or destabilize, or are likely to supersede, dominant matrices of power.

This book arises from three theoretically informed, empirically based research projects conducted by Jane Kenway, Lindsay Fitzclarence and Chris Bigum during the 1990s, and during 1999 and 2000 by Jane Kenway and Elizabeth Bullen. These Australian Research Council research projects were titled 'Marketing education', 'Marketing education in the information age' and 'Consuming education: contemporary education through the eyes of students'. Some discussion of these projects is necessary as they form the empirical and conceptual background and basis for this book which, in turn, foregrounds those aspects of the projects that relate most to young people. Further, selected passages from the various publications listed below appear occasionally in this book.

The projects were informed by a highly diverse international research and conceptual literature from the range of fields we mentioned earlier. Collectively they included four main sources of data: people, institutions, texts and artefacts. The first project involved the collection of documentary evidence and research literature that demonstrated the range of ways that the market phenomenon had become an integral part of educational policy and administration in Australia and elsewhere (see Kenway *et al*. 1993a, 1993b, 1993c; Kenway 1995; Kenway *et al*. 1995a; Kenway and Epstein 1996b; Fitzclarence and Kenway 1998). It classified the range of meanings that are implied in the use of the market meta-narrative and traced the intellectual heritage of these different meanings in other fields of knowledge such as neo-liberal political philosophy and economics. It tracked the political heritage of marketization in the discourses of the various interest groups that helped to shape education in the late 1980s and 1990s. It also explored how adequately different theoretical frameworks explain the rapid momentum and acceptance of the market motif in education in Australia and beyond. This project alerted us to the fact that those policy sociologists who had analysed the rapid embedding of the market form in education were largely located on the conceptual terrain of political, institutional and economic theories. They had largely overlooked the cultural dimensions of this policy trajectory and, thus, the merits of the theoretical frameworks outlined in Chapter 1. This first project also alerted us to the emergence of a parallel policy trajectory concerned with new information and communications technologies (ICT). While at first glance these seemed unrelated, at second glance the potential synergies between the two became apparent, as did the need for further inquiry. It was thus that the second project emerged.

The second project involved the development of a large representative archive of all the educational formations that come together at the nexus of markets, education and ICTs – including TV and other ICTs in Australia, the USA, the UK and Canada (see Bigum *et al.* 1993; Kenway *et al.* 1993b, 1995b; Bigum and Kenway 1998; Kenway 1998). This archive allowed us to map the field and then to select for closer scrutiny 'ideal types' that differed according to the ways in which they combined the three foci of the research. From here we produced cameo portraits of selected examples of different forms of educational practice that integrate markets and ICTs. The data here included the print and image texts and artefacts involved, both real and virtual, and telephone interview data from key participants in the worlds of education, commerce, information technology (IT), entertainment and advertising. Much of the data assembled here in Chapters 3 and 4 around the hybridization of education, entertainment and advertising, children's and adults' culture and the behaviour of corporations emerged from this project. As it developed, we became acutely aware that children's perspectives were an absent presence, both in the marketization of education and the research on it. Hence, the final project sought a kid's-eye view in the context of their schools.

This final project involved interviews and participant observation in and around seven schools (all anonomized here) in Geelong, a provincial city in Victoria, Australia (see Collier *et al.* 1994; Kenway and Fitzclarence 1998a, 1998b, 2000). Students were interviewed and their schools' promotional activities and cultures were observed. The male and female students of this study came from different age groups (8–9 years, 10–12 years and 13, 15, 16 and 17 years) and social classes, and from schools with different orientations to the marketing of education. Through participant observations, the project team studied the role of commodity markets in these schools, the schools' construction of themselves as educational commodities and, through the interviews with students, it identified their readings of the commodification of their schools and their constructions of themselves as consumers. Of central concern was how students' educational consumption connected with their other consumption patterns, their identities and their relationships.

This book offers an eagle's-eye view of consumer kids/consuming culture in the now hybrid worlds of entertainment, advertising and education, and it shows the ways in which adults are differently positioned within the matrix. In so doing, it brings together for analysis fields that have not commonly been brought together before and deploys a range of theoretical resources that often stand apart. Given the wide scope and intricacy of the matters addressed, this view from above is necessary. A heavily data-based account of each point made and all the issues involved is not possible. Neither is it necessary, for our intention is to document and interpret the big cultural shifts involved. We seek to provide readers with a way of comprehending the big changes that hold together the apparently unconnected and multiple small cultural changes. Many of these small changes have been well documented in the literature, but not in association with each other. That said, we also offer illustrative examples from our various data banks, from the research-based literature and from advertising and marketing industry trade journals and magazines. In addition to offering a marketing perspective – a perspective not usually included in academic discussions of these topics – examples from these sources are intended to bring alive and make more meaningful the more abstract points.

The manner in which we understand young people is of great consequence for schools and, indeed, for all those who care for and work with the young. Young people's histories, locations, affiliations and identities must not be relegated to the margins of the mind as programmes are developed and put into effect. An overarching implication of this book is that social and cultural understandings of children and youth must inform how and what we teach. As we will show, consumer–media culture is a central feature of young people's lives in complex and contradictory ways. We will also show that it generates both possibilities and predicaments for today's kids, parents and teachers. In Chapters 6 and 7 we build on these understandings and suggest some powerful *and* pleasurable pedagogies that are likely both to engage consumer kids and to address some of the dilemmas that consumer culture invokes. Our overarching concern is to provoke others to ponder the role of the school in the 'age of desire', and to consider what all this means for the nature and purposes of contemporary schooling. Indeed, we ask readers to contemplate the purposes of schooling if the distinctions between education, advertising and entertainment diminish.

(1) Devouring theory

◯ Introduction

No one knows quite what to name contemporary times, but one thing is certain and it is this: markets and information and communication media *together* hold a powerful and privileged position in today's culture, society and economy. Kincheloe (1997b: 254) calls the combination of corporate influence and technological innovation 'techno-power'. Further, he argues that: 'The convergence of the growth of international megacorporations and the expanding technological sophistication of the media have prompted a new era of consumption' (p. 259).

Indeed, consumption is now recognized as a defining characteristic of the lifestyle of the western world. As Humphery (1998: 6) says, 'consumption is an important part of our lives' in the late twentieth century and 'frames' the ways we are in the world. We call the cultural form, which arises from this blend of consumption and information and communication media, consumer–media culture. Furthermore, as we will show throughout this book, consumer–media culture in its various forms has transformed the lives of children, the institutions of the family and the school and, ultimately, the 'nature' of childhood.

This chapter provides the historical and theoretical backdrop to the book. It begins with a glimpse of the key moments in the history of consumer–media culture. This is followed by an outline of the different ways in which social and cultural commentators have theorized consumer–media culture. The final section outlines theories of advertising.

◯ Consumer–media culture: a taste of history

Our purpose in this section is to identify the key changes over time in consumer–media culture in the so-called 'developed' countries of the 'West'. We acknowledge that what we offer is 'thin history', but our purpose is not to do the work of a historian (see Slater 1997 for a more generously endowed history of consumer culture). Rather, it is to historicize the present and, thus, to go against a strong tendency in consumer culture to erase history. In Chapter 2, however, we will offer a more robust history of the emergence of the young consumer.

First, what do we mean when we use the term 'consumer culture'? Michael Featherstone (1992: 114), one of Britain's leading sociologists, argues that:

> one of the central features of consumer culture is the availability of an extensive range of commodities, goods and experiences which are to be consumed, maintained, planned and dreamt about by the general population. Yet this consumption is far from being just the consumption of utilities which are addressed to fixed needs ... Rather, consumer culture through advertising, the media, and techniques of display of goods, is able to destabilize the original notion of use or meaning of goods and attach to them new images and signs which can summon up a whole range of associated feelings and desires.

As is implied here, advertising, the media and other meaning-making (semiotic) practices are central to consumer culture. To put it simply, they remake the meaning of goods in order to sell them. The print media, then radio and TV and, more recently, the new ICTs associated with computer networks have dramatically expanded the reach and power of the commodity form.

There is ongoing historical debate about the emergence of consumer culture. Much of it swings on matters of definition. We agree with Featherstone (1992: 113) that if the term 'consumer culture' 'refers to the culture of consumer society', then history must point to the times and places at which 'the movement towards mass consumption was accompanied by a general reorganization of symbolic production, everyday experiences and practices'. Or to put it another way, when and how 'the concerns of industrialism shifted from production to selling, from the satisfaction of stable needs to the "invention" of new desires' (Humphery 1998: 25).

Many historical overviews point to the long-term development of consumer culture and the different times at which it emerged in different countries and for different social classes. For instance, Ewen (1976) argues in his classic text, *Captains of Consciousness*, that consumerism in

the USA can be traced to the industrial planning and scientific management of the corporate sector in the 1920s. This was accompanied by the
ascent of advertising, the motion picture, fashion and cosmetic industries and the mass circulation of tabloid newspapers and magazines.
Featherstone (1992: 113–14) points to the work of other historians who
argue that for the middle classes in Britain, consumer culture began in
the eighteenth century. However, historians claim that it began in the
nineteenth century for the working classes in Britain, France and the
USA, 'with the development of advertising, department stores, holiday
resorts, mass entertainment and leisure' (Featherstone 1992: 113–14).

Speaking very generally then, the first stage or birth of consumer–
media culture can be associated with the production, promotion and
consumption practices which were part of the symbiotic development of
industrialization, the advertising industry and the print media. Together
they delivered mass-produced goods and mass markets largely on a
national scale, and a proliferation of consumer sites and experiences. By
the end of the nineteenth century, newspapers and consumer magazines
had become major locations for advertising. Later, radio played its part.
Through radio the privileged relationship between sponsorship and programming began and developed. Advertising, the print media and radio
helped to facilitate the creation of a new kind of being, the consumer,
and a new kind of ideology, consumerism. The arrival and continuation
of consumer culture also meant the emergence of a number of specialists
engaged in the production and circulation of symbolic goods. New sites
for consumption also helped to produce and sustain the consumer.

The department store holds a central place in this history of consumer
culture as it was 'within the department store that this new concern for
selling took on a life of its own and in which shopping finally became
completely detached from necessity, while the merchandise was transformed into a spectacle' (Humphery 1998: 25). This gave rise to: *dreamworlds* – a changed pattern of personal and social consciousness in which
life was given meaning through consumable things, and the meanings
offered were ones that drew on the inner fantasies and desires of the
consumer' (p. 25). Drawing on the work of a number of historians,
Humphery observes that a modern European consumer culture was
cemented though the opening of Paris's Bon Marché in 1869. This was
seen as 'both a reflection of an encroaching bourgeois culture and a
vehicle for the construction of a modern culture of mass consumption
which would increasingly affect all social classes' (p. 25).

The second major stage of consumer–media culture can be associated
with the production, promotion and consumption practices that are part
of the symbiotic development of 'post-industrialization', the advertising
industry and the image media. Together they are delivering niche-
produced goods and niche markets, but on a global scale. Post-Fordism

is a term often used to describe these recent tendencies in the economy. (See Harvey 2000 for a full discussion of the differences between industrial and post-industrial paradigms and of the moments of transition from one paradigm to the other. See also Kenway 1994 for discussions of the contentious term 'post-Fordism'.) Commonly, post-Fordism refers to an unevenly emerging movement away from the mass manufacturing base and assembly line practices of the Fordist era towards 'flexible' and decentralized patterns of work brought about by rapid technological developments. This is accompanied by the 'contracting out of functions and services; a greater emphasis on choice and product differentiation, on marketing, packaging and design [and] the targeting of consumers by lifestyle, taste and culture' (Hall 1988: 24).

Post-Fordism is also associated with significant changes in international economies. These include the growth of world trading blocs and transnational corporations, the internationalization of the labour and money markets, and the rapid growth and extensive application of new ICTs which have facilitated the development of a global economic village (Probert 1993).

In Fordist economies, most market activity and growth involves consumer staples such as food and clothing and consumer durables such as cars and white goods. In contrast, an increasingly large proportion of market exchange activity in post-Fordist times involves: 'cultural technologies (stereos, VCRs, telephones, computers), cultural goods (games, theatre, music videos, toys, sports equipment) and social services (restaurants, theatres, personal advice and welfare services, information processing, management services)' (Kline 1993: 5). Clearly, then, cultural and service markets have become increasingly important in the second and most recent stage of the development of consumer–media culture. They represent the dematerialization of the commodity form, and the rise of what Lee (1993: 135) calls 'experiential commodities'. These include cultural events, enterprise culture, the heritage industry, theme parks, commercialized sport and other public spectacles. Lee suggests that there has been a rapid growth in the development of such experiential commodities in recent times and that this represents 'the push to accelerate commodity values and turnovers' (p. 20). It is also part of the more general move 'to make more flexible and fluid the various opportunities and moments of consumption' (p. 137).

It is self-evident that the expansion of production depends on the expansion of consumption. Across both these stages we have seen the restless search for ways to extend current markets and identify and develop new markets. As Lee says:

These range from the export of consumer capitalism to many regions of the Third World and the construction of an *enormous children's*

market in the First, to the deeper commercial penetration and commodification of the body, self and identity in the form of new health
foods, and expanded cosmetics and fashion markets.

(Lee 1993: 131, emphasis added)

The expansion and ever-increasing complexity of the children's market
is the subject of Chapters 2 and 3. Chapter 4 shows how it is expanding
into schools.

There are a number of new production practices that assist in this
process of market expansion. Obsolescence, product senility or decreasing
the lifespan of goods is one set of methods with which those who use
computer software are all too familiar. We also have aesthetic obsolescence involving the rapid turnover of style and fashion. Lee argues that
another method is the 'the liberation of consumption' from certain time
and space restrictions (1993: 133). This involves the ability to use and
consume goods in a variety of locations and timeframes. As Lee explains,
we now have mass-produced portable stereos and CD players, telephones,
recording devices and computers. Further, many such devices have been
adapted so that time schedules need not matter (Lee 1993: 134).

This latter shift is made possible by the application of new micro-
technologies. The time spent consuming certain items may now be
compressed to make that time free for other forms of consumption.
Miniaturization or the reduction in the size of items not only means that
they can go anywhere with us, but that they make more space available
for other goods. Further, retailing has also been reorganized and shopping
is no longer so limited by time and space. Many large chains are open 24
hours a day and we can shop and bank any time, increasingly from
home through our smart machines – the TV and the networked computer.

Also worth mentioning is the growth of more and more sophisticated
methods both of reaching consumers and of providing them with finance.
In the 1980s the former included 'tactically targeted mail shots, the birth
of tele-shopping and a rebirth of mail-order retailing' (Lee 1993: x). The
latter included 'in-store credit facilities and credit cards generally, personal loans and hire purchase schemes' (p. x). This has been facilitated
by, and has facilitated, the proliferation of new forms of media and communication. Overall, we see the growth of increasingly diverse settings
and techniques that provide opportunities to promote, sell and shop.

At the same time, consumption has so transformed the material landscape at all levels that people now talk of the 'aestheticization of everyday life' and 'sign-saturated landscapes' (Lash and Urry 1994). Shopping
complexes, malls, strips and retail parks have shaped the character and
functions of our urban landscapes and streetscapes. Public space has
been colonized by commercial interests. Along with this, we witness the
growing emphasis on product design and image. Haug (1986: 50) draws

our attention to the packaging of the commodity – its 'second skin' – which, he argues, is usually 'incomparably more perfect than the first'. He claims that the form and functionality of the commodity are detached from its surface or countenance which now, through its 'amorous glances', does the work of seductive selling. Indeed, he claims that no commodity can now keep up with its perfect packaging.

In Chapters 4 and 5 we will argue that school education is now emerging as a new site for consumption and as a new children's market within the expanding terrain of cultural markets. In many ways it has become an 'experiential commodity' which represents another development in the restless search for new markets.

◯ Consumer–media culture: a taste of theory

Definitions such as Featherstone's (1992) are a useful place to begin to conceptualize consumer culture and its relationship to media forms. Indeed, many studies of consumption focus on the consumption of media technologies and products and, more recently, post-television technologies in particular. However, a fertile understanding requires an appreciation of the various ways in which social and cultural commentators have considered the topic and how their views change as consumer culture itself changes. So let us provide a little more theoretical background on consumer culture as a basis for the discussions to follow, keeping in mind that it is beyond the scope of this book to give a detailed and critical account.

First let it be said that although the 1980s and 1990s saw a minor avalanche of work in the area (Humphery 1998), there have been bodies of literature in social theory with a much longer-term interest. While the earlier literature was dominated by critical theory and neo-Marxist perspectives, more recent work sweeps across a range of theoretical orientations including feminism and postmodernism, and a wide range of disciplines (for example, cultural studies, media studies, sociology, history and anthropology). It might be argued that academics have been devouring theory on the topic. Trends in the academy are also subject to theoretical fads and fashions. Indeed, some of the imperatives which analysts discuss with regard to consumer culture apply equally to theoretical fashions. Theories become over-used, and new trends date their predecessors.

Featherstone (1992) identifies three main orientations in the literature on consumer culture. These are (a) the production of consumption approach, (b) the modes of consumption approach and (c) the approach that emphasizes the consumption of dreams, images and pleasures. It is our view that each of these offers a valuable lens through which to view different aspects of children's consumer–media culture and its implications for both adult/child relations and schooling. Indeed, despite the apparent epistemological incoherence of combining these perspectives, we believe that together they offer both a holistic and suitably complex account. We will thus outline each view here and draw on them where appropriate later in the book.

The production of consumption

This point of view emphasizes the ways in which consumer culture helps to reproduce the different stages and forms of capitalism that we alluded to earlier (see pp. 10–11). It originated in the 1920s with European Marxism and the neo-Marxist critical theory associated with the Frankfurt School, and referred particularly to the USA. For instance, in *History and Class Consciousness* ([1923] 1971), Lukàcs focused on the explosion of the commodity form, the rise of consumerism and the implications for the social psyche and its broad structure of needs – consumption being understood as the path to gratification. By the late 1930s, Horkheimer and Adorno (1972) had developed their critique of mass culture, arguing that it enfeebles non-commercial culture and thwarts the possibilities for revolutionary social change. Subsequently, many more academics from Europe and the USA, and many non-Marxists or non-academics, further developed such ideas. The stress has been on large-scale forces that mould history, social configurations and selfhood, and that script individuals along the lines of dominant ideologies.

Most people who write from this position draw in one way or another from Marx's *Capital* ([1867] 1976), and are critical of consumer culture and what is also referred to as 'mass culture'. Consumer culture is seen variously to control, manipulate, segment and debase society, to contribute to the breakdown of local communities and to produce harmful forms of individualism and materialism. Some also suggest that it contributes to bland cultural forms which cater to the lowest common denominator, thus undermining individuality and creativity.

One strand of thought within this set of perspectives focuses on 'the logic of the commodity' – that is, the ways in which the original use value of commodities has been dissolved under capitalism and commodities released to take up secondary use values with many possible and often arbitrary meanings. This freedom has led to the manipulation of signs in the media and in advertising. Through such cultural agencies, signs float free from objects and services and are then used in a multiplicity of seductive ways unconnected to the original product.

While such a line of thinking began with Horkheimer and Adorno (1972) of the Frankfurt School, it was most fully developed in the work of Jameson (1979) and, in particular, the early work of Baudrillard

(1975, 1981, 1983b) who talks of 'commodity-signs' and the 'consumption of signs'. Indeed, it is Baudrillard's view that much Left analysis overprivileges the role of sites of production, labour and exchange value as the determining factors in social relations. His early view is that social relations are formed in the sphere of consumption. The shared view of Jameson and Baudrillard is that consumer culture and TV together have produced an excess of images and signs which have led to a world of simulation. This process of simulation has obliterated the distinction between the real and the imaginary and has led to a 'depthless' illusion of reality to such an extent that the 'real can no longer be grasped' – virtual reality is the outcome (Humphery 1998: 146).

Indeed, Jameson and Baudrillard argue that the current saturation of signs, images and simulations has led to an aestheticization of reality, an endless flow of incongruous juxtapositions and to a loss of referents, stable meanings and a sense of narrative, time and history now referred to as 'hyperreality'. The shopping mall or centre provides one example of this transformation of reality 'into a series of fleeting images and disconnected locales, an environment in which we become lost in a seemingly timeless and disorienting commercial space of countless levels and endless aisles' (Humphery 1998: 146).

Hyperreality and its simulations are seen to have implications for both individuals and groups. Individuals' experiences are isolated, disconnected, discontinuous and incoherent in the 'perpetual present'. Coherence and a sense of self are replaced by intensity and 'a mysterious and oppressive charge of affect' (Jameson 1984: 120). In an attempt to describe the feeling of living in such a hyperreality, Jameson uses the term 'schizophrenia'. Further, as Lee (1993: 149) points out, this is said to lead to the 'loss of the solid and coherent structures of collective social meaning that once characterised other, more stable, cultural moments'.

Jameson and Baudrillard eventually suggested that the capacity of capital to manipulate and the susceptibility of the people to be manipulated have, therefore, also disappeared. In a fragmented and continually changing culture there is no such thing as a dominant ideology. Both the author and the subject are deemed 'dead'. Featherstone (1992: 55) observes that:

> For Baudrillard, then, the logic of commodity production has produced a particular reversal in which culture once determined, now becomes free-floating and determining to the extent that today we can talk about the triumph of signifying culture, to the extent that we can no longer speak of class or normativity which belong to the prior stage of the system as people are reduced to a glutinous mass which refuses to stabilize in its absorption, reflection and cynical parody of media images.

Such views are seen by some to represent a 'nihilistic embracement of the consumer present' (Humphery 1998: 147).

Of course, simulation, hyperreality, schizophrenia and the overall triumph of signifying culture have a strong 'spatial fix' (Harvey 2000). Not only are they associated with geographies of plenty, but also with the highly differentiated global distribution and reception of images and information in postmodernity. However, theorists of the triumph of signifying culture do not attend to such differentials, let alone to uneven economic development or the triumph of globalizing and regionalizing economies and polities. According to many current theorists of globalization, attention to such matters is essential to any analysis of the triumph of signifying culture in what Lash and Urry (1994) call globalizing 'economies of signs and spaces'. So, too, then is discussion of the intersections between cultural and economic resources and, thus, of the economic exploitation, marginalization and deprivation that underwrites semiotic society.

The manner in which 'Third World' labour markets (within both the 'Third' and 'First' World) support 'First World' economies of signs is a central part of much current commentary (Mitter and Rowbotham 1995; Sassen 1996). So, too, is an analysis of the unevenness, directedness and purposefulness of configurations of power, its 'hierarchies and headquarters'. Here, attention is paid to the economic and ideological strength of transnational corporations and macro-institutions such as the International Monetary Fund (IMF), the World Bank, the World Trade Organization (WTO) and regional alliances such as the European Union and the North American Free Trade Organization (NAFTA) (for example, Rodrik 1997). The discursive ascendancy of neo-liberal economics and political philosophy and of corporate management thought and practice in business and government organizations worldwide is now widely seen to have contributed to the current global triumph of the metanarrativity of the postmodern market. Further, the triumph of the postmodern market is also evident in the major aesthetic and cultural trends and the constant slippage between local and global, public and private, commerce and culture which typifies postmodernity.

The broad frameworks we have outlined so far inform different aspects of the chapters to follow. They help us to recognize the overarching economic forces that lie behind the emergence and expansion of the children's market as outlined in Chapter 2. They assist us in seeing the role that the consumption of a wide variety of signs plays in the formation of adult–child relationships and in the construction of differences among young people. Further, they provide frameworks with which to critique the consumer cultures within which children are immersed and to comprehend the character of their immersion, particularly in the case of contemporary young people. These young people are the first generation to have experienced, from their infancy, what Lyotard (1984) calls the 'computerization of society' and, thus, the effects of hyperreality.

Despite their acumen, the perspectives outlined here have attracted some criticism. It is pertinent to mention some examples of this, as they lead us into the second and third ways of analysing consumer culture. The argument is made that such views ignore the particular in favour of the general and thus fail to see the specificity of particular contexts and sites of consumption and specific consumption practices. To many, such views are deterministic, overly negative and blind to the ways in which differently situated and psychologically complex people actually respond to and use consumer goods and services. The case is made that such views underplay human agency and fail to recognize active consumers and their potential resistance to, and subversion and transgression of, the messages encoded in consumer texts.

The critiques revolve in part around the power of the market/media to make meaning in relation to, and in comparison with, the power of the consumer/reader/viewer. Such critiques have led to modes of analysis which either focus on what Featherstone (1992) calls a 'modes of consumption' approach or an approach which focuses on 'consuming dreams, images and pleasures'. Melancholic and somewhat moralistic accounts of alienation and exploitation give way to more detached ethnographic accounts in the case of the former. In the latter case, the amoral embrace characteristic of the later Baudrillard appears to have become quite standard.

Modes of consumption

The modes of consumption approach has led to many studies of particular consumption practices of particular social groupings. Such studies explore how the consumer becomes active as a producer of undesigned and unanticipated uses and meanings, and how practices of consumption can provide the location for 'personal empowerment, cultural subversion, and even political resistance' (Humphery 1998: 7–8). This orientation points to the complexity of both consumer culture and consumers. The emphasis here is on mediation, on how ideas are received and transformed during the negotiation and construction of culture identities. The work of de Certeau (1984) is influential here. He emphasizes the 'guileful ruses' or 'tactics' that people employ in their 'practices of everyday life' to allow them to respond creatively to dominant cultural 'strategies' that would position them otherwise. At the more extreme end of this body of work, Fiske (1994: 95) developed the notion of 'semiotic democracy', arguing that many current market/media texts provide a 'menu of meaning' which users can freely select from to produce their own meanings. His emphasis is on such texts as 'rebellious spaces'.

A particular focus is on the ways in which consumption is used to maintain, strengthen and challenge various social and cultural boundaries including those associated with class, gender and race, and various subcultural groupings. Here we see the different ways in which people use consumption to create identities, social bonds or distinctions and distances; to display and sustain differences; and to open or close off opportunities for themselves and for others.

Much of the early literature investigating the use of cultural goods for the purposes of communicating differences has focused on social class. For instance, writing at the turn of the twentieth century, Thorsten Veblen ([1899] 1970) talked of the development of an American leisure class which derived its social status in part through 'conspicuous consumption' and the meanings attached to the goods it consumed which entirely lacked necessity or function. Given that social class is one of the 'differences' under consideration in Chapter 5, we will expand a little on some of the key ideas, drawing on the work of Douglas and Isherwood (1979) and Bourdieu (1984).

Prestige economies, the goods that constitute them, and the ways that they communicate the ranks of social class relationships, are the focus of much analysis here. For instance, Douglas and Isherwood (1979) show how three sets of goods are used as markers in this way: staple goods (e.g. food), technology goods (e.g. capital equipment) and information goods (e.g. education, arts). The poor are usually restricted to the consumption of staples, while more affluent and prestigious class groups invest time and money in developing the 'natural' competencies associated with the consumption of the information set of goods. In so doing, they come to know the principles and hierarchies of classification; they can signal and read the status of the bearer of the commodity. These competencies feed into employment and further status opportunities and distinctions. Taste plays quite a central role here, and can be understood as: 'the discriminatory judgement, the knowledge or cultural capital, which enables particular groups or categories of people to understand and classify new goods appropriately and how to use them' (Featherstone 1992: 17).

In *Distinction* (1984), Bourdieu says 'Taste classifies, and it classifies the classifier'. In other words, taste in cultural goods operates as a marker of class or class fractions. In *Distinction*, Bourdieu maps several fields together: ' "high" cultural practices (museum visits, concert-going, reading) as well as taste in lifestyles and consumption preferences (including food, drink, clothes, cars, novels, newspapers, magazines, holidays, hobbies, sport, leisure pursuits)' (Featherstone 1992: 88) along with class/ occupational structure. Cultivating the fine distinctions of 'taste' is a disciplined and difficult educational process. So, too, is learning the unemotional and detached bodily deportment which accompanies the performance of good taste. Good taste is what separates the cultured élite from the masses whose tastes are seen as cheap, undemanding, unimportant, uncivilized and possibly even vulgar. As Bourdieu points out, the tastes of the masses are seen to be 'too closely linked to bodily pleasures and sensual desire', 'to animality, corporeality, the belly and sex'. Cultivating 'good' taste involves developing a distaste for 'those who wallow in pleasure, who enjoy enjoyment' (Bourdieu 1984: 489).

Bourdieu's interpretation of the French working class is that they have to make do with 'the choices of necessity' and are thus denied access to cultural and educational capital. For them, goods must perform both a material and symbolic function, and he argues that this becomes the determining criterion of cultural judgement. Lee (1993: 35) explains that:

> Working-class taste in food, for example, is generally governed by the capacity of individual foodstuffs and meals to satisfy hunger and provide plentiful protein. This is transformed unconsciously by the habitus to a symbolic level where the typical working-class meal objectifies a deep-seated struggle to escape the yoke of economic scarcity. This is why, wherever possible, the meal, and more importantly perhaps, its mode of cultural consumption within the working-class lifestyle so often embodies a sense of material substance, abundance and elasticity: 'soups or sauces, pastas or potatoes . . . served with a ladle or spoon to avoid too much measuring or counting' (Bourdieu 1984: 194).

Closely related to taste is style. Style is a key ingredient of consumption, and can be understood in a range of ways. Style 'is a way that the human values, structures, and assumptions in a given society are aesthetically expressed and received' (Ewen 1988: 3). It can be seen to provide the impetus for markets in appearances, surfaces and mystifications. But style can also be understood as providing tools for 'constructing personhood', as a statement about who one is and wishes to be. Style allows people to imagine themselves differently; it provides an opportunity to define and redefine themselves; it can be an expression of fantasy – to quote Barthes (1983) 'a dream of identity', and even a 'dream of wholeness', in an age of fragmentation and alienation.

Current studies of style tend to be less concerned with class and more interested in what is referred to as the 'stylization of life'. This process foregrounds the importance of the aesthetic. It promotes the notion that the pursuit of commodity aesthetics and the new are what constitute the good life. Here is Featherstone's (1992: 86) reading of this:

> Rather than unreflexively adopting a lifestyle, through tradition or habit, the new heroes of consumer culture make lifestyle a life

project and display their individuality and sense of style in the particularity of the assemblage of goods, clothes, practices, experiences, appearance and bodily dispositions they design together into a lifestyle. The modern individual within consumer culture is made conscious that he speaks not only with his clothes, but with his home, furnishings, decoration, car and other activities which are to be read and classified in terms of the presence and absence of taste.

Ironically, while on the one hand consumer culture promotes the idea that 'life should be a work of art', it also makes it clear that the enchantment of the new is unsustainable. This is underwritten by the market dynamic with its constant search for new fashions, new styles, new sensations and new experiences (Featherstone 1992: 86).

As this suggests, there is a fundamental tension between the market dynamic and the agency of consumers in the modes of consumption approach, and this is particularly evident in recent reconceptualizations of gender and race. We will explore this theme by means of theorizations of gender and consumption in the context of the segmentation of the consumer market in Chapter 2. Here we offer a general overview of race and style; we look more closely at youth subcultural style in urban multiracial communities in Chapter 7.

Style has been a central premise in contemporary reappraisals of the relationship between race and consumer culture. Celia Lury (1996: 162) describes two competing trends in the representation of race, the one tending towards racial homogenization or sameness and the other towards heterogeneity or difference and, 'In both cases, race is represented as a matter of *style*'. This tension is produced by what has come to be called the 'seriality of commodification'. At the same time as 'differences between political, moral and cultural values' are levelled, 'the market requires novelty to stimulate demand', thus creating a 'standardized variation' or 'serial commodification' (Lury 1996: 162). This is reflected in the way representations of race variously efface and emphasize racial differences. In early advertising, 'colonized peoples were represented, not as historic agents, but as *frames* or *figures* for the exhibition of the commodity' and thus their presence in an advertisement 'was not necessarily a reflection of, or an address to, a black person' (Lury 1996: 159–60).

The reconfiguration of race as an aesthetic or cultural rather than biological category has created the 'fantasy of the potential of commodities to change race'. This is reflected in Benetton advertisements where 'Skin colour, a key marker of race, is not simply displaced, but replaced and reworked as an act of choice' (Lury 1996: 167). Lury says that the colour coding of skin and product colours in the United Colours of Benetton campaigns present race 'not as a biological category, but as a question of style' (p. 168). Such representations arguably commodify race and deny the political reality of racism. They remain largely aimed at a white audience.

Indeed, this perspective on race falls into the category of 'production' of consumption discussed earlier (see pp. 14–17). A richer reading may be gained by looking at the ways in which people of colour have used cultural goods to challenge their marginalization in western society. Lury refers to Gilroy's (1987) contention that the consumption practices of black people subvert the seriality of the commodity to construct alternative and oppositional understandings of race, often mediated by art and culture. For example:

> in many black consumption practices, there is a refusal and reversal of the dominant white tendency to privatize consumption, to make it a matter of individual preference, carried out in the domestic sphere. In black culture, consumption is celebrated, not as a private or individual practice, but as a collective, affirmative practice in which an alternative public sphere is brought into being.
>
> (Lury 1996: 170)

According to Gilroy (1987) the black community's creative appropriation of recorded music has contributed to this process. He has argued that such black cultural practices have contributed to the dissolution of the boundaries between high and low culture, performer and audience, art and life.

Lury (1996: 175) points to Andrew Ross's argument that such 'plagiaristic commerce between black and white' cultures is an 'everyday phenomenon'. However, the traffic between them is neither even nor equally weighted. At issue here are questions of imitation and authenticity. Ross (1989: 67) suggests that black authenticity is 'part and parcel of the long transactional history of white responses to black culture, of black counter-responses, and of further countless and often traceless negotiations, tradings, raids and other compromises'. Because it has been historically weighted in favour of whites, it could be said that '"imitation" may be better understood as "theft" and "appropriation", and that black authenticity has very different meanings in the two cultures' (Ross 1989, cited in Lury 1996: 175–6).

In fact, as the consumption of recorded music suggests, many contemporary black cultural phenomena are commercially mediated. The association between commerce and culture is conventionally understood as a feature of white culture and usually regarded as negative. Manufactured cultural commodities like the Spice Girls, for instance, are not taken seriously because they are not regarded as 'authentic' (see Driscoll 1999). Lury explains that white culture's nostalgic insistence on black authenticity blocks black people's claim to 'the economic capital . . . which their cultural practices create' (1996: 177). At the same time, it has also been of importance to black people 'who seek to lay claim to an autonomous identity, uncontaminated by white racism' and consumer practices (Lury 1996: 182). Humphery (1998: 159) provides an example of this in Australia when he reports Aboriginal activist Gary Foley's view that consumerism is 'damaging to the fundamental Aboriginal values of communality and non-materialism'.

Mercer (1994: 63) argues that the identity of diasporic peoples is inevitably 'imbricated in Western modes and codes' and that the question is not about 'the expression of some lost origin or some uncontaminated essence [but] the collision of cultures and histories that constitute the very conditions of our existence'. She suggests that there may be another solution to the problem of expressing authentic identity under conditions of colonization and diaspora. This, she says, is evident

> in aesthetic practices of everyday life among black peoples of the African diaspora in the new world of the capitalist West, which explores and exploits the creative contradictions of the clash of cultures. Across a whole range of cultural forms there is a *syncretic* dynamic which critically appropriates elements from the master-codes of the dominant culture and *creolizes* them, disarticulating signs and rearticulating their symbolic meaning otherwise.
>
> (Mercer 1994: 63)

Imitation, or what Homi Bhabha (1994) calls 'mimicry' in reference to interracial borrowings and Amit Rai (1994) calls 'hybrid-mimics', does not function 'as a strategy for overcoming domination, but as a form of resistance which survives or negotiates its domination' (Lury 1996: 187). However, as Lury points out, the implications of these views of race and consumer culture have been little examined in the dimensions of social life outside the domains of leisure, recreation and relaxation.

Such ideas lead us back to the notions of hyperreality and schizophrenia that we mentioned in the previous section. They raise some provocative questions about the implications of hyperreality and schizophrenia for the racial and class practices outlined above. For example, when symbolic goods and consumer commodities are in abundant supply and rapidly change and circulate, how readily do they signal rank or culture? Does postmodernity's propensity for the eclectic mixing of codes and for un-chained signifiers defy our ability to write and read social scripts about race and social class? To put it another way, does the irregularity of signs mean we are now in a period of cultural declassification, or do new irregular rules apply? In response to such questions, Lee (1993: 143) argues that:

> a postmodern aesthetic . . . plagiarises, and therefore effaces the significances of histories, to the extent that previous styles, symbolic codes, cultural movements and artefacts, now stripped of their

original contexts and meanings, are juxtaposed into a bricolage or 'pastiche' of retro-chic and nostalgia. Such an aesthetic also invites a fascination, rather than a contemplation, of its contents; it celebrates surfaces and exteriors rather than looking for or claiming to embody (modernist) depth; . . . and it erases several of the key boundaries of separation that have previously existed between discrete cultural forms. In short, the postmodern aesthetic transforms all cultural content into objects for immediate consumption rather than texts of contemplative reception or detached and intellectual interpretation.

The bodies of theory discussed in this section inform our later analysis of the manner in which children, youth and adults inscribe themselves within consumer culture and deploy the resources available therein to craft their diverse identities and relationships. They also inform our understanding of the current hybridization of entertainment, advertising and education.

Consuming dreams, images and pleasures

Much of this third body of literature has come from cultural and media studies and in the latter case, in particular, the emphasis is on consuming images. However, in contrast with those theorists outlined above, the utopian or positive moments of consumer culture are identified and celebrated along with the aesthetic potential of popular culture. Indeed, people writing within this frame seek particularly to erase the distinctions between high and low cultures of consumption.

This genre focuses on the aesthetics of desire. The most common objects of inquiry are particular sites of consumption or images for consumption and the pleasures, desires and dreams which they evoke. Walter Benjamin, whose fragmentary and incomplete *Das Passengen-Werk* or 'Arcades Project' (1982) centres on the image of the nineteenth-century Parisian arcades as a figure for mass culture and its commodification, calls such sites 'dream-houses'. For Benjamin, the arcades were the 'primordial landscape of consumption' (cited in Gilloch 1996: 123) and the commodities they housed were the utopian dream-wishes of the social collective. Benjamin's exploration of this landscape extends to include all public places of the metropolis or 'dreamworld' and the typologies of those who occupy it – the *flâneur* (male stroller or street reader), the gambler, the ragpicker and the prostitute. The arcade itself is the prototype of the modern aesthetic that combines art and technology, fantasy and function, innovation and obsolescence.

Those who have followed Benjamin have concerned themselves with the ever-changing dreamscape of mass consumer culture and its development over time. Yet, according to Humphery (1998: 64), 'arguably, only Walter Benjamin really went beyond the condemnation of mass culture – and into everyday shopping environments – to analyse the manner in which people were drawn into a different mode of participation under conditions of consumer modernity'. Benjamin saw that consumer culture involved a 'manipulation of the masses, but equally, that these cultures gave rise to a popular creativity and a new democratic aesthetic' (Humphery 1998: 64).

According to this dialectical vision, mass culture does indeed give rise to 'the phantasmagoria of false consciousness', but within it lies 'the source of collective energy to overcome it' (Buck-Morss 1991: 253). Although, like Adorno, Benjamin described consumerist modernity as 'Hell', he resisted a 'totalizing critique', attempting instead 'to rescue the utopian moments locked in the commodity' (Gilloch 1996: 122).

The central premise of the 'Arcades Project' is that 'under conditions of capitalism, industrialization had brought about a *re*enchantment of the social world . . . and through it, a "reactivation of mythic powers"' (Buck-Morss 1991: 253–4). The producers of this new mythology were its 'photographers, graphic artists, industrial designers, and engineers'; its mythic forces, the new technologies; and its muses and heroes 'the stars of the stage and screen, billboard advertisements, and illustrated magazines' (Buck-Morss 1991: 255–6). This mythic reenchantment cast society into a dream sleep but the concept of the dreamworld is ambivalent, simultaneously an image of loss and redemption.

These two aspects of the dreamworld are related to the generational differences between adult and child discernment. According to Benjamin, it is through the child's perception of the discarded dream images of the previous generation – his or her ability to 'discover the new anew' (Buck-Morss 1991: 274) – that the spell can be broken and the dreamer awakened. As Gilloch (1996: 83) explains, whereas adults seek to view the world from a position of superiority, the 'child enjoys a privileged proximity' and, as such, a view that 'problematizes the habitual, forgetful vision of the adult'. The child both participates in and negates the myth of modernity through play. Benjamin identifies three dimensions of play: transgression, mimesis or imitation, and collecting. As we shall later see, these have come to be manipulated by advertisers.

Bakhtin (1968) explores similar themes in his concept of the carnivalesque. Many contemporary theorists draw on his discussion of the pre-industrial carnival and show how certain forms of consumer culture have drawn on this tradition which evokes the pleasures of various forms of excess. They document the cultural impulse towards play, sensation, immediacy and transgression. They revel in considering disorder, ambiguity, artificiality, the strange, the exotic and the spectacular, and the capricious mixing of codes that produces stylistic promiscuity. Decentred subjects, sensory overload and aesthetic immersion are their *cause célèbre*.

For example, some writers have shown how, in the second half of the nineteenth century, such environments as the music hall, the urban market-place and the department store incorporated the exciting and giddy aspects of the carnival. Others have shown how these elements persist in many contemporary media (advertisements, rock videos and cinema) and sites (holiday resorts, theme parks, video arcades, shopping complexes and sports tournaments). As Featherstone explains, yet others have shown how such ideas are incorporated 'into conspicuous consumption by states and corporations, either in the form of "prestige" spectacles for wider publics, and/or privileged upper management and officialdom' (1992: 22). As he says, these are sites of 'ordered disorder which summo[n] up elements of the carnivalesque tradition in their displays, imagery and simulations of exotic locations and lavish spectacles' (p. 23).

In its original form, carnival represented an opportunity for the population to temporarily transcend the social relations and moral and economic imperatives that organized everyday life. Typified by the consumption of fattening foods and alcohol, and promiscuous sexuality, it celebrated the grotesque body and thus inverted the privileged position of pure over impure, mind over body, beauty over ugliness, abstemiousness over consumption and high culture over low. As Featherstone (1992: 79) explains:

> The grotesque body and the carnival represent the otherness which is excluded from the process of formation of middle-class identity and culture. With the extension of the civilizing process into the middle classes the need for greater controls over the emotions and bodily functions produced changes in manners and conduct which heightened the sense of disgust at direct emotional and bodily expressivity . . . In effect the other which is excluded as part of the identity formation process becomes the object of desire.

However, this inversion is only ever temporary and the carnivalesque has been theorized as a socially sanctioned transgression that is ultimately instrumental in compelling conformity with the social status quo.

Julia Kristeva charts similar territory in her psychoanalytical theorization of the abject and abjection in *Powers of Horror* (1982). Modelled on the mother's mapping of the infant body into clean and unclean zones, the processes of abjection are integral to the formation of the boundaries demarcating individual identity. Thus, clean and unclean are paralleled by the oppositions of self and other, subject and object, inside and outside, healthy and diseased, culture and nature, proper and improper (McCann 1997: 146). Abjection involves the expulsion of identifications that contradict, pollute or exceed the identity of both individuals and cultures and is typically represented by bodily waste. In essence, it is opposed to the object of desire and, as the expelled element, to incorporation or consumption. Ultimately, it is the maternal identification that is expelled as the condition of the individual's entry into language and the social order, both of which are associated with the paternal principle. Yet, like the grotesque in Bakhtin's carnival, the abject is a pole of both attraction and revulsion and an aesthetic in so far as music, art and poetry evoke the maternal semiotic.

In an essay concerned with the delineation of childhood boundaries in a domestic context, Sibley (1995: 127) points out that there are

> Two aspects of abjection which are crucial to an understanding of the role of boundaries in childhood (and adulthood), boundaries separating the pure and the abject. First, the abject is an expanding category that includes people and places through the elision of the biological and social. Bodily residues become social residues . . . The second, related, feature of abjection is that it is learned.

Accordingly, the concept of abjection has been used recently to explain the social positioning of class, race and gendered minorities. Their categorization as abject acts to compel adherence to often repressive social and cultural norms. The abject has also been used to explore modernity's preoccupation 'with the marking of safe, purified or domesticated territories' (McCann 1997: 146). Abjection theory offers a means of conceptualizing the adult opposition to the 'polluting' aspects of consumer culture and the push to keep schools as commercial-free zones. However, what is considered abject by some social groupings or cultures will be acceptable in others. Adults are just as likely to be the abject others of children's and youth culture.

The ways of thinking discussed in this section direct our analysis to the role that enchantment, pleasure, fantasy, disgust, anxiety and rejection play in children's culture and in adults' responses to it.

The mundane and the profane

It is now quite commonly accepted that the second and third approaches noted above have their limits. For instance, some commentators argue that ethnographies of consumption have become rather formulaic and 'correct' in their concentration around the 'narrow conceptual repertoire [of] meaning, identity, distinction, pleasure' and thus, to some extent, have remained isolated from wider debates (Robins 1996: 109). Humphery says much such work involves thick description but thin conceptualization, and he makes the compelling point that consumption is not only connected to dreamworlds, fantasy, excitement and pleasure. He claims these are 'overly written in' in analysis and that scholars must also consider the ways 'in which everyday life is altered in deep but quite unspectacular ways . . . Consumption not only transforms life through spectacle, but through far less exciting processes such as routine and the physical reconstruction of everyday public space' (Humphery 1998: 26).

Robins is also concerned about the overemphasis on identity, pleasure and such popular cultural products as soap opera and music. He asks how well such emphases are able to address a wider human motivational range associated with screen consumption, particularly when such consumption involves the death and violence on 'realist' TV. He offers the following to complement the focus on pleasure: 'Consumption may . . . be seen as one of the institutionalised strategies of social defence that we have developed to cope with the real world; it serves to evade or to insulate against the anxieties or fears provoked by our relations to the world' (Robins 1996: 111). He acknowledges that consuming realist TV is in part about the desire to see, know and develop an opinion. But he argues that other cognitive processes are also going on and that these are associated with the desire not to know or to feel too much. As he says, 'Consumption activities may be driven by the desire to create defensive barriers and to avoid and minimise anxiety' (p. 125). He observes that, as the images of the world proliferate, the TV screen extends our information, impressions and 'experiences'.

Many of these can be disturbing, frightening and disruptive. As a result, accompanying them is a desire to escape the awfulness of such knowledge and to fend off the force of the feelings such images might generate, if they were to be fully assimilated; to fend off their 'disturbing or threatening realities' (Robins 1996: 118). TV, Robins says, has the capacity to put us in touch with reality but, at the same time, to veil reality. This is because of the 'weightlessness' of the image, because the small screen contains and minimizes the shock of the real. This induces a sense of detachment and remoteness from what is seen. The screen becomes a kind of technological shield or fortress which produces an 'anaesthetized kind of knowing'. The result is 'the numbed quality of the witness' and 'dispassionate proximity, intimate detachment' (p. 118).

Robins is interested in consumption as a strategy of survival – how it is used to ward off a sense of vulnerable existence, how it becomes a withdrawal from the complexities of experiencing 'the shocking and exhausting' reality of life in postmodernity. He further suggests that virtual reality may be the 'ultimate consumer environment' allowing full engagement at a distance. It allows one to do the impossible or the prohibited, overcoming physical and moral restrictions in comfort and security.

More generally, the current view is that emphasis on the active/ powerful consumer has become somewhat uncritically populist and politically bland, ignoring wider forces at work. Of particular concern is the failure to acknowledge the exploitation and injustice involved in the 'night-time of the commodity' – the economic modes and practices associated with production and consumption. Many warn against the quasi-romantic idea of the fully knowing, fully calculating sovereign subject or consumer, freely able to produce meanings and pleasure from the raw material of the text. Indeed, it is suggested that such a view echoes much neo-liberal ideology and fails to see that 'some consumers are more sovereign than others' (McGuigan 2000: 297). The active consumer is not necessarily the powerful consumer.

There is now some debate about the directions that studies of consumer culture should take. Humphery (1998) and others say that this debate is caught up in the false polarization of attraction/resistance, choice/manipulation, self-expression/conformity, pleasure/guilt. Some are now calling for a return to structural and macro perspectives or at the very least a return to a concern for the complexities of social and historical contexts. Yet, the most astute recognize that swinging between two opposite perspectives is not the best way to proceed. At the very least, a both/and approach is necessary, one which is sensitive to the vertical dimensions of power and ideology and the horizontal dimensions of contexts and everyday life (Robins 1996). As Featherstone (1992: 84) insists:

> To use the term 'consumer culture' is to emphasize that the world of goods and their principles of structuration are central to the understanding of contemporary society. This involves a dual focus: firstly, on the cultural dimension of the economy, the symbolization and use of material goods as 'communicators' not just utilities; and secondly, on the economy of cultural goods, the market principles of supply, demand, capital accumulation, competition, and monopolization which operate *within* the sphere of lifestyles, cultural goods and commodities.

The current trend is to understand that consumer culture powerfully frames but does not wholly define people, and that people engage in it in a range of ways in different sites and circumstances. Thus, they can be within, against, distant from and, indeed, can sometimes also refuse it.

Humphery (1998: 11) believes that the emphasis on the resistant or active consumer and the pleasures of consumption has muted political analysis and left little ground to construct critique. He insists that we explore further the question of critical distance whereby

> people stand back from the market, feel anger at its presence, refuse to participate or, at the very least, question its relevance to other aspects of their lives. This process of standing back is not a process of 'making do' but of 'thinking through', of imagining an

'outsidedness' and an oppositionality which is embedded in a process of 'distancing' rather than participation. It is this outsidedness, and people's attempts to actively delimit the areas of their lives that are commodified, which has been almost completely ignored by the celebrants of the resistant consumer.

It is to questions associated with the 'cultural dimensions of the economy', the 'economy of cultural goods', 'popular participation', everyday 'outsidedness', the 'wide motivational range invoked by consumer culture' and the 'night-time of the commodity' that we will return throughout this book. We will develop the argument that a political engagement with consumer culture is vital for young people in schools; and in the final two chapters we will consider what forms such engagements might take and whether consumer culture might provide some of the educational modalities. Students do need to understand how consumer culture works with and against them, and when and how to oppose it. They need to comprehend what else is possible and how these possibilities may be made real.

However, for now let us consider the role of advertising, because the impact of advertising confronts young people almost everywhere, including schools, in 'semiotic society' (Wexler 1987).

○ Theorizing advertising

There are many sides to advertising. Raymond Williams (1980) argues that we must appreciate both the cultural influences *on*, and the cultural effects *of*, advertising. Obviously, commercial interests are the primary cultural influence *on* advertising. Advertisers' work is central to the process of market exchange and, patently, advertising provides the vital link between production and consumption. It has been pivotal to the development of consumer–media culture. The point here, however, is to comprehend the complex ways in which this happens. As Kline (1993: 36) points out, advertising was historically

> conceived as more than a simple technique for organizing distribution and sales; it was an organizational technique directed towards managing the whole system of capitalist production through promoting consumerism . . . for managing and solidifying the psychic structure of industrial society, for reorganizing the experience of desire, for channelling protest and subduing the alienation of capitalist economy.

That said, it is also important to make it clear that the cultural influences on, and the cultural effects of, advertising are not one and the same.

There are different sources of power for the determination of social meaning. As we made clear earlier, commodities have various uses. Some are defined by the economy and are largely about profit and maintaining and developing the economic system. As we also showed, some uses are defined by consumers and may take a rather different form from those intended by the cultural intermediaries who seek to construct uses for consumers. It is thus that Kellner (1989) talks about commodities *for* consumption – their ideal use value and imagined meaning *vis-à-vis* the producers, promoters, distributors and objects *of* consumption in everyday life and lived experience.

Since its inception, advertising has been built on the recognition that selling is a matter of motivation through strategic communication. Clearly, advertising will advocate and seek to persuade. As Young (1990: 291) says, 'Advertising is a particular form of discourse where only the best side of a case is put forward so that the virtues of the topic are presented, to the relative neglect of the vices'. It is about *face value* and *best face*.

With the rise of postmodern advertising, so powerfully analysed by Brown (1995), it is not so clear what best face is or, indeed, how exactly the advertisement connects to the product. Postmodern advertising transgresses many of advertising's standard rules in highly creative and eye-catching ways. Its developers understand advertising as innovative art and their work involves anti-realist, surrealist and avant-garde formats, non-linear narratives, pastiche, nostalgia and overall glossy visuals and stylistic effects. This reflects the broader cultural shift to a concentration on style, form and image, and away from use value, substance and direct address.

Whether taking a modern or postmodern form, advertising – and indeed marketing and public relations (increasingly named collectively as 'promotional culture' after Wernick 1991) – involves a wide range of semiotic practices. These include such things as product design – packaging and imagery, product differentiation/positioning and repositioning when necessary, and product renewal involving redesign and redefinition. It may involve developing a corporate image. It may also involve market segmentation and associated population and lifestyle building and targeting. It is now commonly accepted that there is no longer a mass or middle market, 'just diversity and continual change' (Humphery 1998: 156). Advertisers now target micro markets, market niches or segments and in so doing stress differentiation and positioning. All of this may include the impression management associated with such concrete matters as location, architectural design, floor layout and display. It may also involve the abstractions associated with sponsorship and media buying.

Print and electronic media have been central to marketing's semiotic work, its strategic communication. The media has vastly enhanced the processes of exchange and is the most powerful and wide-ranging information infrastructure. Its institutions, policies and meaning-making practices are systematically and strategically geared to consumption. As Sut Jhally (1990) points out, commercial media play a twofold role in consumer culture. The media is used by producers to sell products to consumers and, equally, media audiences have become commodities sold by media organizations to producers – hence we have *a process of double exchange*; that is, the media acts as a two-way delivery system.

The cultural effects *of* advertising are wide ranging. It facilitates, mediates and arbitrates society and culture. Kline (1993: 30) argues that advertising 'forcefully communicates about the nature of social relations and ultimately asserts its place in shaping those relations'. It is through advertising and marketing that commodities acquire certain cultural meanings or 'sign value' and it is thus that advertising participates in the social construction of our needs.

Advertising, then, is the 'art of social and cultural influence'. It involves an appreciation of the *dual nature* of commodities as both objects and symbols. In other words, the utility role of goods and services in people's lives is acknowledged. But possibly more importantly, advertising involves understanding the social, cultural and psychological role of goods and services in the lives of consumers. Advertisers are interested in the role of objects *of* consumption in everyday life and lived experience. Drawing on the discussion of consumption in the previous section, let us consider this point further with regard to advertising.

Advertisers are expected to understand that for consumers, consumption performs a number of purposes above and beyond necessity. As we have indicated, it plays an important role in identity development, in group formation, in distinctions, differentiations and relationships. Advertisers are also expected to understand that relationships of power and status are refracted through practices and patterns of consumption. As Lee (1993: xi) observes, commodities and the meanings constructed around them through advertising are used to 'make visible personal affluence, to suggest sexual potency and physical attraction and, perhaps more than ever before, to function as the index of intelligence, education and social literacy'. Lee explains that 'the powerful and often overwhelming imagery and language of sexuality, power, guilt, envy and, above all, glamour [are] the key discursive fields' of advertising (p. 18). Advertising seeks to generate dreams and desires, fears and fantasies, repressions and displacements. Baudrillard (1988) calls this process whereby, through advertising and marketing, commodities acquire certain cultural meanings, 'sign value'.

Williams (1980) observes that advertising is a *social narrative*. It tells fictional tales about social identities and relationships, and implies that the purchase of goods will fulfil the story's promise. It inscribes goods with a 'narrative capacity' – the goods themselves are eventually seen to tell the story and thus to fulfil the fantasy. Advertisements, it seems, are not expected to fulfil their promises but rather to connect to their readers' fantasies about themselves and their futures. Drawing on Berger and Haug, Lee (1993: 19) argues that advertising is judged by the spectator/ viewer according to its relevance to fantasies or yearnings rather than its capacity to fulfil its promises or its connection to use and reality. 'Seduct- ive illusion' is what sells. Advertisements also have the potential to provoke *plaisir*, the pleasure which is derived from a recognition that 'the text' acknowledges a group's distinctive values and aspirations (Barthes 1975).

How then does postmodern advertising work? After all, it involves 'a plurality of reading positions based upon an unstructured combination of signifiers and a narrative form that does not invite ideological recogni- tion, identification or closure' (Lee 1993: 156). Lee goes on to argue that advertising invokes a different sort of pleasure from *plaisir* – that which Barthes calls *jouissance*. Lee explains that '*Jouissance* is produced by an intensity of experience that has less to do with an act of cultural recogni- tion and more with a quasi-erotic interaction with the text' (1993: 157). Connected with the pleasure of the body rather than of language, with physical sensation rather than semiosis, *jouissance* is invoked by 'A text where we can hear the grain of the throat, the patina of consonants, the voluptuousness of vowels, a whole carnal stereophony: the articulation of the body, of the tongue, not that of meaning, of language . . . [*Jouissance*] crackles, it caresses, it grates, it cuts, it comes: that is bliss' (Barthes 1975: 66–7). *Jouissance* depends on the reader consuming rather than interpreting the text – consumer hedonism. Again, no expectation of fulfilment with regard to the product is offered or, presumably, ex- pected. The advertisements are fulfilment enough.

Advertising, packaging and commercial product design have become a form of 'commodity aesthetics' and increasingly define their purpose in terms of fantasy, desire and sensation. Advertising's and marketing's role within consumer–media culture then, is to ensure that the desire to consume becomes a primary motivating force. Consumption is thus offered as 'the best way to achieve success, happiness and well-being' (Kline 1993: 11). Further, according to Lasch (1979), advertising seeks to evoke a restless narcissistic pursuit of pleasure, of self-indulgence – it promotes the id of society. Because women and children are the main consumers they are often also cast as the irresponsible id. We will de- velop this point further in the next chapter.

As these various perspectives imply, if the influences *on* and *of* advert- ising and consumption are considered together, then it is clear that com- mercial and corporate interests play a major role in shaping personal and social meaning and identity. However, as indicated, that is not all there is to it. Neither advertising nor consumption are just about manipulation, deception and irrationality. They also offer and invoke a certain creativity – a certain choice within constraint. Lee (1993: 49) explains:

> In essence, the culture of consumption is never simply a mere symbolic echo or the purely functional realisation of product positioning by advertising and marketing strategies. Similarly, the market is never a simple reflection of consumer tastes and needs... This suggests that consumers have clear limits placed upon the range of meanings and uses which they may assign to commodities by the fact that those commodities are already adapted, both functionally and symbolically, by advertising and their design to meet the imagined needs of an ideal market. Likewise, the design and symbolic contextualisation of commodities by producers and advertisers are structured by the lived meanings and uses of commodities as they have passed over into the status of cultural objects in everyday life.

Advertisers, then, produce and disseminate symbolic goods. They can be seen as cultural and psychic mediators teaching 'the art of living', the cultivation of lifestyle: 'helping' us to understand, appreciate and consume through the production of 'dream-scapes, collective fantasies and facades' (Zukin 1991: 291). These image and symbolism specialists are called 'cultural intermediaries' (Featherstone 1992) and include people in advertising and also those in media production, design, fashion, public relations and film, radio and music. Much planning and many creative and other resources are directed towards understanding and constructing the consumer's psyche. But ultimately, as Lee says, 'The function of commodity aesthetics is... to accelerate the rate of commodity exchanges and value turnovers' (1993: 20).

Conclusion

Throughout this chapter we have shown that consumer–media culture is continually changing in order to sustain itself and is becoming ever more complex in its composition and processes, and wide ranging in its compass. As we have also implied, one needs to draw on a range of foundational and more recent theoretical resources in order to properly comprehend this complexity. At the same time, it must be recognized that aspects of consumer culture have their own specificity. They have their own particular contexts, producers and real and intended consumers. They vary in their progress from conception to production, from mediation (advertising and promotion) to use and finally in the implications of such use for the duration of the cycle.

Throughout this book we will show that commodities and advertisements have long been used by both producers and consumers to construct the child and to articulate social relationships within families. They have also been used to construct and articulate relationships between adults and children, peers and peers, social institutions (such as schools) and families, the sexes, social classes and races. There may not be a perfect fit between production, representation and consumption, and unruly patterns do emerge and change. In the next chapter, we will consider the historical construction of the child/consumer and the role of the commodity and the media in this process.

2 Inventing the young consumer

In *Shopping with Mother* (1958) Susan and John, the young protag-
onists, experience the excitement of shopping. Leaving Tibby, the
cat, and Mike, the dog, at home, the children visit, under the careful
guidance of 'Mother', the grocer's shop for jam and sugar, the baker's
for cakes, the fish shop, the butcher, the green-grocer's and, finally,
the ironmonger to buy a hammer for Dad. After a couple of hours this
odyssey is brought to an end and Susan, John and Mother return
home to unpack the goods – an event which excites even the animals.

(Humphery 1998: 61)

Introduction

As the child learns to shop, it also learns to be a particular sort of child.
The child is a social construct. To the extent that they exist, histories
of childhood indicate that the 'nature' of childhood, the relationship of
children to each other and to adults, to the family, and to other social
institutions such as work and school, have changed across time and
place. In the so-called developed world, the last two centuries have seen
sweeping changes in conceptions of childhood and children's culture,
child-rearing practices, family life and adult/child relationships. The purpose of this chapter is to consider some distinctive features of evolving
and contemporary childhood and youth. We will make the case that any
adequate understanding of childhood and youth must recognize the
specific role played by consumer–media culture in broader social and
cultural change. Such an understanding provides the basis for a more
nuanced view of the construction of children's and youth cultures and
identities. Focusing on the work of historians with a particular interest

in childhood and consumption, the chapter explores the emergence of the child consumer and the construction of contemporary childhood. This provides the contextual scaffolding for what is to follow.

Poststructuralist historians have pointed particularly to the discursive construction of the child and the multiple discursive fields through which the child is invented (see Meredyth and Tyler 1993). Some have singled out for attention those relatively recent disciplinary discourses associated with the growth of the social sciences – developmental psychology, for instance. In so doing, they have pointed to these discourses' institutionalization in such primary agencies of socialization as schools, health care and legal systems, and in child-rearing practices in families. For instance, discourses associated with developmental psychology have promoted the notion that the movement from childhood through adolescence to adulthood is linear – a transition from irrationality to rationality, from simplicity to complexity (Valentine *et al.* 1998). Such notions inform the structuring of adult/child relationships within such institutions as the school and family. Conversely, schools have played a key role in defining childhood (see Ariès 1973; Hendrick 1997). However, as we will show, histories of the construction of childhood also indicate, first, how social scientific experts have changed their views about the nature of childhood and, second, how such experts' views have been deployed in the process of market expansion.

In order to assist us to develop an understanding of the history of contemporary childhood we will employ in particular two major texts, complemented by others. These are Stephen Kline's study *Out of the Garden: Toys, TV and Children's Culture in the Age of Marketing* (1993) and Ellen Seiter's *Sold Separately: Children and Parents in Consumer Culture* (1995). We have chosen them because of their location within debates in the fields of consumer and media studies. In very broad terms, both are interested in the ways in which meaning is conferred by advertising on media texts and other children's commodities. Together, these two books span the cultural effects *on* and the cultural effects *of* distinction with regard to advertising identified by Williams (1980) and outlined in Chapter 1. However, each employs a different theoretical framework. Kline's emphasis is on the production of meanings in the first instance, and so represents consumer culture as an implacable force which has shaped history, society and individual identities over the past two centuries. In contrast, Seiter focuses on the ways in which meanings are consumed and remade by their 'readers' (another view of production some may say). In a sense, therefore, these books can be seen to represent respectively the 'production of consumption' approach and the 'modes of consumption' approach outlined in Chapter 1.

Kline offers a historical account of the rise of the child's place in the framework of consumption – the evolution of markets for children and the emergence of the child consumer. He argues that consumption (shopping, toys, TV, music, clothing) is now a central part of the 'matrix of forces' that socialize young children. It is just as central to children's development as the family, school and community life. Indeed, he implies that consumption is now an integral, if not overarching, feature of all of them. Elsewhere Kline has written with others (Leiss *et al.* 2000) on the evolution of the bond between media and advertising. We will refer to the various stages in this evolution as we explore the construction of the child consumer.

Seiter's work brings additional feminist perspectives. She stresses the need to understand the rise of consumerism in 'the context of larger social changes – in domestic work, in mothers' labor force participation, and in patterns of child rearing' (1995: 4). It is her view that childhood and parenthood 'are expressed through and mediated by television, advertising, and consumer goods' (p. 6). She foregrounds the need for greater awareness of the ways in which 'television organizes, distorts, and expresses gender and race difference' (p. 6). However, in contrast to Kline, who argues that children's play culture has been largely defined by marketing strategies, Seiter stresses the agency of the child consumer. Thus, together they present quite a comprehensive picture of the young (see also Buckingham 1995).

We will begin by identifying some of the key historical trends in relation to consumer children, concentrating on the factors leading to the construction of young people as a discrete consumer group separate from adults. We will then discuss the segmentation of the child and youth market, focusing on age and gender segmentation. In the final section, we look briefly at the construction of the contemporary child consumer. We acknowledge that these trends have manifested themselves differently in different locations in the western world and that historians disagree on matters of specificity and interpretation.

It should be noted at this point that it is important not to fetishize children's commodities. Explaining what such fetishization means, Lee (1993: 15) draws attention to the 'grubby chrysalis of production' and to 'the mysterious economic dark side of social exploitation which is so effectively concealed in the dazzling glare of the market-place'. Without doubt, the consuming child of the West is the beneficiary of labouring children of such countries as Indonesia, China and Pakistan. The 'dark side' of such celebrated brand names as Nike, Disney and Mattel involves impoverished and highly exploitative sweatshop production conditions for young children in these countries. The distressing story run in *Life* magazine of 'Pakistani kids – looking shockingly young and paid as little as six cents an hour – hunched over soccer balls that bore the unmistakable Nike swoosh' (Klein 2000: 328) represents the tip of this child labourer iceberg. A more complete history of the child consumer than that which follows would show how the consuming children of the West consume the lives of children in the so-called 'Third World'.

◯ Historical inscriptions of the child consumer

The historical disagreement noted earlier is certainly evident in regard to Philippe Ariès's assertion that 'in medieval society the idea of childhood did not exist' (1973: 125). Ariès's *Centuries of Childhood* (1973) and texts following it (for example, de Mause 1974) inform Kline's historical scene setting just as is does Neil Postman's account in *The Disappearance of Childhood* (1994). According to this view, children were integral to the political economy of the medieval household and workplace in the western world. They had no separate sphere, identity or culture and shared work and leisure activities with adults. It was precisely this viewpoint – that children in the Middle Ages were regarded as 'shrunken adults' – that a 1995 exhibition at the Bibliothèque Nationale in Paris was designed to refute. According to Bel Geddes (1997), documentation presented included paediatric manuals and recently excavated toys. Ariès had based much of his theorization of childhood on the absence of such evidence as well as on the representation of children as small adults in medieval art (Gittens 1998).

Cunningham (1995a) draws attention to the controversy among scholars that Ariès's claim generated. Shulamith Shahar (1990) contends that medieval attitudes to children were in some ways more indulgent than those in later centuries. After all, it was hardly a step forward when, in 1719, a child was employed to work in a factory in England for the first time. However, Cunningham suggests that Ariès did not mean that children had the same 'status' or 'role' as adults or lacked any special considerations but, rather, that there were no boundaries separating child and adult worlds. 'The theme of his book', Cunningham explains, 'is the growth of a "*sentiment*" about childhood, and of a separation of the worlds of adulthood and childhood' (1995a: 31). Paradoxically, having played a critical role in both the growth of this 'sentiment' and the separation of child and adult spheres over the past two hundred years, consumer–media culture is now threatening the boundaries of separation. For this reason, then, our history of childhood concentrates on the nineteenth and twentieth centuries.

As Kline explains, by the nineteenth century children were increasingly excluded from the world of production and granted rights of protection. According to Cunningham, when the British Parliament passed the Factory Acts, 'it was effectively defining childhood as a period in which people needed protection by the law' (1995a: 140). In this regard, the State now took on the role which, in broad terms, had belonged first to the Church and later to philanthropic and charitable organizations (Cunningham 1995a). Child *protection* and *control* seemed to be the two guiding motifs, a push-pull dynamic which reflected the legacies of both the Rousseauian conception of childhood innocence which emerged in the eighteenth century and the competing Puritan emphasis on original sin. Thus, protecting the child from the demands and abuses of both family economics and the factory system was only one side of the coin. The other side involved offering him or her up to schools, although this was by no means complete in western countries until well into the twentieth century.

Kline (1993: 50) explains that although

> the school system was being built upon a less harsh vision of child-hood [and] schools were to be a special world within which children could learn at a more leisurely pace, free from the demands and pressures of both parents and industrialists . . . The Victorian state school and curriculum did not provide a children's paradise.

Like earlier Church and charity controlled programmes which, according to Fairchilds, allowed for 'a surveillance of [children's] moral condition' (1976: 83), nineteenth-century schools were driven by an alleged moral/civilizing social purpose. Ironically, however, they were run along industrial lines and promoted the values associated with the factory. They were characterized by regimentation, discipline and obedience, and involved functional, rote-learned literacy and numeracy and the assimilation and repetition of knowledge. It could be said that these schools were Fordist in style. As we will suggest in Chapter 5, markets in education are now drawing schools back towards this model.

By the time the nineteenth century drew to a close, children had become inscribed within the discourses of specialists. In effect, childhood was being constituted as separate and different from adulthood, and as having distinctive capacities and needs. The focus now shifted away from the idea of controlling the child – conceived of as a miniature and potentially recalcitrant adult – to the need for nurturance; the need to cater to the special needs of the naturally innocent and underdeveloped child. Kline suggests that children were regarded as 'symbols of hope' during a period of profound social change (1993: 53). Thus, the role of parents, teachers and schools came to be associated with nurturing the child to full development. A cohort of specialists arose to assist this process. Schools came to be seen as children's spaces catering to and stimulating their developmental needs. At the same time, child-specific organizations and activities developed in the form of such institutions as Sunday School, the Boy Scouts (founded in 1908) and the Girl Guides (founded in 1910). According to Kline (1993: 51), 'Play, it was argued, was not simple idleness but the "work of childhood" – the moral equivalent of labour', and this principle informed the expansion of these organized children's activities.

It was also towards the end of the nineteenth century that children became part of the emerging culture of consumption. Increasingly, consumer goods were becoming part of many dimensions of life and new means were sought to develop interest in consumption. Around this time the department store arose to offer a spectrum of consumer goods to cater for the family, including separate children's products (medicines and foods), and sections with distinctive children's shoes, clothes, furniture, school and club uniforms, books, toys and sports and musical equipment. Child education and health development themes were mobilized to sell such children's products. Childhood was now defined as a specific stage involving specific behavioural traits. Seiter (1995: 24) explains that as child experts advocated increased attention to child development, product designers moved in to assist mothers in their task of nurturing the health and well-being of the child.

At this stage children were not usually directly addressed by advertisers. The child was 'a symbol of consumer aspirations – a way of interesting a parent in a product, or of referring to children's growing expanding [*sic*] consumer needs' (Kline 1993: 163). Images of children were thus mobilized in the interests of sales. Childhood was associated with innocence and moral purity and such imagery came to dominate the advertising landscape. Images of children used in nineteenth-century advertising, such as the famous Pears' soap advertisement showing the Millais painting, 'Bubbles', were designed to promote the equation between moral purity and cleanliness (Kline 1993: 53; Gittens 1998: 131).

The 'therapeutic ethos' took up this theme, with Jackson Lears (1983: 23) noting the 'nostalgia for a pristine, natural state' in the following example: '"Mothers, do you not know that children crave natural food until you pervert their taste by the use of unnatural food?" a Shredded Wheat advertisement asked in 1903. Unnatural food develops unnatural and therefore wrong propensities and desires in children' (quoted in Kline 1993: 54).

However, by the early twentieth century, the marketing of soap and other hygiene products carried a further subtext. It reflected what Cunningham describes as the 'medicalization of infancy' that resulted from the international infant welfare movement. Infancy, he writes, was constituted as 'a medical problem in which mothers were the front-line defence against germs' (1995a: 153). Mass-produced products were promoted as providing the ammunition.

This reflects Seiter's point that 'Expert advice about child rearing exists in a complex relationship to marketing. The lines between advertising and advice are blurry' (1995: 24). She shows that the mode of address in a wealth of popular women's magazines and catalogues of the time was an 'advisory voice' shot through with self-help and self-improvement themes associated with matters of child health, education and care. These advertisements also reflect the preference for 'a persuasive informational approach' in advertising which Leiss *et al.* (2000: 249) suggest typified the first phase of advertising (1890 to 1925). They call this first stage 'the product-orientated approach' and link it with the commercialization of print media.

Although somewhat differently inflected according to country and class, these themes were replayed with greater intensity in the twentieth century, in spite of the interruptions of the wars and the 1930s depression. The trend towards the 'purchase and use of commodities in place of home-made goods' (Lury 1996: 125) intensified, with the family a targeted unit of consumption for standardized food, cars, houses, furniture and appliances. The mass production of Fordism depended on the creation of mass consumers and mass consumption. Here the development of consumer culture has also been 'identified with what has been called a domestic revolution in the making of the modern home, or what Game and Pringle [(1984: 120)] . . . call a "major shift from housework as production to housework as *consumption*"' (Lury 1996: 124).

The family and home were also targeted as a social dynamic involving different production and consumption patterns. Lury links the constitution of the home as a 'haven from a heartless world' with what she refers to as the '*emotionalization* and *aestheticization*' of housework (1996: 127). She explains that 'By the mid-twentieth century, housework had become not just a job, but an expression of love and warmth performed by each woman for her own family' (p. 127). Housework became 'aestheticized' in so far as the standards by which it was measured related not only to 'hygiene and efficiency, but also . . . [to] . . . style, harmony and "atmosphere"' (p. 127). In the process, the performance of housework and the allied acts of consumption which make a house a home were conflated with the performance of femininity.

At the same time, the intensification of women's work as consumption was extended to child-rearing. As Kline (1993: 58) says: 'In twentieth-century advertising the imagery of childhood became vital in the tapestry of the consuming family – as a motivation for adequate provisioning, as an indicator of family pride and virtue, and as an easily understood symbol of the long-term benefits of continued economic prosperity'.

Advertising continued its didactic role, prescribing correct child-rearing practices. The predominantly behaviourist approaches to child-rearing favoured in the 1920s gave way to developmentalism. Behaviourism recommended the training of children through reward and punishment – a scientific approach simultaneously reminiscent of 'Locke, with his insistence on habit formation, and Puritan belief in the importance of obedience' (Cunningham 1995a: 176). Developmentalism (its most influential proponent being the psychologist Jean Piaget) placed its stress on the naturally developing child (James and Prout 1997) and the need for imaginative play to promote cognitive development. Advertising now exhorted parents – mothers – to buy products promising to ensure their child's maximum development. Good mothering came to be equated with good shopping and good shopping was understood as rational.

Paradoxically, this view of shopping stands in stark contrast to the popular notion of the female shopper as irrational and impulsive. While *buying* was seen to be 'worthy', Lury says that *shopping*, which 'was seen as peculiarly feminine', was not (1996: 128). She traces the construction of the female shopper as 'irrational, fanciful and frivolous' with reference to a range of nineteenth- and twentieth-century literature including housework manuals, women's magazines and department store in-house journals. In doing so, she shows how, 'at the same time that consumer culture was imbued with conventional understandings of femininity and masculinity, it reinforced gendered relations in the family economy of the household' (p. 132).

As Humphery (1998: 95) indicates, notions of appropriate masculinity were also inscribed in the gender of shopping:

> Men were drawn into the terrain of consumption as well. But their source of identity was allowed to remain more anchored within themselves – through what they *did*, particularly in relation to paid work – rather than being dependent for its expression on bought objects and their display. Men too could be drawn into consumption as a process of abandonment and pleasure, such as in the purchase of a house, a car or a lawnmower. Yet even here the activity of consumption was closely linked to production and/or the rational notion of practicality, since the consumer object was a machine or structure that was functional and that could be 'maintained', not just admired, shown-off, cleaned and cared for.

Such assumptions about the gendered patterns of consumption resulted in the targeting of women shoppers, a strategy later 'justified by the fact that marketing experts in the post-war period estimated that women were responsible for up to 90 per cent of consumption decisions' (Humphery 1998: 95).

However, Merle Curti's (1967) account of the development of marketing thought on human nature suggests that the notion of the irrational shopper was more generalized and 'from about 1910 to 1930, "the dominant idea came to be that man (*sic*) is actually more irrational than rational"' (Leiss *et al.* 2000: 247). In their own delineation of the second phase of advertising (1925–45), Leiss *et al.* suggest that 'marketing thought' had begun 'to shift towards the non-rational or symbolic grounding of consumption based on the notion of appeals or motives, putting less emphasis on the product and its uses' (2000: 250). They link the transition from rational to irrational appeal, from a focus on product performance to the 'social motivations for consumption', with radio – in particular the advertising sponsorship of radio plays. The elements of dramatization – dialogue, character development and 'stars' – 'allow[ed] the advertiser to assimilate much more about the social context of consumption as the basis of advertising strategy' (p. 250).

The period beyond the Second World War saw major social changes which included the rise of the age of affluence and accumulation, and changing family forms and patterns of work. It is Kline's view that new patterns of advertising and consumption were carefully articulated to these changes. This was the period of new economic and personal freedoms after the constraints of the wars and the depression. It was less emotionally restrictive and less interested in thrift, delayed gratification, strict moral codes and parental discipline. It was a period of indulgence and the baby boomers were to become the indulged generation.

Discovery learning became attached to developmentalism. Play was appropriated as a pedagogical strategy in kindergartens and nursery schools since 'In play children appear to be less resistant to being taught because they are more intently engaged in the learning' (Kline 1993: 153). The publication of Benjamin Spock's *The Common Sense Book of Baby and Child Care* in 1946 (subsequently published as *Baby and Child Care* – Spock 1976) ushered in a more liberal approach to child-rearing. Children were offered new freedoms of creativity and peers, and new patterns of family interaction although, according to Sommerville (1982: 225), if 'they were to be freed from many of the demands parents formerly made, it was sometimes in order that they could meet their peers' demands instead'.

For children, these new directions included the opportunity to shop. As Humphery (1998) indicates, along with the rise of the supermarket in North America came *The First Book of Supermarkets* (Bendick 1954). This introduced children to the practicalities and pleasures of modern shopping complete with boy/girl couple images. Along similar lines in Australia came the Ladybird Learning to Read book called *Shopping with Mother* (Gagg 1958) mentioned in the opening extract of this chapter. Humphery explains that 'the young readers of *Shopping with Mother* were doing an awful lot more than learning to read. They were learning to consume, learning about what one could buy, about who usually did the buying, and about the pleasures of it all' (1998: 61). The child was inscribed in children's texts as a 'probationary consumer'.

The post-war period also saw the rise of *youth* as a distinct market segment. Hebdige (1988) claims that the teenager was invented in the relatively affluent period of the 1950s, with its stress on consumption, style and leisure. During this time and subsequently, childhood and youth came to be understood as fully separate categories to be expressed, in part, through separate modes of consumption. Lee (1993: 106) elaborates, pointing to the role of mass public education in inventing youthful identities:

> The opportunities made possible by the affluent society opened up fertile teenage markets . . . teenage fashions, recorded music, cars and motorcycles, new forms of meeting places and centres of consumption such as clubs, cinemas and milk bars, all provided a rich source of potentially subversive cultural resources. At another level, the massive expansion within public education provided for some sections of youth culture a powerful political and social literacy from which new insights into the economic and political system could be gleaned. The combination of a radical political consciousness and the easy availability of teenage consumer goods, ripe for use as symbolic markers of a new subcultural status, supplied for youth culture as a whole a powerful means by which they could establish a critical social distance from, and negation of, the values that were espoused by their parent culture – values such as work, sobriety and moderation . . . Youth can be seen here as . . . the children of Marx and Coca-Cola: at once extremely lucrative and immediate marketing opportunities, but also highly volatile in their values and beliefs.

Through a range of 'image clusters' (Hebdige 1988: 30), youth was constructed as a spectacle consisting of contradictory elements. It was understood as fun and trouble, compliant in peer terms but resistant in generational terms. In the latter sense, youth came to be associated with autonomy and rebellion and the idea of the generation gap within families and schools emerged.

By this time, 'Marketing strategy and advertising styles revolve[d] around the idea of a prototypical mass consumer accessible through television, the quintessential mass medium, and characterized by a limited set of traits (interest in convenience, fascination with technology and science, desire for glamour)' (Leiss *et al.* 2000: 251). Yet the period 1945–65 was also distinguished by the trend towards personalization, as advertisers sought to understand the 'ordinary consumer'. By the mid-1960s, however, the focus of targeted marketing had shifted, concentrating 'not on personality but on the activities of different subgroups of consumers . . . their consumption preferences and their lifestyle attitudes' (Leiss *et al.* 2000: 251). Linked with the rise of multimedia, the authors characterize the period 1965–85 as one of 'market segmentation'.

Market segmentation performs the role of functional differentiation for commercial products. A major focus of Kline's and Seiter's attention is the rise in recent decades of TV's market segmentation practices and the targeting of programming and associated advertising specifically at or to children. What marks these recent practices as different is the *direct address* from programmer and advertiser to the child, and an apparent commercial concern for children's right to enjoy autonomous leisure and pleasure. Whereas Leiss *et al.* (2000) date market segmentation from 1965, we can trace the development of after-school, Saturday morning and preschool TV audience segmentation patterns and the growth of advertisements directly addressing children about such things as food, toys, games and clothes from the 1950s onwards. These advertisements both run alongside, and nest within, such programming.

Adult/child market segmentation came about, Kline suggests, because marketers were dissatisfied with family viewing. Neither schools nor families were seen by the world of commerce to be adequate providers of consumer skills, knowledge and attitudes. Marketers wanted the market to have a more central place in the 'matrix of socialization' (Kline 1993: 13); indeed, the market wanted to talk directly to children. TV offered them a way. Along with Seiter, Kline (1993: 74) argues that with TV the 'undisputed leader in the production of children's culture', marketing is now a major force within the life of the child.

By the late 1970s new family forms and new approaches to child-rearing had emerged. Many women were moving into part- or full-time paid work. Divorce was common, as were blended and single parent families. Further, as Humphery indicates, 'By the late 1970s retailers began talking of the consumer driven by "time consciousness" rather than "price consciousness"' (1998: 148). Time itself became a scarce commodity as women's work intensified. This happened within the home as a function of changed standards of child-rearing resulting from the advice of child experts, increasing expectations of schools with regard to parental involvement, the increased work of consumption and women's involvement in the paid workforce (Seiter 1995).

During this period, child-rearing was increasingly the province of professional child carers or the TV set. Childhood and, importantly, youth were now understood as fully separate categories to be expressed, in part, through separate modes of consumption. Youth came to be associated with autonomy and rebellion and the idea of the generation gap within families and schools strengthened. Both the family and child-rearing came to be seen as problematic. While time for child-rearing was in short supply, anxiety about the decline of the family and the end of the idea of shared family values was not. This period eventually came to be characterized by a search for new forms of social integration.

In Kline's view, the commodity stepped into the vacuum. He argues that shared family values were replaced by shared things and that children and parents were encouraged to understand that all needs were best gratified through consumer goods. Hence, family life was further commodified. Kline attributes a particular role to TV which he says, as 'a pivotal technology for reorganizing many dimensions of the household' (1993: 72) became the centre of these new family forms and dynamics and the 'ultimate weapon of consumer socialization' (p. 68). TV and its associated cultural apparatuses reshaped parents' and children's preferences and consolidated the children's market.

Kline singles out for particular attention TV advertising and TV situation comedy, as they came together in the notion of family-orientated programming and domestic consumption. He shows how many of the family tension themes noted above were enacted and, indeed, mapped on the screen as the family came to be seen and played out as a site of 'chronic confusion and misunderstanding' (Kline 1993: 67). These tensions were articulated as possession and consumption, offering what Kline calls 'consumerist solutions to parenting problems'. Products could help to assuage such tensions; families could be unified through common brand loyalties. We will pursue this theme further in Chapter 3.

Seiter argues that as a result of market segmentation children and parents came to be 'sold separately'. She points to the selling of children's toys to parents on the basis of their educational and happiness value and to the complicity of the print and later the image media in this process. In contrast, and more recently, TV has sold toys to children on the basis of their 'badge appeal' to peers (Seiter 1995: 5). Indeed, child and youth markets have themselves become segmented. In the next section we consider the reasons for the segmentation of the child and youth markets and how they are segmented according to age and gender.

◯ Further fracturing children

Children's commercial culture appeals so much to children because it takes children's play, pleasure and desire seriously. Clearly it helps to construct their play, pleasure and desire, but it also seeks to understand and tap into them. At worst, it involves the cynical exploitation which Jacobson and Mazur (1995: 26) identify when they quote advertising agency president, Nancy Shalek:

> Advertising at its best is making people feel that without their product, you're a loser. Kids are very sensitive to that. If you tell them to buy something, they are resistant. But if you tell them they'll be a dork if they don't, you've got their attention. You open up emotional vulnerabilities and it's very easy to do with kids because they're the most emotionally vulnerable.

At best, children's commercial culture offers the insights into children's culture of an increasingly reflexive industry.

Hobson (1999) outlines three main strategies which advertisers believe act as triggers for child consumers. She calls the first 'enduring themes', which include: control (getting one over on adults, feeling intellectually superior, mastering skills); aspirational values (wanting to be older); social acceptance (friendship and peer group acceptance); possession (ownership, collecting, privacy, secrecy); and good versus evil (from Brothers Grimm to *Star Wars*). At the same time, children are responsive to innovation and change. The second and third strategies are contemporary relevance and the 'now' factor – the former an updated version of an existing product, the latter a product of its times. As an example of marketing which adapts to the times, Hobson describes the metamorphosis of the Sugar Puffs character from Cuddly Honey Monster to a rapping Sugar Puff Daddy. She makes the point that 'Throughout its evolution, the core values of approachability and being the child's (slightly older and therefore aspirational) friend have been retained while growing and developing in line with children's needs and motivations' (Hobson 1999). Products which capture the 'now' factor are usually novelty-based and likely to enjoy a shorter lifespan. Collectibles like Tazos, Tamagotchis and Pokémon, and associations with current film or television characters are typical of this phenomenon in advertising.

Segmenting by age

Yet, according to Hobson (1999), none of these strategies will make a difference if brands ignore the huge changes which occur during childhood and as kids move through their school life. Products and advertising which appeal to one age group will fail with another. Knowledge of the target audience is fundamental and advertisers have looked to market research for guidelines about what appeals to children, and for profiles of each age group when developing marketing strategies. How, then, do the advertising and marketing industries construct the child consumer?

Between the ages of 4 and 6, children are drawn to fantasy and gender-targeted design: 'They are less concerned with what a product is than how it looks' (Hobson 1999). Though they have little money of their own, their 'pester power' makes them an attractive market. Children aged between 7 and 9 years particularly enjoy collectibles and can be motivated by humour. They have developed reasoning and literacy skills, which means they are more likely to be persuaded by verbal information on packaging. Profiling 9- to 11-year-olds, the *Kids Marketing Report* found that children in this age range: 'like "funny"; they like "stars"; they like "catchy music"; they like sound effects, liveliness, they like "weird" and "gruesome" and they particularly enjoy ads with a twist at the end. Boys especially respond to "action"; girls are more likely to appreciate "mood"' (Steward 1998).

Gender differentiation becomes even more marked in the 10 to 12 year age group, with boys favouring sporting brands and girls fashion. This group is highly subject to peer pressure. These young people want to earn peer acceptance as well as to differentiate themselves from others. Brand clothing can act as a prop which marks their position in their peer culture, earns external approval and confers status. According to Duff (1999), by age 9 or 10, three-quarters of children shop alone or with friends. They have progressed from buying lollies, snacks and drinks to magazines and music. By 10 to 12 years they are expected to be more in control of their parents and have their own money to spend.

According to Hobson (1999) 12 years is the cut-off point of childhood in marketing analysis. However, before we can turn to the youth market proper, we need to consider what Handel (1999) calls the 'tween generation': 12- to 14-year-olds. Whereas brand functions as the currency which buys peer acceptance in the previous age group, brands are now valued for their iconic associations – sporting heroes, supermodels, actors and pop culture idols – and the identities which can be constructed as a result. 'Cool' is an object of desire which can be bought. 'Link marketing' is the advertising strategy.

Identity is also a big issue for this age group. Not only are they becoming increasingly interested in the opposite sex, they have become focused on creating their own sexual identity. They are also seeking to construct identities which distinguish them from their parents and mark their independence from the family. Between 12 and 14 is the age range when parents 'just don't understand', and the age when kids 'want to know what is taboo' but are only just starting to test boundaries (Handel 1999). This age group has high aspirational values. They are eager to 'trade-up' age-wise but are also territorial: 'successful products are designed with them as the sole target' rather than seeking to simultaneously engage the adult consumer (*Kidscreen* 2000). Their product repertoire includes computer games, clothes, fast food, music, drinks, snacks, magazines and personal care items. They have a greater say in large family purchases like computers, cars and holidays. Handel (1999) notes that the 12 to 14 age group is particularly open to sponsorship and 'cause-related' marketing because of 'their curiosity and morality'.

We see many of the characteristics of the 'tween' market in the youth market. The icon remains, but with a difference. Webb (1999) makes this point when he cites the Tango advertisement which went against the trend of creating icons using celebrities to sell its product and, instead, used Ray Gardner, 'a fat bloke with attitude'. 'This is youth marketing at its best', writes Webb, because 'it gives them something to talk about, becomes part of their language and best of all, it informs their culture'. Aspiration is less important now: if youth want icons, they must be icons whose endorsement they can trust, who will 'filter the dross'.

Youth media brands act as style leaders but 'the most successful brands hold up a mirror to the teen audience and above all, act as a non-judgmental friend' (Webb 1999).

Segmenting by gender

As the focus on gender in these brief accounts of age groups suggests, segmentation occurs vertically as well as horizontally. Interestingly (as will become apparent in the discussion on gender to follow), interpretations of the implications of gendered commodities vary. Yet, as Seiter points out, advertisers and programmers have traditionally privileged boy viewers and boy characters. This is because 'the conventional wisdom has it that boys will not watch girls on television but that girls will watch programs for boys' (Seiter 1995: 145). A 1996 *Kidscreen* special report surveying children's TV production and distribution houses suggests that this belief still has currency. As Brian Lacey of 4 Kids Productions put it: 'Why produce just a girls' show? By doing that, you reduce your audience by half' (*Kidscreen* 1996). Michael Hirsch, chairman of Nelvana Limited, which produces animated series including *Care Bears*, *Babar*, *Rupert* and *Little Bear*, explains that with more products targeting boys, the boy demographic is worth more to broadcasters in advertising dollars. More recently, however, the economic clout of the girl audience was driven home by the box office success of the film *Titanic* (1997), the grosses of which were demonstrably influenced by the attendance and reattendance of pre-teen and teenage girls (Robertson 1998a).

Young girls were first recognized as a market segment worth specific targeting by the electronic media in the 1980s. Although girls make up more than half of the children's TV viewing demographic, they were reconceptualized as a 'niche' market, differentiated according to the conventional wisdom about gender difference. While boys' programming focused on action, things and conflict, girls' programming privileged relationships, beauty and harmony. As Seiter (1995) says, girls and boys came to be 'sold separately'. At this time, the market for girls' toys was seen to have much untapped potential. Market research led to the production of licensed toy characters around which toy-based video series for girls were developed. These did not require girls to cross over and identify with males, as was the dominant tendency. By centring on female characters and on the concerns and play of little girls, these programmes offered an attractive fantasy space. Carol Monr'e of Hearst Animation Productions suggests, however, that programmes like *Rainbow Bright* and *My Little Pony*, which were 'thought of as girls' shows were simply very young shows . . . that little boys also watched' (*Kidscreen* 1996). Nevertheless, Seiter observes that in targeting the young female consumer as a separate audience and in doing so in a girl-friendly manner, dominant conventions of children's stories of the twentieth century were challenged. Similar arguments are put by Richards (1995) and McDonnell (1994) who both also stress the importance of fantasy in psychic development.

However, Seiter goes on to say that 'Something was gained and lost when marketers and video producers began exploiting little girls as a separate market' (1995: 157–8). On the one hand, their culture was ghettoized by boys and despised by many adults (particularly male cultural theorists). On the other hand, it freed girls from the ambiguity and psyche-splitting involved in identification with the male characters of the dominant available forms. It offered them, instead, a utopian 'playful world of love and friendship' and 'magical physical abilities' (Seiter 1995: 170) – not a bad choice in the commercial culture of femininity, according to Seiter. We now see similar patterns of gender segmentation emerging in the interactive games industry.

The 1980s and 1990s saw the development of video games, first in arcades, then in homes. This period also saw a rapid growth in TV advertising about computer games, and magazine and shopping mall outlet sales of such games. Computer games came to be seen as the children's medium of the 1990s and, as they became domesticated, access to them extended down to younger children and from mainly boys to include girls. However, even in 1999 the interactive industry's courtship of girl gamers remained 'sluggish', with one media analyst observing that 'Still pretty in pink, girl-specific interactive games aren't branching out much beyond the feminine stereotypes of the kinds of activities girls like – namely, creativity, communication and, of course, fashion' (Barker 1999).

Alloway and Gilbert (1998) argue that video games aimed predominately at boys are also highly gendered. They suggest that while different individuals respond differently to cultural texts, 'the draw and power of hegemonic discourses of masculinity must be compelling' (p. 98) for many boys and young men. Unfortunately, many video game 'texts align masculinity with power, with aggression, with victory and winning, with superiority and strength – and, of course, violent action. They offer positions for young male game players that promise success as masculine subjects' (Alloway and Gilbert 1998: 97). Conversely, because women and subordinate males are positioned as other, gaming texts are often implicitly or explicitly misogynist and homophobic.

The strongly gendered nature of computer games has other consequences. It has been argued that interactive entertainment is reconfiguring the relationship between gender and space. As much of the literature on girls' and youth culture has shown, the home is the traditional site for young females' leisure activities. But, as a function of computers, computer games and the Internet, young males are spending more time indoors. This is leading to struggles between girls and boys over access to ICTs in the home and also to new gendered geographies in cyberspace. McNamee (1998: 197) says that research shows that girls like to play computer games just as much as boys. Given this, the fact that they do so with less frequency may be due to the fact that 'for some girls, their access to computers and video games is controlled by their brothers'. McNamee argues that boys and 'Young men are controlling and policing their sisters' access to computer and video games in the expression of their masculine identity' and, as a consequence, 'girls' use of domestic space as resistance to boys' domination of the streets . . . is now being eroded' (p. 204).

Such moves suggest that the relationship between domestic spaces, gender and leisure is being detraditionalized – and retraditionalized – by young people. It is interesting to note that this relationship between space, gender and consumption is changing in other places too, and not just for children. Earlier, we noted that shopping spaces had come to be identified as primarily female. Humphery (1998: 148) points out that:

> Cultural historians in both Britain and Australia have suggested, however, that by the 1980s men were being purposefully drawn in to the terrain of consumption, and that shopping spaces such as the mall and department store were becoming more sexually ambiguous in line with a postmodern emphasis on diversity and the fragmentation of sexual and social boundaries. As Gail Reekie has argued, within some areas of leisure retailing during the 1980s space and gender were becoming uncoupled.

Meyrowitz works from a similar premise in *No Sense of Place* (1985) where he attributes this 'uncoupling' to the electronic media. He argues that not only has it destabilized traditional gender identities and led to a merging of the masculine and feminine but, as we will argue in the following chapter, it has also destabilized and merged generational identities and relationships.

Meyrowitz suggests that the advent of electronic media, in particular TV, disrupted the construction of gender identities traditionally held in place by the domestic/public split and by distinct gender information systems. TV undermined the segregation of masculine and feminine spheres which supported traditional versions of femininity. This created 'a sharp discrepancy between the traditional image women were offered of their "special sphere" in women's magazines and the wider view of world events offered to them by television' (1985: 211). He suggests that the first generation of child TV viewers grew up to be first-wave feminists.

Of course Meyrowitz's claims are controversial. In contrast, it is often argued that television and advertising continue to be profoundly sexist and have negative consequences for females. Some claim that 'pronounced

stereotyping of the sexes may cultivate distorted views about the character of, and appropriate social and professional, roles for women' (Furnham
et al. 1997: 91). Female characters are offered a narrower range of roles
on TV programmes. Images persist of 'women as dependent, unintelligent
consumers who were concerned with the social consequences of purchasing a product, while men tended to be portrayed as independent,
intelligent, objective decision makers who demonstrated expertise and
authority' (Furnham *et al.* 1997: 92). Male characters predominate in
advertising directed at children and 'gender-typing' also 'occur[s] at a
structural level with male-oriented advertisements containing more cuts,
loud music and boisterous activity, whereas female-oriented advertisements con[tain] more fades and dissolves, soft music and quiet play'
(Furnham *et al.* 1997: 92–3). Giroux (1997, 1999a) has written extens-
ively on the gender stereotyping in Disney movies, as have contributors
to *From Mouse to Mermaid* (Bell *et al.* 1995). How does Meyrowitz recon-
cile such claims with his argument?

He concedes that TV content may reinforce old stereotypes but argues
that the fact that 'both girls and boys are exposed to male and female
role models may weaken the traditional distinctions in socialization patterns' in the long term (Meyrowitz 1985: 214). He says that children
tend to imitate behaviours they perceive to be successful and if 'television tends to reward men more often than women, it is quite possible
that girls begin to imitate the male behavior rewarded on television'
(p. 214). Ironically, the strong male content in TV and advertising trans-
mits information to girls that may have once been offered only to boys,
demystifying male power. If this argument holds, a return to the 'pretty
in pink' stereotyping which typifies entertainment and products targeting
the girl market segment, and gender segregation such as Fox Family
Worldwide's 1999 launch of the gender-specific The Boyz Channel and
The Girlz Channel (Robertson 1998b) and supporting websites, may not
necessarily be desirable.

Meyrowitz claims that TV has led to an 'androgynous' style of behaviour and, theoretically, liberated both genders from old 'sex roles'. However, the impact on girls and boys may not be equal, and given that
certain cohorts of boys are now falling behind girls in their school performance (Collins *et al.* 2000) this has implications for educators. If TV
offers girls a repertoire of behaviours upon which to model their identity, does it offer boys a comparable choice? At the same time as TV has
made it more difficult for men and boys to play traditional male roles,
the negative representation of girls and women continues to discourage
boys from emulating female role models. Boys who exhibit cross-gender
behaviours and characteristics are more likely to be punished by other
children than girls are likely to be (Browne 1998). Indeed, even though
more action-orientated programmes with strong female lead characters

like *The Secret World of Alex Mack* and *Bug Juice* are appearing, 'girl power' is denigrated and girls continue to be represented as the 'dupes' of culture industries (see Driscoll 1999).

Certainly, the commercial culture of femininity continues to address itself particularly to the adornment and display of the female body. As the following remarks indicate, even very young girls are not exempt:

> Marketers increasingly target the lucrative teen and preadolescent market with ads for beauty products. And they are having an effect: Female teens spend an average of $506 per year on cosmetics and beauty salon visits. Most wear make-up by the time they are thirteen, and 26 percent wear perfume every day. Ever-younger girls are being fitted for miniature Iron Maidens: Christian Dior makes bras and panties with lace and ruffles for *preschoolers*. One toymaker produces a Little Miss Makeup doll, which looks like a five- or six-year-old girl. When water is applied, the doll sprouts eyebrows, colored eyelids, fingernails, tinted lips, and a heart-shaped beauty mark.
>
> (Jacobson and Mazur 1995: 79)

The question here, however, is what are the implications of such gender scripts? Different feminists offer different interpretations. While some adopt the view that long-standing sexist inscriptions have matching consequences, others point to the increasing liquidity and multiplicity of the gender positions offered in consumer–media culture and to the 'guileful ruses' people adopt to circumvent the gender strategies of consumer–media culture. Greer fits into the former camp.

According to Greer (1999: 23), 'Magazines financed by the beauty industry teach little girls that they need make-up and they train them to use it, so establishing lifelong reliance on beauty products'. Barbie's 'non-functional' body sends little girls the message that 'The further from the natural a female form, the more attractive it becomes. The further from the natural a female form, the more feminine it becomes' (Greer 1999: 25). As Greer goes on to suggest, given her physical proportions, 'Barbie is unlikely to have been very effective in her career roles as astronaut, vet or stewardess'; she is 'women's liberation in effigy' (1999: 24).

Additionally, commercial culture is increasingly targeting men and boys in relation to bodily adornment. Manufacturers of sport-, surf- and streetwear invite boys to adopt their own specialized look. As Lury (1996: 149) notes, 'masculine and feminine modes of playing with self-identity [are] further complicated by the ways in which, so it is argued, masculinity is increasingly being represented as a sign in contemporary art and popular culture in the same way that femininity has been historically'.

Theorizations of this trend, like Evans and Thornton's (1989) discussion of the representation of gender in postmodernity, lead Lury to suggest that 'femininity has been replaced by, or made interchangeable with, masculinity in recent representations of subcultural style and *haute couture*' (1996: 149). Boys are exploring the previously 'feminine' terrain of 'narcissism' and 'masquerade'.

Masquerade originally referred to femininity as a simulation of gender identity. Butler (1990: 47) says that in Lacan's ambiguous usage it refers to either 'the performative function of a sexual ontology' or 'a denial of a female desire that presupposes some prior ontological femininity regularly unrepresented by the phallic economy'. Recently, masquerade has come to be seen as a strategy of empowerment. Thus, rather than passively emulating the versions of femininity promoted in consumer–media culture, women 'have developed ways of seeing femininity as a *masquerade*, a performance, in ways which enable them to play with their personal identity, and take pleasure in the adoption of roles and masks' (Lury 1996: 144).

The notion of 'masquerade' and its relationship to the masculine gaze have been elaborated in several ways and can be linked to the theorization of consumption practices as a form of narcissism. For example, Radner has argued that while 'the "New Femininity" created through product usage appears to construct a femininity that exists solely to confirm the projection of the masculine gaze, it also "offers women a libidinal return on their investment that is in excess of the pleasure they may or may not receive as the object of the male gaze"' (1995: 63, quoted in Lury 1996: 148).

Grant (1997) applies a Kristevan theorization of narcissism and abjection to fashion, suggesting they offer an alternative to the 'fallacy of internalism' which implies that 'in consuming the products of the culture industry individuals are expressing their adherence to the social order'. Grant argues that the fallacy of internalism makes no allowance for 'partial identifications' nor considers 'what (innocent) pleasures might be at stake' in consumption. By contrast, through the interplay between incorporation and abjection, conformity and transgression, the individual is a ' "subject-in-process" . . . capable of creative self-articulation'.

In his discussion of postmodern marketing, Brown (1995: 138) implies that all postmodern identities are similarly 'fluid' and 'easily changed through the acquisition of new repertoires of products', though not necessarily with the same degree of agency as Grant assumes. He links this aspect of identity construction with current marketing practice and advertising imagery which, he says, reflect the postmodern preoccupation with hyperreality, pastiche, liminality, carnivalesque, heterogeneity, spectacle, ambiguity, nostalgia, hybridity and fragmentation (p. 156). As products are increasingly separated from their consumer context (including gender specificity) and the market broken down into smaller and smaller segments (implying a plurality of masculinities and femininities), gender representation, and thus gendered market segmentation, are problematized.

While the long-term impact on children of these changes in the representation of gender identities remains to be seen, the construction of the current generation of children and youth reflects some other aspects of the postmodern consumer culture that Brown describes. In the final section of this chapter, we look at the construction of children, childhood and youth in postmodernity and, in the process, we both employ the concept 'generation' and problematize some of the current ways it is used.

◯ The postmodern youthful consumer

Since at least the 1970s, the social sciences have addressed issues of generation. Across time, understandings of the concept 'generation' have varied, as have the debates within which it has been immersed. Within much current analysis a 'generation' is often defined as 'a group of individuals who were born at about the same time, or in the same era, and who have been subject to common social, cultural and economic influences' (Mackay 1997: 3).

Viewed in this way, generations can be seen to represent different cultural phases in the development of particular societies. It is notable that the concept seems to come into prominence in inquiry during periods of dramatic social and cultural change – particularly technocultural change. It seems that at such times the understandings, practices and mores of one generation are not easily applied to or accepted by the upcoming generation and vice versa. Hence, intergenerational relations, dynamics and differences, tensions and uncertainties are often stressed in analysis just as they are in this chapter and those to follow. It is also unfortunately the case that an emphasis on generations may blur differences within them. In picking up on issues of difference we will seek to avoid this problem.

Contemporary postmodern, post-Fordist times and their associated social and cultural features, which we outlined in Chapter 1, have generated both considerable debate about generations and numerous labels for contemporary young people, as Buckingham's (2000) analysis of such debates indicates. Many such labels are associated with innovations in the media or the consumer form. It is thus that today's children and youth have variously been called the Supermarket Generation, the Screen Generation, the Computer Generation (Papert 1993); the Nintendo Generation, Techno-kids and Cyberkids (Sefton-Green 1998). However, other labels such as the Lost Generation (Green *et al.* 1998), Generation X (Coupland 1994) and Generation Y (O'Leary 1998) move beyond such technological reductionism by pointing to wider sources of identity. For example, witness the following titles with regard to Generation X: *Sex in the Time of Generation X* (Morrissey 1996), *Gen X TV: The Brady Bunch to Melrose Place* (Owen 1997) and *Generation X Goes to College: An Eye-Opening Account of Teaching in Postmodern America* (Sacks 1996). But the labels employed also point to some definitional doubt about this sociocultural grouping. They reflect the elusiveness of postmoderity itself.

The questions we will now pursue are these: in generational terms who are today's young people?; what social and cultural forces have impacted on their ways of being?; and how do they differ from their teachers' and parents' generations? In Chapter 3 we will pursue the following question. 'What do these intergenerational differences mean for the intergenerational relations and dynamics pertinent to teachers and parents?'

The latest in this history of labelled generations is what is called the Y Generation, born between 1980 and 1995. They are also known as the Echo Boomers. They are almost as big a demographic (26 per cent of the US population) as the post Second World War baby boom generation which comprised 29 per cent of the population. They are far more numerous than the intervening Generation X (1966–79) which comprises only 16 per cent of the population (*The Dallas Morning News* 1998). A focus for much analysis of the Y Generation is their spending potential and their technological access – in other words, their identities as consumers and particularly as consumers of technology. Discussion barely goes beyond these two features and thus has limitations which we will seek not to repeat.

The Y Generation is said to have more money to spend than Generation X. In 1998, the teenage market, for example, spent almost twice as much as a decade ago (*Maclean's* 1999). As the number of children per household decrease, they are becoming the beneficiaries of the even greater spending of often guilt-ridden and stressed working parents. The Y Generation is regarded as being 'highly consumption oriented and sophisticated in terms of their tastes, aspirations and shopping skills' (Schneiderman 2000). Further, they have more influence over household spending, particularly in regard to technological products (Schneiderman 2000).

For its sheer ubiquity, TV remains the dominant ICT involved in identity construction. As Kellner (1997: 86) puts it: 'This generation was conceived in the sights and sounds of media culture, was weaned on it, and socialized by the glass teat of television used as a pacifier, baby-sitter, and educator by a generation of parents for whom media culture, especially television, was a natural part of everyday life'. However, we might also say that computer and interactive game technology is rapidly becoming the preferred media form of the current generation. The US

1998 Roper Youth Report found that 69 per cent of children aged 6–17 had used a computer in the past month, whether at home or school (Nucifora 2000). In Canada in 1999, that figure was 76 per cent (*Maclean's* 1999). All of these trends are likely to intensify as we enter the age of digital convergence and datacasting.

O'Leary (1998: 49) defines, somewhat hyperbolically, the Y Generation according to their media resources and *savoir faire*. She says that, unlike their parents who

> grew up in the confines of cookie-cutter suburbia, these kids are developing their interests in a world of exploding technological opportunity, learning through computers, video and a bursting array of cable options. This sophisticated, mouse-wielding, joystick-operating group grew up with advanced eye-hand coordination and a low threshold for boredom. Within five years, they are expected to produce term papers with full-motion video. All the conventions that shaped a more traditional past are being left behind as these early adopters rush into ever-changing technology.

Marketers seeking to target this generation are already recognizing the imperative of reaching them through the new media forms. Equally though, as the following quotation indicates, they are being seen as an increasingly diverse and individualized grouping. Nucifora (2000) predicts that:

> Because they spend so much of their time attached to their computers, online marketing and the Web will be dominant strategies for developing a marketing relationship with the Ys. This is also a generation with heretofore unheard of access to consumer information. Couple that with expanded choice and what results is greater individuality and self-expression in how they select and interact with their brands and provide feedback. To that point, communicating through e-mail is essential to this group.

New ICTs and postmodern market forms are certainly changing the contexts in which today's children and youth are growing up and, thus, their consumption practices. O'Leary (1998: 49) suggests that 'There are no rules for this group . . . With all the media stimulus, things like the Internet, there's no one authority for them. Every voice has equal power and you see more fusions and hybrids' of brands, products and marketing strategy.

While one might disagree with O'Leary's claims about equally powerful voices, it would seem that market segmentation is now giving way to market fragmentation. The fragmentation of markets into yet smaller segments is predicated on the expanding range of communication channels and advertising media which, in turn, reinforces fragmentation and diversification. Demographics are no longer a reliable index of consumer interests. Niche markets are becoming the norm. At the same time, Internet technology has also intensified the homogenizing force of corporate culture which now has increasing access to consumer tastes and is thus increasingly able to target consumers in highly individualized and localized ways. This suggests that the evolution of advertising in postmodernity has entered a phase beyond those charted by Leiss *et al.* (2000). But more importantly for our purposes here, this has implications for the ongoing construction of young people.

Marketers link fragmentation to what has become known as the 'new tribalism'. 'In the 1970s and 1980s' argues the journal, *Maclean's* (1999), 'adolescents in Canada could pretty much be divided into jocks, rockers and preps'. In contrast, Sean Saraq of the Canadian Environics Research Group asserts that today 'there are at least a dozen "tribes" defined by their fashion, music and magazines' (*Maclean's* 1999).

If one were to limit an understanding of Generation Y to their consumption of such commodities, then of Canada, the USA and Australia it might be observed that permutations of Generation Y include ravers, rappers, hard-core skaters, goths, hip hop, new Jack gypsy, iconics, twenty-first century soul, rockabilly and nerds. However, as we have indicated throughout this and the previous chapter, products alone do not make identity; gender, race, class and location are major factors in the manner in which consumer products are taken up, reinvented and used as sources of identity, empowerment and subversion.

A compelling example of this process is offered in the recent novel *White Teeth* by Zadie Smith (2000) as she tells a story of the syncretic racial dynamics of inner city London. Here she addresses the creolizing cultures of young people and mentions: 'Becks, B-boys, Indie kids, wide-boys, ravers, rude-boys, Acidheads, Sharons, Tracys, Kevs, Nation Brothers, Raggers and Packis' (p. 200). She describes another group, the Raggastanni, explaining how popular youth culture, ethnicity and masculinity came together for this group (which she says is a 'cultural mongrel of the last three categories') as follows:

> Raggastannis spoke a strange mix of Jamaican patois, Bengali, Gujarati and English. Their ethos . . . was equally a hybrid thing. Allah *featured* but more as a collective big brother than a supreme being, a hard as fuck *geezer* who would fight in their corner if necessary; Kung Fu and the words of Bruce Lee were also central to the philosophy; added to this was a smattering of Black Power (as embodied by the album *Fear of Black Planet*, Public Enemy), but mainly their mission was to put the Invincible back into Indian, the Bad-aaaass back into Bengali, the P-Funk back into Pakistani . . . Naturally there was a uniform. They each dripped gold and wore

bandanas, either wrapped around their forehead or tied at the joint of an arm or leg. The trousers were enormous, swamping things, the left leg always inexplicably rolled up to the knee; the trainers were equally spectacular, with tongues so tall they obscured the entire ankle; baseball caps were compulsory, low slung and irremovable and everything, everything, everything was *Nike*™, wherever the five of them went the impression they left behind was of one gigantic *swoosh*, one huge mark of corporate approval.

(Smith 2000: 200–1)

Predictably, this story of youthful hyperreality and cultural trading and raiding resonates with many others, indicating that this generation defies ready generalization.

The Y Generation has emerged in the context of rapid sociocultural change. It is our view that, in this sense, the Y Generation shares certain qualities with those whom Mackay (1997) calls the 'Options Generation' – born in the 1970s and beyond. Indeed, the indications are that many of the characteristics of the Options Generation are intensified in the Y Generation. We will pursue this point, because Mackay's analysis includes, but moves beyond, matters of consumption and technology and focuses on the implications for the identity of change itself.

Mackay says that although, as in the case of all generations, members of the Options Generation simply respond to the world as they find it, their 'kaleidoscope keeps moving and the patterns are not set for long' (1997: 141). They are not anxious about rapid change or social destabilization: 'constant change is in the air they breathe; the water they swim in' (p. 138). With no alternative but to accommodate change, this generation is patient and fluid. Its members keep their options open, remaining noncommittal for as long as possible and adopting short-term goals and temporary solutions when they are ready. They do not expect stability and predictability. Neither do they fear change. Overall, this generation is highly adapted to change. Its members take 'pride in their individuality, their flexibility, their openness to possibility. They resist the idea of conformity and they hate generalisations being made about them' (Mackay 1997: 171). Thus, it is a generation that 'is *proud* of [its] ability to live in a fluid and hybrid culture' (p. 174). And, given such hybridity and fluidity, this generation's responses are diverse, highly idiosyncratic and individualized.

However, there are some paradoxes at the heart of this generation. While its members stress their independence and flexibility, they are actually dependent on parents, education and welfare, probably more so than earlier generations. Clearly, the family is being reconstituted yet again. Employment is the key to independence but for many it is not readily gained. Thus, identity is gained in other ways, partly, as Mackay

says, through an emphasis on style and image. Any appearance of conformity belies an inner sense of individuality. Searching for a satisfying
code to live by, and code-tasting and testing, are features of the lives of
this generation Y – sometimes a dangerous feature.

But what of the parents of the Options and the Y Generations? We
need to understand something of them in order to comprehend the
intergenerational dynamics to be discussed in the next chapter. Mackay
calls people born between the late 1940s and early 1960s baby boomers
or the Stress Generation. Their worldview, he says, has been shaped by
the continuities and contradictions of the 1950s, 1960s, and 1970s, and
by the dramatic economic downturn and other changes of the 1980s
and 1990s. Mackay says that during their earlier years, the world was
'full of the promise of an endless prosperity' but that in their middle
years they have been faced with 'turbulence and hardship' (1997: 59). In
their early years they experienced the benefits and opportunities afforded
by a long period of economic growth and prosperity. This produced in
them a sense that growth would be unending and prosperity inevitable.
They believed in what Mackay (p. 71) calls 'the over-promise' of the
1960s.

At the same time, they experienced the uncertainty and anxiety associated with the real and imagined dangers of the cold war, the growth of
the nuclear capacities of the two main ideologically opposed power blocs,
and the threat of nuclear war. Together, economic prosperity and the
nuclear threat produced in them a rather contradictory consciousness
associated with the alternative possibilities of a 'rosy, easy future' and
'no future at all' (Mackay 1997: 62). This translated into nihilism and
hedonism; into materialism and the demand for immediate gratification.

It is widely acknowledged that this is the generation for which youth
culture industries and, indeed, mass public education arose and in
relation to which the concept of the 'generation gap' was invented. A
tendency of the baby boomers in their youth was to discard their parents' values 'in favour of hedonism, materialism, consumerism' (Mackay
1997: 113) and to be suspicious of the very orthodoxies and authorities
associated with the abundant social order which made their way of life
possible. Their modes of detraditionalization led to the sexual revolution, changed attitudes to marriage, divorce and the family, and to such
social movements as multiculturalism, feminism, environmentalism and
republicanism.

In their adulthood in the 1970s and early 1980s, the baby boomers
were able to effect some political regulations and moral codes associated
with such movements – since labelled 'political correctness'. In their lifetime there has been a major political move against 'political correctness',
away from the welfare state and towards the values of neo-liberalism
and the corporatized state. In addition, in their later adulthood the Stress

Generation has had to deal with the technological innovations, economic turmoil and uncertainties of globalization, and the associated
restructuring of work and much institutional life. This has meant that
the parents of the Y Generation have had to adjust to uncertainty,
disappointment and stress.

This reading of the baby boomers points not only to intergenerational
differences but also to some considerable potential for intergenerational
tensions and contradictions, which we will explore in the chapter to
follow.

Conclusion

As we have seen, conceptions of the child and childhood, child welfare
and family life in the West have been successively mediated by the
Church, philanthropists, the State and, most recently, consumer–media
culture in its various modalities. We have pointed to the connections
between changing family forms and gender and age relations, and to the
ways in which they have been connected to the commodity form. Or, to
put it more bluntly, and in Kline's words, the ways in which constitut-
ing and reconstituting the family has proved to be a way of 'opening and
maintaining the communicational passageways between the marketplace
and the consumer' (1993: 72). As we have shown, the child as a social
construct and generations of young people have changed along with
changes in consumer–media culture.

Over the course of this evolution, the duration of childhood has been
extended and children and youth segregated from adult life. With the
aid of advertising and new media forms, the market has increasingly
separated children from adults and one another – offering them identities based along a consumption grid. Childhood has been represented as
a time both of innocence and of diminished moral and intellectual agency.
Both of these views still have currency, along with the notion of youth
as threatening (see Giroux 1999b). The title of Kline's *Out of the Garden*
(1993) is a metaphor for a loss of innocence (and secondarily, a reference to the sedentary lives of the children of the television generation),
which he attributes to consumer–media culture. Neil Postman's negative
stance on the impact of media culture in *The Disappearance of Childhood*
(1994) reflects the second viewpoint. As Cunningham suggests, Postman's 'vision of a good childhood is not one in which the essence is
freedom and happiness; rather it is good behaviour, a deference to adults,
and a commitment to learning skills essential for the adult world' (1995a:
180).

The implication is that children have been 'transported back into
that world which Ariès had imagined for the middle ages in which the

boundaries between adulthood and childhood were fluid or non-existent' (Cunningham 1995a: 179). We will explore these themes further in our exploration of adult/child relationships in the following chapter, and look more closely at the relationship between consumer forms and consumer markets, focusing on the increasing convergence of education, advertising and entertainment. In doing so, we will examine the implications of this convergence for young people, adults and cross-generational relationships. We will make the case that these intergenerational relations pose some serious dilemmas for teachers in current school settings. These need to be understood and addressed if we are to properly connect to the young people of today and tomorrow.

3 Polarizing pleasures: the allure of the grotesque

◯ Introduction

Market segmentation and niche marketing proceed apace. At the same time, a number of cultural categories that were once understood as separate are now coalescing. This is the case for entertainment, advertising and education which, we will show, are not converging as one or all at once. Different convergences of the consumer form have different implications for different generations and for different types of cross-generational relationships. In this chapter we clarify how this process of aggregation and disaggregation is occurring.

We will begin by considering young people's culture. In this regard we make two key points. First, we argue that children's entertainment and advertising are converging. This is occurring via the marketing forms of cross-selling and licensed merchandising, programme-length commercials and product placement. These forms mask the true advertising intent and construct entertainment and advertising as playful and pleasurable. In contrast, education and adults are constructed negatively and in opposition to young people's culture and pleasure. Our second point, then, is that consumer culture exploits this opposition by simultaneously exaggerating and collapsing generational differences.

In terms of kids' culture, the generation gap has been exaggerated in order to create a child and youth market distinct from the adult segment. At the same time, the differences between adult and child have been collapsed in order to offer children and youth positions as autonomous consumers. We look, therefore, at the way in which media and consumer culture has offered children identities through the practice of 'othering' adults. We suggest that this has implications for teachers, schools and education.

In the second section of this chapter, we examine adult culture, looking first at how they respond to kids' culture. We argue that adult concerns about children's precocity are cultivated by the media and also entail 'othering' practices. These translate into an adult consumer form which hybridizes entertainment and education, and advertising and education. However, in the concluding section we also argue that the transgenerational address which has constructed these opposing positions for adults and children has also created adultlike children and childlike adults.

⭘ Kids' culture

Hybridizing entertainment and advertising

> *Interviewer:* How do you know what is in, what's fashionable? Where do you get your ideas?
> *Girl:* I get my ideas from television and magazines.
> *Boy:* *The Simpsons.*
> *Interviewer:* *The Simpsons*? Do you get clothes ideas from *The Simpsons*?
> *Boy:* Yes, like the brands, like Nike and Adidas and things like that.
> *Girl:* I get my ideas from *Beverly Hills 90210*.

The boy and girl speaking in this interview are 8-year-olds. When we later asked a group of students aged between 10 and 11 years the same question, *The Simpsons* was again offered as a kids' cultural resource. However, as one student pointed out, the Simpsons 'wear the same clothes all the time'. They do not wear brand label clothing. Yet this young boy's mistake is revealing. The boundary between the programme and the advertising that punctuates it has blurred. Today, young people's culture is dominated by a technologically mediated convergence of entertainment and advertising. Advertisements are increasingly presented as entertainment, as enjoyable in their own right rather than 'as consumer information' (Seiter 1995: 105). Children's and young people's culture/entertainment has its own aesthetic. It is flashy, fast, frenetic, fantastic, funny, fun, colourful and catchy. It privileges visual communication over verbal and so do the commercials that target children.

Indeed, a British qualitative study of children's responses to advertising found that children rarely mention the product – they like particular advertisements because of 'the personalities, the gimmicks, the humour and the songs' (Cullingford 1984, cited in Seiter 1995: 105). These elements constitute, in Williams' (1980: 185) classic words, 'a system of magical inducements' rather than a rational appeal. Market researchers know that children's preferred mode of information processing is visual, their ability to process it far superior to that of adults, and that advertising is most effective when key points are presented to them in this way (Smith 1997: 3). Of course, entertainment is not solely visual, but in TV and online advertising, what is shown has greater impact than what is said. This is because 'The response of children to brand advertising is largely based in its symbolic content, its metaphorical meaning' and how this connects with their world and their aspirations (Dell Clark 1999: 82). According to Dell Clark (1999: 81):

> Often, successful children's advertising uses a symbol, such as a character that literally personifies the brand's symbolic meaning . . . through appearance and behavior [this] demonstrates the effectiveness of both narrative and metaphor as a means to convey higher order constructs through nonverbal means.

Advertising of this sort is a hybrid genre that intersects with kids' emotions, fantasies, desires and aspirations. As many media studies scholars point out, young people's entertainment/advertising is a major resource for pleasure and agency, for building identity and peer communities, and for peer literacy.

The resulting hybridization of entertainment and advertising which distinguishes young people's culture and media manifests in a variety of ways. We will look first at the various ways this hybridization is occurring; second, at how this consumer form reflects and reinforces the generational differences upon which the segmentation of the child market is based; and third, at the implications of this for education.

Cross-selling and licensed merchandising

Girl (8 years): You know the Subway commercial with Jared with the big pants? Well I went to Subway on the Internet. It's got nothing to do with Subways but they've got dolls there. They've got the Shaving Ken Barbie that I really want.

Interviewer: How did you know how to get to Subway?

Girl: It's on the bottom of the [TV] commercial so I went to www.subway.com.

An extension of licensed merchandising, cross-selling refers to promotional partnerships between two or more companies. The alliances between Disney and Nestlé and McDonald's and *The Simpsons* are familiar examples of cross-selling which hybridize advertising and entertainment. The Australian release of *Stuart Little* in April 2000 coincided with the inclusion of *Stuart Little* toys in Hungry Jack's kids' meals. Disney's *The Tigger Movie* was used to promote Sanitarium breakfast cereal and Nestlé individual serve yoghurts and vice versa. At the same time, and in addition to its pre-release promotion for the movie *Dinosaur*, Nestlé hedged its bets with characters from earlier favourites *Toy Story* (1995), *Tarzan* (1999), *A Bug's Life* (1998) and *Sesame Street* on its flavoured yoghurts, *Teletubbies* on its custards and *The Lion King* (1994) on its choc-mud mousse. Like link advertising, cross-advertising encourages the consumer to 'associate a brand automatically . . . with a favoured activity or hobby' or, in the case of children, with a character they admire (Handel 1999).

Characters sell particularly well to kids, and marketers have known this for a long time. The first Mickey Mouse films were released in 1928, and by 1929 the characters were being used to sell Disney licensed merchandise. Among these first products were school writing tablets, with Mickey Mouse dolls being released in 1930 (James 1997: 3). Today, the rights to use the selling power of successful characters are sold to manufacturers who pay a licensing fee. The incentive to do so is apparent in an industry advertisement which invites potential clients to 'Benefit from Mattel's success by becoming a licensee. Barbie is a success story that continues to gather fans with over 90% market penetration' (Consumers Union Education Services 1990: 20).

The conflation between advertising and entertainment is intensified by the way characters, originating in different genres and media, cross over. Characters may originate in books (*Winnie the Pooh*); animated (*The Lion King* and *A Bug's Life*) and live action (*Star Wars*) feature films; TV cartoons (*Rugrats* and *Bugs Bunny*) and puppet series (*Sesame Street* and *Teletubbies*); advertisements (Sam Toucan); computer games (Super Mario and Sonic the Hedgehog); and toys (Barbie). Personalities from other entertainment fields no longer simply lend celebrity endorsement to a product. Sporting hero Michael Jordan, pop group the Spice Girls and Britney Spears have become 'brands' in their own right. Characters are then used to market merchandise as diverse as clothing, jewellery, furniture, food and drink, toys and collectibles, stationery and interactive software. Licensed products may not yet cover every conceivable lifestyle product, but the Hello Kitty shop in Sydney's Chinatown, for instance, stocks everything from erasers to steering wheel covers. The pleasures of entertainment thus become the pleasures of consumption and lifestyle.

Manufacturers of traditional children's toys are also looking to characters to sell their products – *Thomas the Tank Engine* train sets; *Rugrats*, *Teletubbies* and *Bananas in Pyjamas* jigsaw puzzles; Looney Tunes playing cards; *Pokémon* Monopoly – and creating new ones around them. Board games like *Jumanji*; *Rugrats* Guessing Game; Furby – Adventure Game; *Friends*; and Where in the World is Carmen San Diego? use characters of various provenances to target various age groups. Characters have also displaced other traditional consumer goods and entertainment. They form the basis of rides at theme parks and fill sample bags at shows and carnivals. Character-based confectionery is fast superseding the Easter egg.

Programme-length commercials

> *Interviewer:*   Do they have commercials on the Internet?
> *Girl (8 years):* No, no commercials. Say on NaughtyDog.com I went into the toys and I clicked on them and saved them. But they're not a commercial. At Barbie.com you can dress the Barbies.

With characters increasingly marketed as brands in themselves, children's and youth TV programmes now function as full-length commercials for toys (toy-based programming) or for music (MTV). In fact, the toy 'characters' are often created first and the TV programme is then developed around the 'characters'. Music clips have been scripted before the songs are even written (Jhally 1990: 98). In anticipation of the Christmas 2000 release of *Jumanji 2*, Robertson (1999) reported that the cast of hybrid animal characters in the sequel were created expressly for their licensing potential. The original film featured 'traditional', and therefore hard to license, animals. Programme-length commercials benefit both the entertainment industry and commerce. In regard to TV, the toy manufacturer enjoys high exposure for their product, and the broadcaster a 'pre-sold' audience (Jacobson and Mazur 1995: 107). As with cross-advertising, the object is to encourage multiple purchases of the toys and associated licensed merchandise.

Kids can usually recognize the persuasive intent of TV commercials. Children under 5 are able to distinguish between commercials and programmes and, thus, between entertainment and selling intent, even if they cannot articulate the difference between them (Roedder John 1999: 6). Programme-length commercials, however, are designed to make it difficult for children to differentiate content from marketing. The success of this format with older children is evident in the Australian documentary TV show *Popstars* (1999), which followed the manufacture of Bardot, an all-girl band in the tradition of the Spice Girls. Their first single entered the Australian charts at number one, though their subsequent recordings quickly disappeared when the programme finished.

Today, terrestrial, satellite and cable TV and online and interactive games have all intensified the process of character creation. *Pokémon* is the latest in a long line of what are essentially programme-length commercials which include *My Little Pony, Strawberry Shortcake, The Care Bears* and *The Power Rangers*. With a cast of 150 characters and new ones appearing monthly, *Pokémon* takes this practice and its potential for licensed merchandise and cross-selling to new heights. In addition to the TV cartoon series, Pokémon characters 'star' in Gameboy and Nintendo 64 software, Warners' *Pokémon: The First Movie* (1999) and *Pokémon the Movie: 2000*, comics, books and trading cards. Hasbro produces the Pokémon toy range. Pokémon 3Ds have been used to sell Smith's crisps and Kraft

Singles and Pokémon products are offered as prize incentives by Quaker's cereals and Welch's jellies.

Technology has added a further dimension to the convergence of advertising and entertainment apparent in programme-length commercials. Austin and Reed (1999: 591) explain that the 'Safeguards that exist in traditional broadcast media that require separation between programmes and advertising do not exist online', where instead they 'are seamlessly integrated'. As the opening interview extract above suggests, children may be unable to differentiate between the advertising content and the interactive aspects of a website. Austin and Reed also argue that children do not realize that 'product spokespersons or characters are used to develop interactive relationships with them' or 'that in many cases these characters provide hotlinks directly to advertising sites' (1999: 591).

While sites like Nabisco.com tell kids when they are viewing a commercial, Austin and Reed identify a further disturbing aspect of online advertising. 'Fake' advertisements form part of the entertainment on the Nickelodeon.com website and this, they contend, 'could cause children to be misled when they visit other sites that have real advertisements' (Austin and Reed 1999: 596). This is paralleled by the trend towards programmes like *Funniest Home Videos* and *Pets Behaving Badly* in which the line between entertainment and authentic experience is blurred, and programmes like *World's Funniest Commercials* which overtly present advertising as entertainment.

Product placement

> *Girl (9 years):* I reckon McDonald's are good because they are yum and they know what to put in them because *they know what kids like*.

In background action to a scene in the 1997 remake of Disney's 1965 movie *That Darn Cat*, a young girl sitting in a booth in a café tells her grandma that she feels sick. Presumably this is to avoid eating what is on her plate because, almost immediately, the child asks if she can have a Big Mac on the way home. Grandma agrees. It would seem that the girl in this scene concurs with the sentiment expressed above. She also reinforces it. Marketers are increasingly introducing brands into the sets and, as we have just seen, into the scripts of children's films and television, as well as in print, games and toys, for the status they thus acquire. This ranges from the strategic placement of products that are normalized within the setting and add to the illusion of reality, to flagrant advertising like the far from subtle promotion of Warner-licensed merchandise in the movie *Space Jam* (1996). Featuring Michael Jordan and the animated

Looney Tunes cast, the film uses the Warner Brothers logo as part of a sight gag and characters make direct references to Warner merchandise and its child consumers.

Like programme-length commercials, product placement is a covert form of advertising which promotes brand awareness and loyalty. Reese's Pieces (children's sweets) were famously featured as a lure for the extra-terrestrial character in Spielberg's *ET* (1982). Nabisco's Oreo biscuits were the subject of a dialogue in the latest version of Disney's *The Parent Trap* (1998), a switch from Fig Newtons (another biscuit brand) which were mentioned in the original. In the Macauley Culkin vehicle, *Richie Rich* (1994), the main character has his own McDonald's, complete with golden arches, at home. McDonald's placement in *Dick Tracy* (1990) was supported by the fast-food chain's own promotional campaign, clearly linking product placement with cross-promotion. The blurring of boundaries between these strategies is further evident in the placement of miniature replicas of products like Cheerios (a breakfast cereal), Huggies (nappies) and BeechNUT baby cereal and juices in Barbie and Kelly doll sets. A packet of Lays potato crisps and two cans of Coca-Cola to go in Barbie's esky are included with the 'Pop Out Picnic SUV hatchback' set.

Jacobson and Mazur (1995: 69) tell how 'In the mega-hyped *Jurassic Park* (1993), Ford Explorer won a starring role as dinosaur snack food' and, in a prime example of postmodern marketing, 'in another scene, the camera slowly pans a gift shop that showcases the entire line of *Jurassic Park* accessories' which subsequently became available to consumers. They make the point that:

> Many filmmakers are now willing to take artistic advice from manu-facturers. Andrew Varela of Baldwin, Varela and Co. admitted to tinkering with the script of *Home Alone* on behalf of his client, Kraft General Foods. 'We thought it made sense for Macauley Culkin to fix macaroni and cheese for his solo Christmas dinner. The script originally called for him to heat a turkey dinner, but we believed that this kid – left on his own and scared – would reach for some-thing familiar . . . a comfort food'.
>
> (Jacobson and Mazur 1995: 71)

The assumption that Kraft macaroni and cheese is a comfort food is thus reinforced by the film. And so, too, are assumptions about adults and kids and the relationship between the generations.

Pleasing children and othering adults

Children's preference for the entertainment and advertising blend is paralleled by the pleasures they derive from it. Pleasure is at the core of children's consumer culture and the pleasures that it offers are multiple, as we will show. We will also show that in many instances the pleasures it evokes are of a particular sort, which has both benefits and costs for children. Let us then begin this section with a theoretical explanation of different pleasures. We will then show how various pleasures are effected in children's consumer culture, noting the emotional range evoked in consumer culture's processes of othering adults and education. We will conclude with some comments on the implications of such pleasures for the knowledge politics of children's pleasures.

The consumer form blurs boundaries and, we may say, so does the pleasure it produces. What Barthes (1975) calls *jouissance* is a 'pleasure without separation', a pleasure which 'knows no bounds' (Grace and Tobin 1997: 177). Because it involves a 'momentary loss of subjectivity' it is not discriminating. It is a far more voluptuous pleasure than *plaisir*, which 'produces the pleasures of relating to the social order' (Grace and Tobin 1997: 177). By contrast, *jouissance* typically produces the pleasures of transgressing the social order. These are also some of the properties of *jouissance* Kristeva (1982) identifies when she considers it in relation to the psychical development of individuals and societies. She follows in the tradition of Lacan who has stated 'without a transgression there is no access to *jouissance*' (1992: 177, quoted in Fuery 1995: 30).

Kristeva associates the sublime experience of *jouissance* with the primal, prelinguistic and borderless union between mother and child. This union does not distinguish between self and other and precedes subjectivity. Kristeva coins the term 'semiotic' to distinguish the nonverbal signifying practice through which *jouissance* is experienced. Because the semiotic is associated with the drives and the body, it is opposed to language, the father and the social order which it both precedes and exceeds. In this regard, it too is transgressive. Kristeva's concept of the semiotic is the psychical equivalent to, and loosely based on, Bakhtin's (1968) concept of the carnivalesque (Fuery 1995: 63). The carnivalesque 'may be understood as a make-believe over-turning of the law and existing social norms' (Lechte 1990: 105).

Because it contradicts order, the semiotic is ultimately regarded as abject. The abject evokes many of the elements of the carnivalesque. It is irrational, improper, grotesque, unclean, profane, taboo, hybrid. However, unlike the carnivalesque, which is socially sanctioned, the abject is forbidden, unspeakable and repressed. As we shall later see, children's consumer culture, and the 'indiscriminate' pleasures children take in it, are regarded as abject by many adults because they contradict adult ideas about what is 'proper' in regard to children. This is intensified somewhat by the quasi-erotic and transgressive connotations of *jouissance*.

The carnivalesque, like aspects of today's consumer–media culture, evokes *jouissance* in children. Children and youth are encouraged to delight in the impertinent and the forbidden, to transgress adult codes, to live only in the present. Carnivalesque offers them a picture of the world from a kid's perspective. To children, commercials represent resistance and subversion or what McDonnell (1994: 33) calls 'speaking the forbidden'. And, because there is much in consumer and media culture generally which adults see as being unfit for children, they come to represent 'the irresistible aura of power and danger' (McDonnell 1994: 42). Children delight in what their parents may find offensive: the scatological, the macabre and the grotesque. The grotesque is particularly alluring to children because they 'are learning to monitor what is "real" from what is "not real"; what is benign and what is not' (Oates 1994). This curiosity extends to the grotesque body which 'is overflowing and transgresses it own limits' (Grace and Tobin 1997: 172). As subjects-in-progress, children do not feel the revulsion adults experience in regard to the grotesque or abject body. However, as Oates (1994) says, the 'forbidden truth, the unspeakable taboo' of the grotesque is that it 'is not always repellent but frequently attractive', even for adults.

Bazalgette and Buckingham (1995b: 7) argue that in recent times much TV viewing is 'designed precisely to exclude adults' and their values. Walkerdine (1999: 6) makes a similar point in regard to cyberspace. She contends that 'cyberspace offers a new space . . . without the fears attached to public space and indeed without undue interference from adults: it is adult-free, unknown and unsupervised'. Seiter (1995: 11–12) argues that children's consumer culture often involves a

> subversion of parental values of discipline, seriousness, intellectual achievement, respect for authority and complexity by celebrating rebellion, disruption, simplicity, freedom, and energy. [Children's cartoons and commercials] portray an abundance of the things most prized by children – food and toys; their musical themes and fast action are breathtakingly energetic, they enact a rebellion against adult restriction; they present a version of the world in which good and evil, male and female, are unmistakably coded in ways easily comprehended by a young child; they celebrate a community of peers. Children's mass culture rejects the instrumental use of toys and television for teaching and self-improvement preferred by parents.

These practices, according to Seiter, invert many ideas associated with adult culture and bind children together as an audience defined in opposition to adults.

As we have already implied, children's mass culture partakes of the carnivalesque. The concept of the carnivalesque has attracted scholars for the possibilities it holds to explain resistance to, and transcendence and reversals of, dominant discourses. The carnival is characterized by 'subversion, inversion, diversion, and perversion' but, at the same time, represents 'ordered disorder, regulated deregulation, organized chaos, authorized antiauthoritarianism, controlled decontrol of the emotions, and ultimately reinforcement rather than subversion of the status quo' (Brown *et al.* 1999). Postmodern advertising has appropriated many of the elements of carnivalesque. 'Dedifferentiation' refers to the blurring of generational hierarchies focused on here (Brown 1995), but it also partakes of the parodic and the grotesque.

Thus, if consumer culture turns the generational hierarchy upside down, ultimately it is a form of 'ordered disorder' designed to socialize children into consumer culture. With the aid of advertising and new media forms, the market offers children consumption as a primary motivating force and cultural artefacts with which to construct their dreams, set their priorities and solve their problems. It offers them a basis upon which to build their group's commonalities and their sense of others' differences, and upon which to establish their personhood.

Seiter, however, maintains that the desire for the artefacts of consumer culture need not be understood as mainly a function of greed and hedonism. It may also be an expression of desire for common bonds with the child community. She contends that 'Consumer culture provides children with a shared repository of images, characters, plots and themes: it provides the basis for small talk and play' and stresses the agency of the child audiences of children's commercials (1995: 7). She emphasizes the meanings and images which children derive from advertisements, their preoccupation with pleasure, their appreciation of the fantasy element, their enjoyment of the humour and their use of commercials as a cultural resource with their friends. Drawing from the Marxist philosopher, Ernst Bloch, she also identifies a utopian sensibility, noting the way in which children's mass culture represents an escape from or an alternative to the everyday – the image of something better. It stands in direct and extreme contrast to the inadequacies of the real or, as Benjamin would have it, the dreamworld of modernity where genuine utopian longing is distorted.

Given that the purveyors of utopian dreams to children are also the mythmakers of modernity, it is not surprising that media and advertising should simultaneously subvert and reinforce mass-culture's myths. Children are led to believe that they can gratify their needs, wants and desires and solve their problems through consumption. For our purposes the most pertinent feature of this hyperreal utopia is the manner in which it involves separating children from adults, and entertainment from education.

Consumer culture shows children the place they will come to occupy as adult consumers. Read according to Benjamin, it is a place where 'play is transformed into toil, curiosity into fetishism, reciprocity into tyranny, spontaneity into drudgery' (Gilloch 1996: 91). Not surprisingly, then, advertising and TV that break the rules and 'others' adults appeals to children. Consumer culture is likely to appeal particularly to youth, not only because it coincides with the taboo-breaking of many youth cultural forms, but because they are on the verge of entering the 'dystopia' of adult life. Kellner (1997) describes the related emergence of a new youth genre which he calls 'loser television'. Representing 'the revenge of youth and those who are terminally downwardly mobile against more privileged classes and individuals' (Kellner 1997: 91), it is likely to show 'boys behaving badly' and to virulently oppose the political correctness of the older generation. Examples of this genre include *Beavis and Butthead* and *South Park*. Given the desire of the 'tweens' to 'trade up', this genre also appeals to younger segments of the kids' market. Related animated programmes like *Ren and Stimpy* and *Rocko's Modern Life* aimed at a younger audience also capitalize on this desire to trade up.

It is clear that school education, teachers and parents are outside this utopia. They are, at least in part, the real from which escape is sought. In their research, Aronowitz and Giroux argue that 'almost all students grow up in two worlds: one of school and family where they feel that they are not in control of their lives, and the other, with friends and by themselves, which they see as more autonomous' (1985: 54). While teachers and parents may be, and often are, constructed as a problem, they are seldom if ever constructed as providing solutions. Children's and, indeed, youth media represent parents and teachers as dull or too earnest, usually disapproving, slightly ridiculous, unworthy of emulation and as being subjected to well-justified rebellion and rejection. They are only occasionally heroic. Davies (1996) draws on Gerbner (1973) and O'Brien (1990) to show how the representation of teachers has evolved from idealized images of noble professionals – albeit subverted by the 'hidden curriculum' which constructs schools as ineffective – to caricatures of them. As O'Brien (1990: 33) explains, 'The media . . . provide a "hidden curriculum" that supersedes the learning process in school' and caricature teachers 'as incompetent nincompoops or rigid authoritarians. It is bad enough that teachers have been *displaced* by the media, but worse that their image . . . has been distorted' (quoted in Davies 1996: 78).

Advertising and TV construct school as an old-fashioned, puritanical, drab and over-disciplined place where, dreadfully or ridiculously, children must be governed by others or be self-restrained – in other words, as a dystopia. Audiences are exposed daily to the image of Lisa Simpson's jazz saxophone-playing exit from school orchestra practice under the disapproving gaze of a teacher in the opening credits of *The Simpsons* and to the recurrent game of one-upmanship between Bart and Principal Skinner. In images such as these, the generation gap is simultaneously exacerbated and collapsed, and the pleasures of adults and children polarized. In children's culture, entertainment and advertising are constructed as separate from, and superior to, education – at least for children.

Fiske's (1996) analysis of *The Simpsons* offers an insight into both these dimensions of popular culture.

Like Kinder (1995), Fiske argues that, as a subversion of the tradi-tional family, *The Simpsons* engages in a form of transgenerational address (see below). In the early 1990s the show was condemned by the then US secretary of education, banned from schools and, not surprisingly, quickly became 'the mascot of disaffected youth'. Bart, after all, is 'a failure at school and misunderstood at home . . . He is street smart, not school smart: his smarts are those of an oral culture, not a literate one' (Fiske 1996: 122). *The Simpsons'* ratings soared; an achievement all the more significant because the show was scheduled against the overtly didactic *The Cosby Show*. According to Fiske, Theo Huxtable's scholastic difficulties were the occasion for 'constant messages about the value of education' (1996: 123). The Simpson family is additionally significant for their particular racial resonances, in part because of their blue-collar status. Fiske explains that because 'race is often recoded into class, so class difference can be decoded as racial' (1996: 123). Thus, Bart Simpson became a black cultural icon of resistance, 'Black Bart', and a symbol for the argument that the white education system is the cause of black 'underachievement', not its remedy.

If, in this instance, *The Simpsons* 'brand' has been expropriated, mar-keters are well aware that audiences can be amassed and sales gen-erated by imprinting a 'brand' with the values with which the consumer identifies. Commercial culture appeals so much to children because it takes their play and pleasure seriously. Clearly, it helps to construct their play and pleasure, but it also seeks to understand and tap into both. Ultimately, however, cultural differences in attitudes to education and consumption suggest that this is pure marketing strategy. Robertson (1995: 20) explains that if, for example, 'Chinese kids identify with achievement while North American kids prefer play', then 'It's up to marketers to bind achievement with the ownership of brand name products in the mind of those children who haven't yet made the connection'.

Creighton's (1994) study of the role of edutainment in consumer socialization in Japan shows how department stores in particular have exploited the Japanese esteem for education, conflating education with the pleasures of consumption. By contrast, western consumer culture's segmentation of child and adult markets has invited children to regard adults as their negative 'other' and to regard education as oppositional to their pleasures.

Consumer–media culture's implicit and explicit 'othering' of schools and teachers may well have the following effects. First, its othering practices may result in school student populations who get and expect little pleasure from the formal aspects of schooling. Second, it leads students to expect adults not to say anything worth listening to except in purely instrumental terms. Thus, such students are unlikely to take seriously what schools tell them. Third, this 'othering' makes it unlikely that they will construct their identity through schools. Therein lies the rub for commerce and advertising. As we will show in the following sections of this chapter, the commercial world is now trying to ingratiate itself with parents. In the following chapter we will look at how this is happening in schools. Given that commercial culture has hitherto stigmatized parents, teachers and schools and encouraged children to undervalue them, the irony of this move is inescapable. This does not, however, make adults any less avid as consumers, as we will show shortly. But first let us briefly consider some of the implications of *jouissance*, hyperreality and simulation for children's knowledge and reflexivity.

The knowledge politics of children's pleasures

The *jouissance* which children derive from consumer culture is designed to ensure that they unreflexively consume rather than interpret such texts. *Jouissance* is about producing a surge of affect, not the reflexive pleasure of knowing about what is happening as it happens. By its very nature, children's consumer–media culture seeks not to operate at this level of rationality. As Lee (1993: 143) says of the postmodern aesthetic, children's media culture 'invites a fascination, rather than a contempla-tion, of its contents; it celebrates surfaces and exteriors rather than look-ing for or claiming to embody (modernist) depth'. It also 'transforms all cultural content into objects for immediate consumption rather than texts of contemplative reception or detached and intellectual interpretation'. Indeed, consumer–media culture blurs the boundaries between data, information and knowledge, entertainment and advertising. It bombards children with simulations (images) and simulacra (signs) which often have no referents. According to Baudrillard's (1983a) concept of simula-tion and simulacra, hyperreality results when the simulated images or models and signs presented by the media begin to determine reality and our perception of it rather than represent it. Take an example. Giroux (1997: 55) discusses hyperreality in relation to Disney movies, working from Baudrillard's thesis that 'Disneyland is more "real" than fantasy because it now provides the image on which America constructs itself'. He also says that 'Unlike the often hard-nosed, joyless reality of school-ing, children's films provide a high-tech visual space where adventure and pleasure meet in a fantasy world of possibilities and a commercial sphere of consumerism and commodification' (1997: 53–4).

Seldom here are children offered the pleasures of reflexive knowing or of having a sense of agency derived from recognizing how their meanings, identities and affective investments are produced. The potential pleasures of becoming informed and active citizens within the politics of consumption are usually overridden by the pleasures of fantasy. Equally, in anti-political correctness – youthful revenge genres – the pleasures of knowing are outweighed by those of retaliation, reversal and transgression. Further, the historically decontextualizing and self-referential processes of consumer–media culture also mean that the knowledge that children do achieve is contained within the bubble. This means that a critical insider/outsider stance is difficult to gain even when the text itself is potentially what Fiske (1996) calls a 'a rebellious space'. Let us elaborate a little on this point.

Kellner (1997) suggests that much of the satirical intent of TV programmes like *Beavis and Butthead* is lost on young children, and he cites examples of 12-year-olds imitating violent and dangerous behaviour represented in the programme. This is a not only a consequence of immature critical skills. Many younger children have yet to experience the reality that the satire inverts in order to critique it. When an absence of referential experience combines with the decontextualizing effect of hyperreality the textual strategies of satire are taken at face value and the capacity of the genre to successfully resist dominant discourse is neutralized. This is intensified in *Beavis and Butthead* by the fact that the main characters 'derive their entire view of history and the world' from media culture (Kellner 1997: 87).

Hawk (n.d.) identifies a comparable effect in his discussion of MTV. He argues that the musicians who appear on MTV are turned into simulations without a specific spatial, social and historical context and, thus, without resistant meaning. He gives the example of 'gangsta-rap' music, stating that 'when white suburban kids see the videos, they have no understanding of the actual situational context' – that is, of the fact that 'the art was created as an expression of resistance to the feeling of domination in urban life'. Kincheloe believes that the postmodern child cannot avoid the effects of the hyperreality produced by electronic media saturation. As he explains it, in postmodernity 'media-produced models replace the real – simulated TV kids on sitcoms replace real-life children as models of childhood' (Kincheloe 1997a: 45). We may well ask, as Kinder (1991: 35) does, what of 'the impact [on children] of seeing an imaginary world so full of rich visual signifiers before having encountered their referents or acquired verbal language'?

And when it comes to the difference and inequalities of 'real life', the world that media culture presents to children is often already dehistoricized – a place where class, ethnic, race and gender struggles are ignored. Seiter (1995: 134) concedes that in this regard the utopianism of children's commercial TV 'can also serve to mask the fact that participation in the unity and community of entertainment has always been unequal, exclusionary. Entertainment's optimism about community can deny the real hardships discrimination creates'.

Like Seiter, Jakubowicz *et al.* (1994) identify the racial, gender and class hierarchies encoded in media simulations, noting the dominance of images of white boys and blonde girls. They acknowledge the improved representation of African-Americans and Asian-Americans in US advertising – albeit confined to certain positions in the media text – and suggest that, with the easing of regulations on overseas content, this has impacted positively on Australian commercial TV. However, they also point out that minorities including South-East Asian, Aboriginal, Polynesian and Maori groups remain largely unrepresented on Australian TV in much the same way as American Indian and Hispanic actors have been excluded in the USA. Simulation of minority ethnicities in Australian advertising is often stereotypical, with 'almost no-one who looks like a southern European or Arab-Australian unless they are being parodied in some food ads' (Jakubowicz *et al.* 1994: 100).

As these quick examples suggest, there is a politics to children's pleasures that is not necessarily obvious to them. Clearly, as these examples also indicate, there are some very good reasons why kids should be able to adopt the critical insider/outsider stance we mentioned in Chapter 1. Teachers and schools have the potential to help students to develop such a stance, but realizing this potential is difficult. This is due in part to schools' negative positioning within the media's paradigms of pleasure that we noted above, and also due to the moralizing stance that adults often adopt with regard to children's media culture. Both help to take the pleasure out of knowing. In Chapters 6 and 7 we will offer some suggestions which may help schools to realize this potential. Meanwhile, we must say more about adults' culture, children's positioning within it and another politics of pleasure. Beginning by offering the 'adult' perspective on kids' culture, we will consider the adult consumer form that hybridizes entertainment and education, and education and advertising.

◯ Adults' culture

If adults and education are the 'negative other' of children's culture, then the reverse is also true. Children's culture is often constructed by parents' groups and teachers as non-educational and, thus, not as worthy. According to Christian-Smith and Erdman (1997: 131–2):

> In Western societies, children are often regarded as low-status, economically dependent, incompetent individuals who achieve competency and normality through their interactions with adults who initiate children into larger cultural values. Adult society is

constructed as the norm and the desirable state, whereas children's society seems to be different and often aberrant. These notions of childhood are of recent origin.

As we have indicated, consumer culture challenges this central idea.

There has long been a stand-off between these two ideological apparatuses (the media and education) and, thus, between the differently inflected generational or adult/child power relations within which they are both immersed. Schools, teachers, parents and 'child experts' often express anxiety about children's play, pleasure and desire, and about those media which can be said to characterize children's popular culture – in particular, commercial culture on the screen and advertising directed at children. Increasingly, however, educational consumption of various sorts also reinforces children's popular culture. As we will show, many education and entertainment, and education and advertising mutations tap into the particularly contradictory consciousness of the current generation of adults – especially with regard to consumerist 'solutions' to 'governing' children.

Uneasy adults othering children

Many adults are suspicious about the quality of children's media and consumer culture. They fear its effects on reading and print, they object to its hedonism and violence and oppose its race, gender and class stereotypes. They worry that it will lead to the triumph of individualism over community, corrupt children's morals, undermine their creativity and result in passive children. Indeed, they fear it will result in what Postman (1994) has called the 'disappearance of childhood'. In their concern, adults cling to the notion of childhood innocence and ignorance and, by extension, adult wisdom and enlightenment (see Buckingham 1995).

Children's/youth consumer culture is understood to threaten the developmental order of generations: children are seen to 'learn about life out of sequence'. It also taps into the adult generation's concern that children are defiant and hard to control. Adults are concerned about children's individualistic and maverick styles of behaviour. Such matters are of consequence for teachers who are no longer the source of authoritative knowledge and who also have to deal with what they see as children's bad manners, impudence, bravado and egotism. There is a general adult anxiety about the ungovernability of young people.

Holland (1996: 157) suggests that adults' 'Concern about *what* kids know is equalled by concern about *how* they get to know it'. Postman offers one answer when he describes TV as a 'total disclosure medium' (1994: 81) which 'effectively undermines adults' control over the knowledge and experiences that are available to children' (Bazalgette and Buckingham 1995b: 3). According to Holland (1996: 157):

> Many share his [Postman's] fear that knowledge is no longer in the hands of adults who pass it on to children, drip by drip, monitoring its use. Now it is grabbed by them, wholesale and without understanding. They by-pass parents and teachers in the name, not of a children's culture, but of a futurist cyber-culture where the contact is with less responsible adults.

These fears have been exacerbated by the access to adult knowledge which the Internet has given children. Kids' technological savvy makes them 'powerful in a way that kids in previous generations were not' (Bagnall 2000: 24).

Indeed, 'the grown-up world, far from being somewhere children are permitted to graduate only when they have jumped through a fixed course of educational hoops, now appears to be morphing into the image of the Net Generation – fluid and hybrid' (Bagnall 2000: 24). Often possessing greater computer literacy than their parents, children's sense of themselves as 'incompetent and dependent entities' has been subverted (Steinberg and Kincheloe 1997: 17). Advertising's sensitivity to this sensibility is evident in a recent print advertisement for Aptiva (IBM Australia 2000) showing two adolescent girls and the caption:

> i have
> friends I tell everything
> parents I tell enough
> e mail
> an aptiva

As Steinberg and Kincheloe (1997: 17) observe, 'Such a self-perception does not mix well with institutions such as the traditional family or the authoritarian school, institutions both grounded on a view of children as incapable of making decisions for themselves'. Children and youth are not only seen to be in danger, but to be 'dangerous' to themselves and to the integrity of the adult order.

Clearly, there are very real social and economic reasons for the altered face of family life and cross-generational relationships. According to Hugh Mackay in *Generations* (1997), the parents of the current generation of children have had to adapt to new family forms, work patterns and technologies in the context of the declining influence of traditional agencies of socialization like the Church, family and school. At the same time as they juggle the demands of their complicated lives, they try to 'connect' with their children, to give them 'quality time' and 'the good life', to be 'responsible parents' and also to lead fulfilling lives of their own. However, their parenting is also plagued by anxieties. Indeed, their anxieties about their own lives inevitably get transferred and projected onto their children who then become their 'worry targets' (Mackay 1997: 82).

As we noted in the introduction to this book, parents express a range of concerns to do with the 'welfare, whereabouts and well-being of their children' (Mackay 1997: 81). Because they are time-poor, they worry that their children receive too little of their time and energy. They thus involve them in more and more supervised activities. They also worry that their children need more protection from a world that is losing a sense of belonging and increasingly seen as hostile as a result of drugs, heightened violence and abuse. And they worry that their children will not gain paid work and an adequate income. Overall, they believe that life may be even tougher for their children than it was for them, and they feel unsure that they can provide what their children need.

Because they have raised their children on the principles of child-centredness, they worry that they have been perhaps *too open, too permissive* and somehow contributed to the difficult-to-deal-with behaviour noted above. They fear that they have *overindulged* their children, *overcompensated* for their own parental deficiencies through consumer goods, *overexposed* them to the more adult themes of life. They fear that they have left their kids to grow up too fast and *without clear moral codes*. Some question the merits of materialism as a system of personal and family values but find it hard to retreat from it themselves or for their children. They thus turn with nostalgia to their own childhoods which, even if dull and conventional, they associate with clear intergenerational codes and values, including respect for elders and clear discipline.

It is Kinder's (1995) contention that these understandings have been exacerbated by media culture. She argues that an 'exaggeration of generational conflict and conflation' (p. 77) has come to serve as a form of transgenerational address for commercial TV, film and advertising. The dual process of exaggerating and conflating age differences performs the role of functional differentiation for commercial products. By exaggerating generational warfare so that transgenerational products can 'come to the rescue', the same product can be marketed to multiple age groups. The focus on generational conflict, Kinder argues, has many unfortunate effects.

With its focus on the white, middle class, heterosexual family as the norm, the transgenerational address represses matters of class, race, gender and sexuality. It implies that generational wars and dysfunctional families are at the heart of such major social problems as crime, drug abuse and even national productivity. Kincheloe (1997a: 39) makes the point that 'the battle to ascribe blame for family dysfunction in general, and childhood pathology in particular, plays out on a variety of landscapes', including popular culture. In his analysis of *Home Alone* he identifies the mother as the target for blame. These themes produce and promote parental guilt and anxieties about their children and their parenting, and enhance the attraction of consumerist solutions. Kinder reports fears that 'the simultaneous exaggeration of generational conflict and conflation' also 'threatens to erode the formerly "naturalised" boundaries between adults and minors, parents and children, and the patriarchal laws and incestuous taboos that are propped on these distinctions' (1995: 77).

As Sibley (1995: 132) has argued, ' "family" tensions represent a clash between adults' desire for order and young people's for disorder; and between adults' preference for firm boundaries in contrast to young people's disposition for more lax boundaries'. These tensions are part of the negotiation of identities as the subject-in-progress moves towards independence. As we have seen, representations of transgression of boundaries in media and consumer culture can be a source of *jouissance* for children. However, adults tend to believe the blurring of boundaries leads to contamination and the corruption of innocence. These effects have been exaggerated by consumer–media culture, producing the ambivalence, if not the horror, which characterizes abjection. When an individual experiences abjection, *jouissance* is replaced by ambivalence at best, horror at worst. It is this horror which means the abject can simultaneously threaten and constitute the boundaries of identity based on the psychoanalytic triad of the mother–child–father. This is paralleled by the 'kinship imaginary' based on the consolidation of the family unit/ education (paternal principle), consumer culture/entertainment (maternal principle) and the child, which McLaren and Morris (1997: 116) have identified.

The transgenerational address used to manipulate adult consumers has a number of contradictory effects in relation to education. One is the way in which parents have responded to the representations of students, schools and teachers in mass culture. In seeking a sense of the order and stability associated with the authority of dominant ideology, an increasing number of parents are trying to purchase discipline and traditional values by sending their children to private schools. This places educators and education in the role of rescuing children from consumer–media culture, which they do by imparting media literacy skills, at best.

The considerable ambivalence with which schools treat children's and youth consumer–media culture is a flow-on effect of this. Many teachers mirror the 'othering' practices of the media towards education, offering an image of the media as trivial and/or manipulative. While not all teachers respond like this – particularly in primary schools where toys and TV may be used unproblematically as learning aids – schools often relegate children's/youth culture to the field of low culture and image, and locate education within high culture and print. For some parents, these positions may seem to confirm negative media representations of teachers and schools which we have already described. Such parents are vulnerable to marketing that picks up on fashionable educational arguments about such things as the urgent need for new technological literacies and the generational technology gap between kids and parents, students and teachers.

This suggests that it is not just a question of adult controls over children, but of which adults control them and for what purposes. Clearly, these various stances adopted in relation to children's consumer–media culture both challenge and mask certain adult/child power relations as well as power relations between adults themselves. These paradoxes are reflected in the hybridization of entertainment, education and advertising and the commodification of children's education and school life.

Hybridizing entertainment and education, and advertising and education

Whereas children are more attracted to a blend of entertainment and advertising than education and entertainment, adults prefer children's entertainment to be educational. This imperative is evident in the names of toy lines like 'Playskool', the 'Lamaze Infant Development System', 'Learning Curve' and 'Let's Learn Educational Toys Inc.' as well as those of online companies selling them: Right.start.com, EduMart.com and ToySmart.com. According to the promotional brochure for a children's toy shop in New York, 'Our mission is to provide families with a HUGE selection of creative and stimulating products in a customer-friendly entertaining and interactive shopping environment because we believe kids learn best when they're having fun'. Children's TV programmes such as *Sesame Street* promote the comforting belief that they are educational as well as entertaining. Parents buy their children lunch-box snacks that have been marketed as 'nutritious' treats or as making good nutrition fun. Goods and entertainment are sold to parents for their instrumental, cognitive and motivational value in the child's educational development – as Block (1997: 154) says, 'fun *with a purpose*'.

'Fun with a purpose' suggests a particularly adult conception of pleasure. The pleasures of 'fun with a purpose' are much more like *plaisir* than *jouissance*. Grace and Tobin (1997: 177) explain the distinction between these two types of pleasure:

> Plaisir represents conscious enjoyment and is capable of being expressed in language. It is more conservative, accommodating, and conformist than jouissance. Where plaisir is a particular pleasure, jouissance is more diffuse; it is pleasure without separation – bliss, ecstasy, pure affect. Jouissance is an intense, heightened form of

pleasure, involving a momentary loss of subjectivity. It knows no bounds. Fiske (1989) sees the roots of plaisir in the dominant ideology. Plaisir produces the pleasures of relating to the social order; jouissance produces the pleasures of evading it.

Grace and Tobin argue that much of that which passes for 'fun' in school conforms to Barthes' definition of *plaisir*. We suggest that while children may experience *plaisir* as a consequence of the way they use consumer culture to construct a sense of community and solidarity, adult and child pleasures are polarized along the axes of *plaisir* and *jouissance* respectively.

Parents are persuaded to buy goods more for their serious utilitarianism than the pleasure factor. Adults use entertainment to sell education to children. Conversely, marketers use education to sell goods and services to parents including books, toys, technology and software. The educational paraphernalia that fills the shelves of supermarkets at the beginning of the school year is one small example of this imperative. Purely functional goods such as lunch boxes and stationery are enhanced with *Star Wars* and Barbie images. Sportswear brands like Nike and Adidas market footwear to target the education market. The networked computer, its extensive range of entertaining educational software and the CD-ROM are the most recent and most 'hyped' example of this trend. Microsoft's 1999 campaign, aimed at schools as well as parents, claims: 'Technology is a tool . . . Software is a tool. When you give kids tools, you give them choices, and that's the best reason we can imagine to make software' (Johnson 1999). Referring to computer advertisements of this ilk, Lumby (1997: A11) writes: 'I can only imagine the impact these ads must have on anyone with a child. Their message is quite clear: computers are the future of our world, and if your child doesn't have one, they have no future in this world'.

Like much before it, the computer has been sold to parents on educational and family entertainment grounds. This is a strategy that is working very well. Given the ambivalence many adults express about children in the information era, it is ironic that 'Education is the cover that gives kids their passport to play in the digital world' (Bagnall 2000: 24). An Australian Bureau of Statistics survey of Internet use (June 2000) reveals that families with children are almost twice as likely to have Internet access at home than families without children (Bagnall 2000: 24).

Homes are the prime site for the sale of new information and communication media, and parents are being subjected to a hard sell, particularly in the popular press. A home-based education software expert, and also marketing director for the Learning Company in the USA, says:

The biggest growth area for us . . . has been in home-based education. Right across the US parents are buying PCs, laptops and a range of educational software for use at home because the local schools, hamstrung by financial cutbacks, cannot provide intensive computer education training for their children.

(McIntosh 1993: 27)

Advertising targeting the home computer market in the 1990s capitalized on such alleged educational inadequacies. A campaign by Apple, for instance, promoted its product by way of contrast to the pleasureless, print-based learning of the traditional school. Its series of advertisements placed in the weekend magazines of major newspapers in Australia in 1994 had this to say:

Imagine if your kids were as interested in homework as they are in video games. Unfortunately school books don't have the appeal that video games do, but school work certainly can. If you take the sound, moving graphics and interactive nature of video games and add them to education an amazing thing happens. Kids actually become enthused about learning.

(Apple Computer Inc. 1994)

The implicit message is that parents should take charge of their children's education because schools no longer have the equipment or the credibility to do so.

Parents were initially persuaded to see computer games as the first step to computer literacy. A number of private tutoring services emerged to assist students to develop their computer skills. Futurekids is one instance. This is a US franchise which has been purchased in Australia. Our data indicate that children as young as 3 have been enrolled. By the mid-1990s, however, parents were 'no longer satisfied with entertainment-only products that might, at most, be giving their youngsters an edge in "computer skills" or other peripheral areas' (McLester 1996: 46). They demanded titles with direct links to the curriculum. Cunningham (1995b: 191) says that in the UK

Nintendo increasingly markets itself as a console which can be used for both entertainment and education functions. 'Edutainment' is the word used in their promotional leaflets to parents. The 'Mario Edutainment Series' of software is promoted as relevant to the National Curriculum, and it also has other titles which are promoted as educational for preschool children.

However, in buying such goods and services, parents clearly demonstrate a contradictory consciousness. As Mackay's research indicates, they act out their anxious and nostalgic concerns about 'the responsible parent' and 'quality time', and their fear for their children's futures. Through consumer goods they not only over-provide and overcompensate, but seek consumerist solutions to parenting problems. At a more subtle level, they also act out aspects of the hedonism and materialism of their own youth.

Cunningham points out that, given 'Neither young people nor the games manufacturers want to lose their street credibility by being seen as too educational' (1995b: 191), edutainment software did not rate highly in the games charts. More recently, companies have begun to adopt more covert approaches to the marketing of computer hardware and educational software. Director of multimedia buying and Internet marketing at J&R Music and Computer World, Jack Warman, is quoted as saying 'More companies are doing a subtle job of covering up the educational part of their programmes so that kids don't know they're learning while they're having fun' (Traiman 1998).

In spite of the fact that educational software publishers look first to the home market, schools have also always been part of the schema. An advertisement published in 1993 on the flyleaf of *Educational Leadership* (Computer Curriculum Corporation 1993) by the promoter of Success-Maker, the Computer Curriculum Corporation, reads: 'Imagine if our kids' test scores were as high as their Nintendo scores'. It promises a 'Guaranteed learning advantage: It's like education insurance'. Introducing its iMac desktop movie technology seven years later, Apple offers 'an inspired new way to stimulate curiosity, encourage exploration and make learning fun', and opportunities for both students and teachers to 'present their ideas and tell stories in ways they never could before' (Apple Computer Inc. 2000). Marketing of this sort is subtle. The idea that new information technologies will automatically add value to the curriculum has been so well sold that many parents and teachers still automatically expect new technologies to give their students 'the competitive edge'. The fact remains, however, that schools remain 'relatively marginalised from kids' exploration of and growing expertise in the digital world' (Bagnall 2000: 26). In 1998 the Australian Bureau of Statistics estimated that children in typical Australian homes were using a computer between one and five hours a week. In 2000, it was estimated that Australian kids use a computer at school for about thirty minutes a week, if at all (Bagnall 2000: 26). As we will show in the following chapter, this discrepancy, and the assumptions that surround it, has given corporations bearing gifts of technology ready entry to the classroom.

◯ The adultlike child and the childlike adult

Girl (9 years): I like that chocolate ad where there's kids' voices and adults eating it because it is funny and it is also cute. I like the chocolate ad because of how they do it and

you can't imagine a parent doing what they do on
that ad. Yes, it is so babyish and parents do it.

The *Home Alone* (1990, 1992 and 1997) movies are typical of the trend in
entertainment and advertising that shows adults as irresponsible, immoral
and, above all, easily outwitted by kids. This in itself is nothing new.
Fairy-tales and literary classics abound with adult characters who are
wicked, foolish or neglectful and child characters who get the better of
them. If such child characters transgress the rules of the social or
generational order, it is to expose the folly of adults or the corruption of
society. It is implied that the moral purity of the child characters gives
them access to more fundamental 'truths' or values. This is not always
the case in the particular world of children's consumer culture of which
the *Home Alone* films are representative. Young people today are offered
identities as pleasure-seeking, self-indulgent, autonomous, rational decision makers. They are more often precocious than innocent. Kinder
(1995) and Kincheloe (1997a) regard the *Home Alone* movies as emblematic of postmodern childhood and the social and generational relationships which underpin it. Kinder discusses these films as typical of the
transgenerational address we defined earlier. Kincheloe foregrounds what
he describes as the adult ambivalence towards children.

As we have indicated, much in child- and youth-targeted marketing
contradicts the values of the adult world. This is in part due to the fact
that:

> market values have themselves come together with childish values.
> The marketing of goods, particularly toys and other goods which are
> purely for fun and make no pretence at usefulness, depends on the
> creation and potential gratification of desires. The belief that libidin-
> ous pleasure is indeed possible and the ability to throw off con-
> straints in the interests of pure enjoyment are seen as characteristics
> of childish spontaneity.
>
> (Holland 1996: 161)

Children's and youth culture are emblematic of the childhood identifications expelled in order to construct an adult identity and, thus, often
evoke a sense of nostalgia and loss. Seiter makes the point that the fact
that many of the foods advertised to children 'are held by adults to be
repulsive, inedible "trash" or "junk" is a sign that children's culture
inverts and confuses the roles of adult culture' (1995: 116). Such foods
are abject to adult culture, or sometimes a 'forbidden' pleasure.

It is a property of the abject that it is both a pole of attraction and
revulsion, and adults today are increasingly encouraged to indulge in the
libidinous pleasures of its sublime aspect. The transgenerational address
has created:

subject positions for a dual audience of infantilised adults and precocious children. These subject positions seem to provide an illusory
sense of empowerment both for kids who want to accelerate their
growth by buying into consumerist culture and for adults who want
to retain their youth by keeping up with pop culture's latest fads.

(Kinder 1995: 77)

Both Postman (1994) and Meyrowitz (1985) attribute the rise of the
childlike adult to the effects of electronic media. In Postman's view, the
presentation of information as entertainment and the irrational appeal
of commercials have led to a 'dumbing down' of adult sensibilities. He
defines the childlike adult as 'a grown-up whose intellectual and emotional capacities are unrealized and, in particular, not significantly different from those associated with children' (Postman 1994: 99). Children,
on the other hand, are depicted in the media as 'miniature adults' whose
'interests, language, dress or sexuality' do not differ substantially from
adult tastes or style (Postman 1994: 122–3).

Meyrowitz (1985) offers a more critical reading. He argues that at the
same time as electronic media has offered children 'adult' knowledge,
demystified adult authority and wisdom, and invited children to 'revolt',
it has also created 'the feeling among adults that they cannot maintain
their traditional adult performances' (p. 154). As a result, 'both adult and
child roles shift towards a "middle region", all-age role' (p. 154). While
the representation of precocious children getting the better of adults
may be more pronounced today than in the early days of TV, Meyrowitz
says that TV has always subverted adult roles. Unlike Kincheloe (1997a)
and Postman (1994), Meyrowitz argues that even programmes like
Father Knows Best exposed children to the hidden aspects of adult life,
showing them the 'backstage reality' of adult 'fears, doubts, anxieties,
and childish behaviours, and "privately" discuss[ed] techniques for hand-
ling children' (1985: 236). Today's parents were, of course, the original
child viewers of such programmes. *Their* perception of adult authority
has also been undermined.

These feelings of uncertainty have been compounded by the massive
social, economic and technological changes which have occurred during
the second half of the twentieth century. As their lives have become
increasingly complex, the morals, values and mood of the current generation of adults have become ambiguous. Many who expected to be in
stable jobs and relationships, comfortable, happy and even prosperous,
find themselves short of time and energy and plagued by feelings of
uncertainty, insecurity, anxiety, disappointment and stress.

It is little wonder that today's adults not only experience doubts about
the parental role, but also an 'envy of children's impulsive egoism and
their ability to indulge without guilt in pure, selfish pleasure' (Holland

1996: 161). They are likely to take advantage of the 'greater license to explore emotions, act "spontaneously" and depart from former stricter controlled parental roles' (Featherstone 1992: 59). Featherstone says that theme parks are 'good examples of sites in which this emotional de-control and appreciation of sensations and adoption of behaviour once restricted to children take place' (1992: 60). According to Mackay (1997: 65), this generation of adults is bent on enjoying what he calls their 'elastic adolescence'. They use consumer goods and services in the attempt to stay young for as long as possible. Mackay says baby boomers are currently preoccupied with sex, travel, food, health, diet, personal growth and self-therapies and information.

In the advertising industry, this phenomenon is referred to as 'extended youth'. Wood (1999) explains that youth is a matter of attitude and behaviour rather than age. He writes that:

> an obsession with music, experimenting with stimulants, interest in fashion, night clubs, sexual experimentation, driving fast cars, the cinema, fast food, banal television and computer games is no longer the preserve of the adolescent. They are also the preserve of the adolescent's mum and dad.

This is reflected in the trend towards shock advertising by online companies. The use of horror in advertising targeting adults trades on the fact that 'Ghoul is gold to marketers'. The irony of this is that this catchphrase traditionally refers to the child market where 'the appeal of the "dark side"' has been noted in children 'as young as eight [and] peaking (with some encouragement) by late adolescence' (Robertson 1995: 23). As we have seen, market profiles suggest 'gruesome' and 'weird' appeal most to 9- to 11-year-olds. Yet, the jellyfish snorting advertisement for monster.com.au increased site traffic by 300 per cent, more than the conventional commercial screened by the company in the USA during the Superbowl (McKenzie 2000: 27).

At the same time, the boomer generation's nostalgia for their own youth and for the heady and mythical days of the 1960s and 1970s is reinforced by the market success of feature-length movie versions of popular TV series of their childhood and youth. Examples include *The Flintstones* (1994), *The Brady Bunch* (1995), *Mr Magoo* (1997) and *Inspector Gadget* (1999), as well as updated versions of Disney films like *Flubber* (1997) and re-released animated classics like *Sleeping Beauty* and *Bambi*. As Giroux says in relation to Disney's films, they 'work because they put children and adults alike in touch with joy and adventure. They present themselves as places to experience pleasure, even when we have to buy it' (1997: 57). However, such films do not merely provide 'the fantasies through which childhood innocence and adventure are produced, experienced, and affirmed. Disney now produces prototypes for model schools, families, identities, communities, and the way the future is to be under-stood through a particular construction of the past' (Giroux 1997: 55).

In its ideological conservatism, Disney offers a reassuring alternative to the post-traditional world, in the guise of entertainment. It is part of a cultural pedagogy which, Giroux says, parents and teachers underestim-ate or, like children, uncritically consume. Through this hybridization of advertising, education and entertainment the consumer form reflects a complex process of detraditionalization and retraditionalization in which not only children, but also adults, are invited to invest, psychologically and financially.

◯ Conclusion

As indicated, for parents, play and entertainment are seen to be most acceptable when they have a serious educational purpose. Advertise-ments, on the other hand, are not seen to have any redeeming features. The reverse is true for children. As Seiter (1995) observes, parents and children are 'sold separately'. Moreover, it would seem that while edu-cation and entertainment can be sold *together* to parents, usually they are sold *separately* to children. Indeed, not only are education and entertain-ment sold separately to children, they are constructed as both separate and *oppositional*. The apparent but problematic child-friendliness of con-sumer–media culture stands in stark contrast. Addressing the complex array of issues outlined in this chapter requires schools to reconsider their pedagogies, indeed their *raison d'être*. However, as we will show in the next two chapters, there are moves afoot in schools that make it unlikely they will rise to this challenge.

④ Promiscuous corporations: desiring schoolchildren

◯ Introduction

In separating child consumers from their parents, consumer culture has constructed children and youth in opposition to adults. As a result, the child and youth market has grown into one of the most profitable and powerful market segments. The young are prized not only for the influence they have over adult spending, but also for their own burgeoning spending power. We have already seen how child consumers have been further segmented from each other by age and gender, reflecting the way in which the search for new markets leads to the production of new consumer goods, new sites for promotion and consumption, and new consumers. Schools are seen to provide a further means to segment the market and to reach young people.

Of course, schools have long been markets for educational goods: textbooks, stationery and the like (see Wilson 1992b). Today, however, they are seen to represent new opportunities for promotion and profit via sponsorship, philanthropy and commercial opportunism – call it what you will (Battaglio 1987). More and more commercial enterprises without an educational dimension are giving themselves an educational gloss and 'targeting' schools, promoting goods which are not necessarily designed to meet the specific needs of the school environment. Therefore, they must 'destabilize the original notion of use or meaning of goods and attach to them new images and signs which can summon up a whole range of associated feelings and desires' (Featherstone 1992: 114). Thus, if they are to succeed in tapping the school market, they must remake the meaning of the products they sell by targeting the desires of this new consumer market. To do so, corporations have enlisted the aid of advertising agencies, market research and specialized educational marketing companies.

The school setting problematizes the interplay between the entertainment and advertising blend conventionally used to woo child and youth consumers, and the entertainment and education blend used to court parents. In the school context, education rather than entertainment becomes the principal channel of distribution. Given that adults have been positioned as the 'gatekeepers' of the in-school market, the generation gap constructed by consumer–media culture can no longer be exploited. Corporations targeting the in-school market have focused on engaging students, parents and schools simultaneously. Yet, there is little to suggest that marketers have been able to engage the dreams, desires and fantasies of the child and youth market in the school setting. As the following survey of the literature on in-school advertising and our interview data suggest, the views of schools and their students tend to converge with regard to the hybridization of education and advertising in schools. None the less, in-school advertising is becoming more commonplace and so, too, is its sophistication.

In their disregard for the traditional boundaries between school and commerce, promiscuous corporations have raised many moral and ethical dilemmas for schools, teachers and parents, the more so because today educational institutions have reason to be seduced. Yet, despite the moral panic which surrounds children's consumer culture in general and in-school advertising in particular, schools have become implicated in the process of double exchange we described in Chapter 1 (see p. 31). At the same time as the school is used by producers to sell products to consumers, school students have become commodities sold by schools and systems to producers. This is a further dimension of what Australian broadcaster, social commentator and former advertising executive, Phillip Adams, calls 'corporate paedophilia', his term for 'the mass molestation of the innocents as mighty corporations turn youngsters into economic units' (2000: 32). In this chapter we ask why corporations are targeting child consumers through schools, and why and how schools and their students are responding.

◯ The lure of schools

Marketing manager: Obviously people recognize, from a marketing point of view, that it is important to get into schools to reach children because they are a fairly difficult bunch to reach through other forms of media. So, it is a question of coming up with a method whereby one can actually get into schools.

Why has the commercial world turned its predatory eye on schools? Our analysis of advertising trade journals found a number of reasons, among them concern over the future of children's TV advertising. However, there are a number of other equally compelling reasons why the non-educational commercial sector is embracing in-school marketing. A+America, a loyalty marketing programme which helps schools earn free educational technology equipment and software by collecting proof of purchase items from sponsoring companies, points to some of these advantages in its online corporate brochure (www.aplusamerica.org/Brochure-04.cfm). These include access to a vast, networked and age-aggregated market; a cost-effective and less competitive alternative to saturated markets and advertising channels; and opportunity to enhance corporate image – all in the context of helping local schools. As a loyalty programme, A+America is also able to promise potential clients a 'national volunteer sales force' through its 'Moms network', and 'passionate consumers' since 'A+America families will go the extra mile to benefit their children and community'. Let us look at each of these inducements in a little more detail.

Audience reach

The possibility of stricter control over children's TV advertising – if not outright bans as in the case of Sweden's pledge to ban all TV advertising to under-12s during its presidency of the EU in 2001 (Hood 1998: 15) – has been one catalyst for marketers to look for alternatives to TV as an advertising medium.

While TV typically retains up to 90 per cent of the advertising dollar, one industry commentator has suggested that 'ban or no ban', its pre-eminence is no longer assured (Eastwood 1999). Eastwood identifies the following reasons why this is so: the impact of the Internet; increasing channel fragmentation; a decline in the quality of programming; the rise of what he calls new 'ambient' alternatives to TV viewing; and the pressure of societal change – including the 'erosion of the family unit' – on children's disposable leisure time. These reasons reflect the evolving relationships between advertising and consumer culture, technological innovation and the media form, and the construction of childhood and family life. Like it or not, this evolutionary process suggests that, whether TV declines or not, the effects of consumer culture are likely to intensify rather than abate.

In 1995, for example, Jacobson and Mazur (p. 72) predicted new VCRs capable of automatically editing out commercials in taped broadcasts. Today there are programmes for blocking unwanted online advertisements and once 'digital television comes in, such approaches could well be extended to the broadcast media' (McKenzie 2000: 27). However,

Jhally's (1990: 89) analysis of the impact of the remote control and video fast-forward suggests that such facilities are unlikely to thwart advertisers. The resulting fusion of entertainment and advertising in programme-length commercials like MTV and much of children's animated television programming clearly demonstrates the capacity of consumer culture not only to adapt to technological change, but to capitalize on it.

For people from industry like Eastwood (1999), having to think outside the literal and metaphorical 'box' has meant reappraising not only traditional non-broadcast media like cinema, comics, videos and cultural events, but computer games, the Internet and the emerging 'in-school' media industry. His own company, UK-based JazzyBooks, is a case in point, producing free sponsored exercise books for schools. Eastwood reports success in attracting otherwise TV-dependent advertisers including Tomy, Hasbro, Weetabix, the BBC and the Royal Mail. One of the virtues of this strategy is that daily use of exercise books sustains brand awareness.

Market reach

As we noted in Chapter 1, 'marketing experts in the post-war period estimated that women were responsible for up to 90 per cent of consumption decisions' (Humphery 1998: 95). While children and youth today may not have achieved the same degree of clout, statistics like Dan Acuff's estimate that 72 per cent of food and beverage purchases are influenced by kids (Nucifora 2000) show just how powerful a market they have become. In 1999, A.C. Nielson research figures showed Australians aged between 7 and 18 spent A\$3.8 billion (Hornery 2000). The teenage demographic in the USA alone spent an estimated US \$153 billion in 1999, including \$48 billion in family purchases (Schneiderman 2000, quoting Teenage Research Unlimited figures). In the UK, the average weekly expenditure of kids under 12 equated to £95 million a year in 1999 and they influenced family spending to the tune of £31 billion (Parker 1999), while in Canada in 1998, 9- to 19-year-olds spent \$13.5 billion (*Maclean's* 1999). These figures will only rise as the younger members of the Y Generation mature. 'Today, kids are a much-coveted consumer group' (Jacobson and Mazur 1995: 21) and schools, where they spend much of their day, offer a potentially captive audience for marketers.

No longer merely 'a symbol of consumer aspirations', as Kline (1993: 163) writes, 'a way of interesting a parent in a product, or of referring to children's expanding consumer needs', the child is now addressed directly by advertisers. The notion of the 'irrational woman shopper' has been displaced by 'pester power'. Children are the advertising industry's active if unwitting allies and the nagging child its ultimate weapon (Jacobson and Mazur 1995: 21). For instance, they have been strongly positioned both as the objects and subjects of the technological utopia. As an industry spokesman says, they are 'the Trojan Horse of the home market' (*Consumers* 1994: 8).

The managing director of a UK-based school media and sponsorship company estimates that the market segment comprising school-aged children and their parents 'accounts for almost half of the UK population' (Rossiter 1999). A+America put its market reach at 70 million consumers in 1999, the composition of which is very likely to extend beyond children and their immediate families. In Japan, for instance, the declining birth rate has given rise to the 'five pocket child' who is indulged not only by parents, but by grandparents, aunts and uncles, neighbouring households and others. This child metaphorically needs a 'pocket' for gifts such as *otoshidama*, or New Year's Money, from each of these sources (Creighton 1994). Such children are not only the beneficiaries of adult spending; they have spending power of their own. They provide access to profitable 'secondary' markets and are a niche market in their own right.

If the targeting of children through school offers a means of accessing a mass audience hitherto the preserve of the broadcast media, schools also offer the potential for 'narrowcasting' – that is, for customization. A mass audience does not necessarily equate to a mass market, and the traditional broadcast media is confronted with the further problem of audience fragmentation. Molnar (2000) says that 'children, particularly teenagers, represent a notoriously fragmented and thus difficult to reach market', watching far less TV than, say, the over-50 age group. Schools not only neutralize the negative effects of fragmentation by offering a captive audience; they present opportunities to turn fragmentation into an advantage. According to Calver (1999), 'more and more retailers are identifying the need to merchandise their products in ways which recognize the "tribal" nature of children's interests'. As the headline of one industry article puts it, peer group pressure is more influential than ads in brand decisions (*Advertising Age* 1997b). In schools, where peer groups are forcibly concentrated together, classmates provide a further advertising channel through which children and youth learn about brands.

There may not yet be the same degree of sophistication in streaming according to social, demographic and psychographic or lifestyle classifications in marketing to children as there is to adults (Calver 1999). However, the 'division of children into schools and grades potentially allows for very refined and specific targeting and message segmentation' (Curran 1999: 534). Schools offer convenient aggregations of age-coded children and, potentially, market segments which can be identified according to gender, class and ethnicity as well as curriculum. What better place than an all-girls school, for instance, for gender-targeted marketing such as

Johnson and Johnson's 'Follow Your Dream' promotion? The tenuous link between following your dreams and the contents of its sample bags (trial-size products of the teenage Clean and Clear skin care line as well as tampons and pads) was not lost on the adolescent recipient who brought us her bag. Nevertheless, Johnson and Johnson accessed almost 1000 young women in the private girls' school she attends.

Agencies targeting schools, such as US Modern's TeenPak who coordinate product sampling programmes like the 'Follow Your Dream' promotion promise 'clients that they can select their preferred audience by gender or by school type' (Consumers Union Education Services 1990: 8). Cover Concepts, which places advertisements on school textbooks, collects demographic data directly from schools and students. This enables them to 'target specific groups of, say, junior high school kids who live within a few blocks of a certain fast-food franchise, and distribute that company's ads on the covers to schools that most fit the bill' (Mormon 1997).

The growing recognition of 'distinctive use and buying patterns among minorities' has seen the development of advertising targeted according to ethnicity. Although the UK industry remains wary (Clegg 1996), this is a growth area in the USA with agencies specializing in targeting Hispanic, African-American and Asian-American households (*Precision Marketing* 1996). According to ethnic marketing research, these so-called 'minorities' have more kids and Baker (1999) suggests that 'the influence of the urban ethnic market cannot be understated, especially in the youth market'. Companies that have directly targeted the ethnic market in the USA include McDonald's, Coca-Cola, Reebok, Nabisco and Hallmark. In entertainment, the Hispanic market has been targeted by CTW with *Plaza Sesamo* and in 1999 Nickelodeon announced plans for a *Rugrats* spin-off featuring its African-American character, Susie Carmichael (Baker 1999). Kidpositive of Largo, Maryland released its first African-American children's title *Tell Me Who I Am* in 1998, while Pennsylvania-based Schlessinger Media, which has strong sales in the educational market, produces and distributes children's documentaries on African-American history and culture (Ashdown 1998).

In schools, curriculum materials provided by the manufacturers of the American Girl Collection now incorporate African-American Addy and Hispanic Josefina in a set of six dolls representing various periods in American history. Historically accurate clothes, accessories and accompanying books are available. Not only does this curriculum promote a rather dubious version of history and gendered multiculturalism, as we will later show, it promotes a product. In 2000, one doll, accessories, furniture and books cost $395 although, as Brady (1997) indicates, the books can be ordered at school through Scholastic Books for a more modest outlay.

As this implies, curriculum offers a further opportunity for customized advertising. Whereas broadcast media is able to sustain 'only a loose compatibility between programmes and commercials' (Jhally 1990: 91), narrowcasting blurs the distinction between programmes and commercials or, in the case of schools, education and advertising. Tampax's 'Mysteries of Me' lesson plans and activities, and Proctor and Gamble's *Changing: A Booklet for Girls* are good examples of ways in which manufacturers are able to heavily promote their products at the same time as delivering information (Consumers Union Education Services 1990: 10). By way of a brief account of the rise of in-school marketing in the UK, Rossiter (1999) points to the way industries and business have been able to identify subject areas in the National Curriculum and target their products to suit. UK Times Newspapers' and Time Computers' 1999–2000 'Software for Schools' promotion offered software linked to the National Curriculum in exchange for tokens. We return to look at how curriculum has been appropriated for corporate image work later in this chapter.

Much of the unsolicited advertising material delivered to schools which we collected is also targeted according to curriculum. (Over 100 items were delivered to one Australian school over the course of an eight-week period in 1996 either through the mail or included with teachers' professional publications.) We also found that advertising was addressed variously to principal or teacher by name or title, according to year level, subject area or department, and also to ancillary departments and fundraising committees – including the quaintly anachronistic 'Ladies' Auxiliary'.

Cost effectiveness, category exclusivity and brand awareness

With 'ad glut' or 'clutter' a major problem, advertisers are finding it increasingly difficult to make products appear distinctive in a marketplace saturated with ads. As they are relatively commercial-free, schools offer advertisers a largely competitor-free environment. Of course, the extent to which this remains true varies considerably both locally and globally. Nevertheless, in comparison with other advertising channels, schools are not only cheap but in many instances they offer opportunities for free advertising and direct access to the target audience.

Indeed, the population of entire school systems can be delivered for very little outlay on the part of the company. In 1997 the Peel Board of Education west of Toronto gave approval for ScreenAd Digital Billboards to run screensaver advertising on school computers (*Advertising Age* 1997a). In 1993 the Toronto Board of Education sold Pepsi Cola exclusive pop and juice vending rights in 115 Toronto schools teaching 87,000 students for $1.14 million. Pepsi threw in student-of-the-month plaques and prizes for students – Pepsi T-shirts and hats (Klein 1994). In 1998, the Coca-Cola Corporation offered the Seattle school district a ten-year, $6 million contract for exclusive rights to stock school vending machines. An editorial in *The Seattle Times* (1998) which weighed the pros and cons of in-school advertising concluded that few corporate–school partnerships are educationally benign and a deal with Coca-Cola is no exception. It cited the example of 'Coke Day' at one school in Georgia where 'home-economics students baked Coca-Cola cakes, chemistry students analyzed Coke's sugar content, the student body formed the shape of the word "COKE" for a group shot, and one boy was suspended for wearing a shirt with a small Pepsi logo'.

Corporations are interested in schools for the opportunities they present for the creation of a new generation of consumers. By reaching children from an early age, marketers are building brand awareness and brand loyalty. According to Jacobson and Mazur (1995: 21), research indicates that even 6-month-old babies are already forming mental images of corporate logos and mascots. Although their brand loyalties are still open to influence, by the time they are 3 most children are making specific requests for brand-name products (Jacobson and Mazur 1995: 21). Indeed, at age 3 more than four out of five know that McDonald's sells hamburgers (Kincheloe 1997b: 255). In its brochure, Lifetime Learning Systems, one of the growing number of agencies targeting the education sector, says that: 'school is the perfect time to communicate to young people directly . . . the ideal time to influence attitudes, build long-term loyalties, introduce new products, test market, promote sampling and trial usage and – above all – to generate immediate sales' (Consumers Union Education Services 1990: 8).

One reason young people are so attractive to advertisers is that 'they have a lifetime of spending ahead of them' (Jacobson and Mazur 1995: 21). David A. Adair, public relations director for the Pittsburgh Children's Museum, suggests that 'It is to the advantage of any company in any industry to associate itself with an organization which proves to be a first memory for many children' (Jacobson and Mazur 1995: 105). As one industry analyst commented, 'Catch them young and you've caught them for life' (Whitworth 1999).

As Sheila Harty's now classic study *Hucksters in the Classroom* (1979) shows, corporate promotion through curriculum materials has been underway for some time, particularly in the USA (see also Consumers Union Education Services 1990, 1995). Calvert and Kuehn (1993: 62) quote a study that indicates that nearly two-thirds of America's largest corporations provide schools with free curriculum materials. In *Giving Kids the Business* (1996), Alex Molnar describes the development in the USA of marketing firms that specialize in 'pitching' products at students in classrooms. Hence many companies now develop custom made, sometimes expensively produced learning materials bearing their corporate logo to be provided free to schools. Molnar's close analysis of these materials points to their increasing pedagogical sophistication and suggests that the application of educational ideas from education experts is becoming a 'natural' part of the process. The purpose here is usually sales and 'building brand and product loyalties'. This is usually overlaid by some apparent educational purpose – for example, 'to teach students nutrition' (see also Deveny 1990).

Jacobson and Mazur (1995) tell a similar story when they describe marketing companies like Lifetime Learning Systems (LLS) of Fairfield, Connecticut. LLS provides curricular material for schools on behalf of the likes of the American Nuclear Society, the Coca-Cola Company, the National Frozen Pizza Institute, the Snack Food Association and even the government of Saudi Arabia. Its sales kit invites potential clients to 'Let Lifetime Learning Systems bring your message to the classroom, where young people are forming attitudes that will last a lifetime' (Jacobson and Mazur 1995: 31).

Future workforce

Schools not only offer industry a means of grooming young people as consumers, but also as their future workforce. If it is the case that the Y Generation and the Options Generation are as open, fluid, non-committal, diverse, idiosyncratic, individualized and adapted to change as Mackay (1997) suggests, then this makes them rather difficult for both employers and marketers to pin and hold down. Further, having grown up in the long shadow of economic and job insecurity, they do not gain their identities from their worlds of work (or no work) and this is a problem for employers who want committed and disciplined, if flexible, workers. The suggestion that they do gain their identities through consumption is not necessarily satisfying to producers of goods and services given the possibility that young people may just as readily switch to lifestyle codes which undermine their capacity to consume and/or their interest in sustained consumption. Market involvement in schools and the marketing of schools helps the world of commerce to address these dilemmas. As US education writer, Jonathan Kozol (1992: 8), explains:

> When business enters education . . . it sells something more important than the brand names of its products. It sells a way of looking at the world and at oneself. It sells predictability instead of critical capacities. It sells a circumscribed, job-specific utility. 'I'm in the business,' says Elaine Mosley, the principal of a corporate-sponsored high school in Chicago, 'of developing minds to meet a market demand'.

By 1999, the Burger King Corporation had expanded its chain of Burger King Academies to 24 and it is just one of a burgeoning number of entrepreneurial education programmes in the USA, Australia, Canada and Europe (see Martin 1997). Working in conjunction with Communities in Schools, Inc., the academies offer tuition, including employment skills and on-the-job training to students 'failed' by the traditional school system. According to the company website (www.burgerking.com.community/bkacademies.htm), Burger King franchisees 'also develop and coordinate a variety of exemplary education programs in their own communities. These local programs create strong bonds between Burger King Franchisees and local students'.

However, an interview published by *Corporate Watch* (1998) suggests that private educational initiatives like the Burger King Academies and public/private partnerships between schools and corporate sponsors raise issues of equity. According to Libero della Piana of the Applied Research Institute in Oakland, California, they are designed to appeal to 'urban communities of colour'. He says that this boils down to unequal funding which 'plays out racially [and] creates opportunities for corporations to influence schools'. However, corporate influence is itself unequal:

> In poor communities you have Burger King Academies. Burger King comes in to help 'at risk' kids and provides them a job opportunity flipping burgers if they have a certain attendance record. But in rich communities you have Microsoft Academies which prep kids for high tech jobs and track them into the best colleges.

This is a reflection, della Piana argues, of corporate America's attempts to reform education to meet the needs of the new job economy through privatization. The long-term outcome suggested by his claim is supported by Gabriel's (1994) data on racial representation among staff of McDonald's UK. In spite of its equal opportunity policy, 'most McDonald's workers of black and ethnic minority background are in low-paid work with minimal skill requirements' (Gabriel 1994: 109).

Equity issues of a different sort were raised in Australia in 1997 when McDonald's announced a scheme to directly link its workplace training programme with the public education sector. Members of its largely school-aged workforce are now able to gain credit towards their High School Certificate and receive bonus points towards their Tertiary Entrance Rank score. This scheme is the most recent of a long line which link education directly with business and, more recently, schools with private training providers. It marks yet another stage in the process by which education is drawn into what Sharp has described as the 'vortex of the commodity' (1985).

The McDonald's scheme has raised many matters of concern which include the following. It privileges one enterprise over others in the fast-food industry and McDonald's students over other non-apprenticeship/traineeship students who work part time while at school. It thus opens the floodgates to similar demands from other such outlets, and to a loss of quality control by education systems. It allows a US multinational company to provide an Australian education credential which is not open to public scrutiny or revision by Australian educators due to 'Commercial in Confidence' claims. This leaves schools and systems in an awkward position with regard to their responsibilities to students and raises questions about the ways in which redress might be addressed once such VET (vocational education and training) has been outsourced. It also raises questions about the distinction between vocational education and vocational training and the extent to which such students will ever get the opportunity to address any of the contentious issues associated with the world of work and with their rights as worker-citizens. Further, it raises questions about where the connections between education systems, schools and McDonald's might stop.

The McDonald's scheme allows school students who work part time in fast-food outlets to gain training accreditation (with global portability) while at school – and at no financial cost to the school or student. For these reasons it has been welcomed by certain students and in certain education circles. There is no doubt that governments and the world of business and industry have decided that schools must be more directly involved in skill formation for the world of paid work.

Corporate image

Given the popular perception of the corporate sector as greed-driven and uninterested in the wider public good, corporate public relations activities are increasingly designed to counteract poor reputations. Schools are a particularly good place for corporations to do this sort of ideological work and to establish a philanthropic image (see, for example, McDonnell 1994). Not only do schools offer a way to establish and maintain a high public profile, but an opportunity for businesses with doubtful reputations or bad publicity to practise some reverse psychology. As Marylyn Collins (1993: 53) argues:

> Even if a firm has not made some well publicized antisocial gaffe in the past, it can no longer safely assume a neutral position. Active social involvement in the form of some kind of philanthropic action is becoming a way of reassuring the public of their good intentions, while at the same time creating a stock of goodwill and separating the 'saints' from the 'sinners'.

This is especially likely when a company's negative work, employment or environmental practices are exposed or when its product is seen to have negative implications for people's health.

Hence, it is not at all unusual for companies to produce curriculum materials which directly address these problems or practices by offering students a positive spin. McDonald's, for instance, has attractive materials on the environment to try to counter the bad publicity it received over its role in the destruction of rainforests in South-East Asia. Molnar (1996: 28) cites environmental education material distributed by the American Forest Foundation and The Plastic Bag Association as well as a video produced by Exxon which minimized the environmental impact of the oil spill in 1989. According to Brady (1997: 224), historical revisionism of this sort is not about mere deception; it is about rewriting history 'as a unified chronological record of events [which is] exonerated of its contradictory, complex and seamy sides'.

A more positive example of this trend is Rethinking Drinking, a drug education curriculum that utilizes a harm minimization approach. This curriculum employs a variety of problem-solving scenarios – for example, a video story entitled *The Party*, and information-based activities related to the alcohol content of different standard-sized drinks. The curriculum does not assume that students do not or will not drink. Rather, it assumes that drinking is a part of everyday experience for many people, including young people, and thus claims to be preparing students for the times when they *will* drink. The curriculum has been prepared by health education curriculum consultants and distributed in association with the Australian Council for Health, Physical Education and Recreation. The irony remains, however, that it is a curriculum development that has been funded by the Australian Brewers Foundation.

Corporate reputations are not only salvaged by the content or appeal of glossy curriculum materials alone. By their very presence in the classroom, corporate-produced curricular materials assume authority. Lifetime Learning Systems is explicit about this: '"Coming from school", promises the sales kit, "all these materials carry an extra measure of credibility that gives your message added weight" . . . "IMAGINE millions of students discussing your product in class. IMAGINE their teachers presenting your organization's point of view"' (Jacobson and Mazur 1995: 31). Furthermore, as Whitworth (1999) points out, 'On the whole, parents trust schools', and endorsement by association is a powerful advertising tool. Needless to say, this is no guarantee of educational value.

The trend towards philanthropy and sponsorship reflects the centrality of image or attitudinal benefits in differentiating products and services in the face of the homogenizing impact of technology and globalization. According to Parker (1991: 23), consumers expect companies to 'substantiate' their claims to be 'good corporate citizens'. Avon, for example, supplies Australian schools with free sunscreen. However, there are other reasons why educational philanthropy/sponsorship is such an effective, if not opportunistic, marketing strategy.

Schools have long been the traditional sites of fundraising for charities and non-profit organizations. When the MS (multiple sclerosis) Readathon, for example, was introduced into Australia in the 1970s, there were very few school-related fundraising ventures. Today, there is not only much more competition in this sector, but increasing pressure on schools to fundraise to meet their *own* needs. These competing interests have offered a window of opportunity for corporate advertisers and point to one of a number of reasons why many schools are responding to rather than resisting the overtures of corporations. In the next section we look more closely at corporate 'philanthropy' in the guise of educational sponsorship and how it is designed to counteract opposition.

◯ Seducing schools

Predictably, many school principals, teachers and parents remain deeply ambivalent about the incursions of commerce and advertising into schools. Much of this opposition stems from the desire to maintain at least one commercial-free zone or sacred space for young people. However, schools have been placed in a difficult and ambiguous position. High ideals tend to fade away as State-provided school finances decline and as the State 'encourages' closer partnerships between education and industry. Educationally sound and attractively packaged curriculum materials fill the hole in the resources budget of schools and offer technologically sophisticated 'solutions' to the pedagogical problems of overworked teachers. These pressures have created a conflict of interest between schools' mandate to educate, and their moral and ethical duties to protect children from exploitation by consumer culture. Corporations have recognized and taken advantage of this dilemma.

First, corporations have positioned themselves as supporters of education through sponsorship programmes. Educational 'sponsorship' takes a wide variety of forms beyond gifts, donations and financial support of school events. It includes many of the strategies we have referred to over the course of this chapter: curriculum materials, exclusive agreements, sponsored programmes and activities – in short, privatization. It also includes making available corporate facilities, expertise and equipment; subsidizing exhibitions, concerts and conferences for pupils or teachers; purchasing advertising space; and holding competitions and voucher and incentive schemes. Second, corporations have constructed themselves as both good corporate citizens and guardians of traditional values in order to mask their principal goal of accessing a consumer market.

This does not necessarily mean that schools are naïve and hapless victims of these strategies of seduction. Analysing interview data collected from Australian school principals, Collier *et al.* (1994) identify five categories of response to the commercialization of the classroom. These range from absolute philosophical rejection at one end of the spectrum; expressions of resentment, contradiction and pragmatism in the mid-range; to active and enthusiastic support at the other. These positions are reflected in the variety of approaches to commercialization, with schools variously accepting and actively soliciting commercial support, and initiating commercial activities of their own. In this section, we counterpoint the responses of principals with the strategies commerce and advertising have employed in order to gain entry to school communities, focusing first on how the ethical opposition to in-school marketing has been co-opted as a marketing strategy, and second on educational sponsorship.

'Ethical' marketing

The very idea of sponsorship, of the commercial, is abhorrent to me. I will, if I am able, resist it.

(Primary school principal)

As a school we do not accept sponsorship as many see it as an insidious form of exposing children to commercial advertising.

(Primary school principal)

As these comments suggest, much of the opposition to the colonization of schools by consumer culture is ethical (see Consumers Union Education Services 1995 for a comprehensive summary of the arguments for and against in-school commercialism). Unfortunately, such principled resistance is based on the fantasy that social institutions can remain separate from social and cultural trends. Indeed, it ignores the extent to which, for decades, schools have been targeted with commercial products associated with food and books, banking and insurance. Press coverage of and controversy over the extent of advertising on Channel One which is broadcast in US schools has drawn attention to commercials in the classroom and 'create[d] the illusion that schools resist the commercialization of the classroom' (Consumers Union Education Services 1990: 8). Identifying educational policy in regard to advertisements on sponsored educational materials as early as 1929, Molnar (2000) notes that advisory committees in the 1950s 'warned teachers against uncritical acceptance of sponsored materials, but also recommended that they not reject such offerings outright'.

However, 'schoolhouse commercialism' has increased dramatically in the 1990s. According to Molnar's (2000) research (he tracked citations registering in-school commercial activity through various databases), there was a 303 per cent increase overall between 1990 and 1999 in the USA. At the same time, the circumspection with which schools regard in-school advertising has also increased. According to this Australian school principal:

> The main problem of accepting sponsorship arises when attitudes of parents, staff, and/or (especially) students are likely to be altered in some way which is counterproductive to the ethical functions of the school (moral, academic, nutritional, etc.). As a school we . . . do not seek sponsorship (nor accept it) if we consider it to be counter-productive to the broader education we are trying to provide.
>
> (Primary school principal)

Points of view like this have led some industry 'players' to reframe the discourse surrounding in-school marketing in ethical terms, suggesting that it is a more ethical way of reaching children than mainstream advertising because it is: 'a non-emotional and non-emotive form of advertising. There is no mental pressure put on children with the products because they are just brand products in their hands' (marketing manager).

For others, like Rossiter (1999), such points of view have meant adopting an 'ethical stance' towards in-school marketing. Based on industry experience, he makes a number of recommendations that businesses might follow if they are to get the 'ethics of in-school activity right':

- seek endorsement by a recognized educational body;
- clearly communicate the ethical nature of the programme to teachers;
- build a long-term partnership with schools;
- provide benefits to schools and pupils;
- arrange independent vetting and checking of marketing material;
- establish feedback mechanisms to identify whether schools are happy;
- run a pilot scheme before rolling out nationally.

This approach is clearly successful. Despite the ethical reservations of the principal quoted above, his school had participated annually in almost every major promotion including Heinz's 'Sportz for All Sortz', Coles Supermarkets' 'Apples for the Students', Pizza Hut's 'Book It!' and Pizza Hut's 'Sport It!'. Cover Concepts reports that 90 per cent of schools they had contacted by 1997 had accepted their advertising-emblazoned book covers, giving them a market reach of almost half the school children in the USA (Mormon 1997). Co-founder, Steve Shulman, said 'we get letters all the time [from schools] asking if we have any more free stuff to send. Sometimes the teachers and schools don't understand why they're getting the covers free'. The bottom line, however, is as Rossiter explains:

For companies engaged in any form of promotional activity in the school environment, the challenge is to harness the power of marketing to the benefit of education. A successful scheme must have educational value which will help teachers do their jobs, save the schools money, get the children excited, and make parents happy *while still achieving the brand's strategic objectives.*

(1999, emphasis added)

In seeking to target the desires of the whole marketing audience – parents, teachers and children – these recommendations reflect industry awareness of the complexities of the in-school market. It is clear, however, that some of these 'ethical guidelines' are not just good marketing practice, but marketing strategies in themselves. If products in schools are just brands in the hands of children as the marketing manager quoted above suggests, they are differently positioned in relation to adult feelings and desires.

Corporate advertisers are increasingly positioning themselves as promoters of traditional values in the consumer age and winning over schools in the process. Describing why his school participates in corporate-sponsored fundraising activities, one school principal said 'Our goal isn't so much raising the funds but creating empathy, awareness and a caring attitude' (*The Sunday Age* 2000a: 17). A primary school principal we interviewed described the Coles Supermarkets/Apple campaign as the best promotion he had experienced 'because it gave the school community a common goal that could be achieved' but, somewhat naïvely, felt that 'whether it was successful for the Coles group is debatable'.

In the lead-up to the Sydney 2000 Olympic Games, the Westpac banking group ran a TV advertising campaign promoting its in-school programme designed to promote among its participants Olympic ideals like fair play, goal-setting, achievement, teamwork, focus and friendship. Clearly, promotions of this kind cultivate a good corporate image by implying that these qualities are valued and aspired to by, if not actual attributes of, the corporate advertiser. However, inspirational messages appear to be an effective way of masking the real advertising intent and disarming those critics of educational sponsorship who argue that it 'creates materialism and hinders the development of moral and ethical values' (Bennett and Gabriel 1999: 43).

For example, a panel of parents, teachers and administrators who reviewed advertisements to be run in a Canadian school district by ScreenAd Digital Billboards approved a Pepsi ad that advised students to 'develop a thirst for knowledge' but rejected a fast-food ad asking 'Hungry? Get the taste now!' (Salkowski 1997). A marketing manager for Imagination for School Media Marketing which places advertising in UK schools said 'We would not allow things like sugary fizzy drinks. We wouldn't entertain computer games or sportswear, or selected confectionery. But if let's say Cadbury's came up with an anti-litter campaign, then we'd certainly look at it' (Whittaker 1998).

The co-founder of the US equivalent to Jazzy Books, Cover Concepts, says that the majority of their covers have a public service message: 'Nike with a racial harmony cover, or celebrities telling kids to stay in school, not to smoke, or covers promoting recycling' (Mormon 1997). We suggest that these messages function as a form of cross-selling which commodifies both non-commercial participants and consumers. The same can be said of the related practices of bringing together corporate, government and charitable bodies as multiple sponsors (Rossiter 1999) and of generating a market for fundraising products by dividing the profits equally between the school, a charity and the company. Otherwise known as cause-related marketing, these are instances of the way in which, as we explained in the introduction to this chapter, new images and signs are attached to the meaning of goods in order to adapt them to new markets and channels of distribution. We argue that in many cases what corporate advertisers attempt to pass off as ethical marketing is, in fact, cause-related marketing.

Educational sponsorship

Ultimately, the acceptance of corporate sponsored fundraising and philanthropic programmes is not just about inculcating good civic values or the naïvety of consumers. It is driven by wider social, technological and economic forces. According to Lindsay McMillan, chief executive of the MS Society of Victoria: 'Generation X's attitude is that if you can't do something yourself, bad luck. Two difficulties involved in fundraising with children are that it may be seen as not cool, and general community attitudes are making it harder to ask people to contribute' (*The Sunday Age* 2000b).

These factors affect not only professional fundraising bodies but schools as well. In a society which has become highly protective of its children, young schoolchildren are no longer encouraged to door-knock in their neighbourhood to get sponsors or to sell raffle tickets. Corporate sponsorship bypasses such impediments. Indeed, cake stalls and quiz nights seem pointless in comparison with initiatives like AOL Europe's and Bertlesmann's joint investment of $75 million to provide free Internet access to 900,000 teachers and to 10 million students at the special rate of $5 a month, and Deutsche Telekom's offer of free Internet access and ISDN connection to 40,000 schools (*Advertising Age* 2000). While Deutsche Telekom said its initiative would not feature in its advertising campaigns, a philanthropic image can only be created if it is communicated to its consumer audience.

Given this, companies purporting to benefit schools have favoured campaigns in which tokens, wrappers or vouchers are collected and redeemed for educational equipment. Neither pure sponsorship nor pure promotion, such incentive programmes are also a form of cause-related marketing which allows the company to represent itself as making it possible for schools and students to acquire what they need and want, and thus generates goodwill. It also allows companies to exploit the greater publicity potential of competitions and, crucially, to generate immediate sales. These competitions typically offer rewards for both the school and the student.

Most marketers understand that offering expensive equipment, such as computers, is an incentive for both schools and students. Coles Super-markets' 'Apples for the Students' in Australia which ran until 1993, Tesco's 'Computers for Schools' scheme in the UK which started in 1992 and the 25-year-old Campbell's 'Labels for Education' campaign in the USA are attractive to schools who want or need the equipment. Mirror Group Newspapers and Times Newspapers both launched similar schemes in 1999, seeking to boost circulation figures by providing millions of pounds worth of free equipment to schools (*Kids Marketing Report* 1999). Mirror Group Newspapers linked with McVitie's biscuits and KP snack foods to run the government-backed education scheme 'Maths Stuff for Schools'. Tokens could be exchanged for goods ranging from a protractor to a PC. Interviewees from all groups in our surveys, marketers, teachers and students, commented that many schools are unable to afford expens-ive equipment and, for some, participation in promotional competitions such as these is the only way to obtain it.

However, this viewpoint is often undercut by concerns about social justice and equity issues relating to the capacity of some schools to win sponsorship or participate in promotions due to their remote location, school image or student population. In spite of the experience in the USA where schools with high populations of disadvantaged or minority students are the most likely to accept corporate sponsorship deals (see, for example, Consumers Union Education Services 1995), this appears to have some foundation. Research by the Department of Business Studies at one UK university found that 'schools located in prosperous areas were far more proactive in their approaches to sponsorship and employed headteachers with more positive attitudes towards marketing and sponsorship than schools in poorer neighbourhoods' (Bennett and Gabriel 1999: 41). A reason for this discrepancy is suggested by Kennedy's (2000) discussion of school budgets in the USA where educational budgets are comprised of differing ratios of federal, State and local funding. He says 'School districts are not created equal' since funding will be relative to the prosperity of the citizens who comprise a district's tax base and, thus, to 'demographic, political and geographical differences, varying

levels of commitment to education and the traditions of local control'
(pp. 17–18).

According to Townsend (1998) many of the problems of school equity
and efficiency resulting from cuts in educational funding have coincided
with the international trend towards self-managing schools (for the
Canadian perspective, see Kuehn 1996). Alleged devolution of school
management to communities and principals lies at the heart of educational reform implemented by the Clinton administration in the USA,
with its charter schools, and by the Thatcher and subsequent Blair governments in the UK, with their locally managed schools and education
authorities. Australian academic, John Smythe, argues that experiments
in devolution in Australia like the 'Schools of the Future' project in the
State of Victoria are 'about removing support structures, cutting them
away and leaving schools to market forces' (quoted in Heaney 1994:
17). As one secondary school principal we interviewed observes: 'The
current initiative of "Schools of the Future" will force schools to seek
funds and sponsorship more vigorously. Currently I am contemplating
the hiring of a professional fundraiser and the establishment of a formal
marketing plan'.

In being forced to look beyond traditional sources of funding, schools
and students are being transformed into 'products' to be 'sold to businesses
in order to generate new capital to meet education demands' (Curran
1999: 534). It is ironic that funds will need to be diverted from immediate education needs to marketing, as the above comment implies. This is
a 'luxury' we doubt all schools will be able to afford. Nevertheless, as we
shall argue in Chapter 5, the ability of schools to survive is becoming
dependent on their own marketing expertise.

Often 'strapped for cash' and 'on the make', many schools are likely
to be receptive given the new strains, freedoms and compulsions associated with school deregulation and local school management – one such
compulsion being 'partnerships' between schools and industry. For some,
like this primary school principal, the emerging symbiosis between schools
and business is a positive development: 'At X, the local community is
clearly supportive of our school and its programmes and [sponsorship]
serves as a vehicle for placing the school in the heart of the business
activity in the area'.

Indeed, many schools are jumping on the commercial bandwagon,
accepting or actively soliciting advertising and school business partnerships as well as initiating commercial enterprises of their own. These
vary greatly in sophistication. In the UK, for instance, a scheme launched
in 1998 offered schools £5000 a year to carry poster advertising in
school corridors, gymnasia and playgrounds, and on dining chairs (Bennett
and Gabriel 1999: 41). The global online student newspaper publisher
HighWired.com allows schools to sell banner space to local advertisers

and keep 100 per cent of the profits, turning participation into a revenue raiser. A primary school in rural Victoria made the press in 1994 when it accepted a local grower's offer of A$5000 to harvest the annual grape crop (Painter 1994). The proceeds went towards helping to pay for curriculum specialists, field trips and the school's minibus. In the effort to generate their own revenue, schools are also becoming entrepreneurial. Such initiatives range from short courses in painting, woodwork and small business practice to full business ventures such as language, adult literacy and technology training centres; and from offering school facilities for hire to ambitious construction projects. For example, an expensive private Adelaide school, Trinity College, built the A$7.7 million 'Starplex' with the express view of raising revenue. Consisting of four basketball courts, two swimming pools, an 1100-seat theatre and a gymnasium, it has already paid for itself through subletting (Fewster 2000: 14). It is argued that such steps will allow schools like Trinity to maintain affordable fees – even though the existing fees are in fact out of the reach of the average parent.

Yet, in many cases the argument of financial need with which many schools justify their marketing relationships with corporations is not reflected in actual monetary gain. Molnar (2000) cites the case of the partnership deal struck by Colorado Springs District 11. In 1996–7, the programme raised $140,000 selling advertising space on school buses and in school buildings and grounds. Aimed at raising funds for musical instruments, computers and staff training, the actual revenue realized equated to $4.35 per student – as Molnar says, 'hardly enough to make a dent in the $4.8 million District 11 announced it had to trim from its budget in March of 1999'. Curran (1999) makes the case that because sponsorship is an 'easy' way for schools to raise funds, corporations are able to take advantage of schools. The reason for this, she argues, is that 'Corporations are well informed of the schools' need for revenue, yet school administrators are ill informed or do not fully comprehend the value of exclusive access to the children, an information asymmetry that apparently leads to an undervaluing of this access' (Curran 1999: 535).

In hard times, with school budgets strained to the limit, 'cash hungry' (Giroux 1994: 53) schools and education systems are often very willing accomplices to the corporate push into schools. But as Calvert and Kuehn (1993: 58) point out, 'Charity from business, rather than taxation of business, puts power in the hands of business to set the agenda for education'. Giroux (1994: 48, 49) takes this line of argument further when he points to the extent to which donations to education cannot only put businesses in the position to influence the development of curriculum, they can also save business substantial amounts of money in on-the-job training programmes. He goes on to say:

Corporations play a double role here. On the one hand they aggressively support tax cutting measures . . . On the other, they then
offer the financially strapped schools 'crumbs' that allow private
business interests to turn the schools into market niches. Of course
if public schools were adequately funded in the first place such
bribes wouldn't be necessary. At risk is both the traditionally civic
democratic function of public schooling and the very nature of how
we define democratic community, critical citizenship, and the most
basic premises of teaching and learning.

(Giroux 1994: 51)

Overall, the main imperative is to commercialize the classroom and
the curriculum – and other aspects of the school such as the canteen, the
sports field, the front office and, indeed, the school administration (Sa
1992; Barlow and Robertson 1994) – in order to establish schools as
legitimate sites for profit and savings, and to produce future citizens who
are dedicated and uncritical consumers and dedicated and docile workers.

◯ Wooing kids

In spite of the concern surrounding the commercialization of schools
and education, many scholars are coming to the view which market
researchers have held for a long time. Kids are highly literate when it
comes to explicit advertising and well aware of its purpose (see, for
example, Buckingham 1998a). Hardman (1998) points to the Children's
Research Unit report, *Youthsight*, which found that:

children from as young as three years old can recognise the persuasive intent of advertising. While at this early age, they can verbalise
the role of advertising as 'they're trying to get me to buy it', by the
age of five or six this has developed into 'they are trying to sell me
something'. By seven, most children are capable of understanding
exactly what advertisers are trying to achieve and, by ten, children
have become adept critics and prove a hard – even cynical – audience to influence.

A *Kids Marketing Report* (Steward 1998) survey of children aged 9 to 11
found:

They know about targeting. They know which ads are aimed at
them and which are more 'grown up' and they also clearly identify
ads that are 'babyish' and therefore are for much younger people
than them. They understand that some ads are aimed at 'the person
who does the shopping' and some are aimed at them so that they
can influence the person who does the shopping!

Children know that advertising is designed to make people buy things and to help ailing products. They take a very moral stance towards TV advertising around the age of 9 to 11 years, not only believing that cigarettes and alcohol should not be advertised, but that anything associated with sexuality like tampons, women's underwear and condoms should not be aired until after young children have gone to bed. They are also aware that advertising cannot always be trusted and that advertising promotes materialism and greed. However, unlike their parents, they do not resist it. They see it as offering information and 'They take it as part of the entertainment being offered' (Steward 1998).

The question we ask in this section is, do children demonstrate the same degree of discrimination and acceptance with regard to commercials in schools? Do they recognize advertising in the various guises in which it appears: curriculum materials, competitions, sample bags, fundraising, canteens stocked with one brand, commercials accompanying broadcast and online educational programmes and corporate sponsorship and donations? We found that as critics and consumers of in-school marketing, kids displayed many of the characteristics identified by *Youthsight*. The interview data which forms the basis of this section show that kids do not resist in-school advertising, accepting it as part of market culture. At the same time, they have a moral sense of what is proper in the school setting. This, and their awareness of the instrumentality of in-school promotions, echoes the adult attitudes we have already identified.

However, our data also suggest that the current advertising and education blend does not tap into kids' desires and pleasures or serve as the basis for identity-building in the same way as the hybridization of advertising and entertainment. Our analysis in Chapter 2 indicates that the fact that children are able to decipher advertising intent in television commercials does not necessarily mean that they will demonstrate the same degree of discrimination in regard to programming which blends advertising and entertainment. Given this, will they be able to decode advertising intent if and when the in-school advertising form blends education with the pleasures of entertainment? We conclude this section with a cautionary look at some of the existing and emergent forms of in-school commercialism which reproduce kids' preferred consumer form in the school setting.

Kids as consumers

We found an inherent acceptance of marketing as a basic feature of everyday life when we put the following scenario to a range of students aged between 8 and 11 years:

Interviewer: Here is a newspaper photo of a classroom. There is a television, video recorder and computer supplied by the Coles docket competition. There are hockey sticks from a sports competition that Pizza Hut ran; footballs from a Hungry Jacks competition; and cricket gear from a Western Star competition. What do you think about having a classroom like that?

Boy (9 years):   It would be awesome . . . because at our school we have all the sports equipment in the room over there and we get to borrow it every morning but by the time I get to school and go to the sports room and I want to borrow skipping ropes, they have closed. So that would be all right because you would get the sports equipment in your room and you can take it out every playtime.

Girl (11 years): Pretty good because they have got all good stuff and they could use it whenever they like.

Girl (10 years): I would feel lucky to get it.

In the photograph we showed to the students, the classroom has been transformed into a site of consumption, abundance and, therefore, instant gratification.

If this is the stuff of dreams for the students of many Australian schools, Tobin (1997: 16) argues that in the USA:

> Consumer desire is reproduced by the material reality of our pre-schools. The variety of things and choices offered by middle-class preschools is overwhelming to many children. We create over-stimulating environments modeled on the excess of the shopping mall and amusement park . . . We have become so used to the hypermateriality of our early childhood care settings that we are oblivious to the clutter; settings that provide more structure and are less distracting seem stark or bleak.

Tobin is here referring only to toys and equipment, not to the advertising to be found in many schools. He argues that this is a form of commodity reification which reflects the consumption-driven nature of late capitalism rather than authentic desire, and which conflates 'things with value' (1997: 16).

We found that this view was reflected in the responses of the students we interviewed. The majority considered in-school marketing and promotional material to be normal and, therefore, acceptable. This was the case even when they were well aware of the advertising intent and said that it neither influenced nor altered their own or their family's consumer behaviour. The most frequent reason they gave for this was:

'If you get them for free it's all right', or, as another student put it, 'I guess it is [okay], because you get stuff out of it, but it isn't costing the school anything'. The notion that 'if it's free it's okay' is a statement about the understanding of commodity values: a tangible return for minimal input means there is some basic value in the exchange.

This was borne out by the answers we got when we asked students what sort of competitions they considered to be the best:

> *Boy (8 years):* Coles.
> *Interviewer:* Why is Coles the best?
> *Boy (8 years):* Because it has the most.
> *Boy (9 years):* And the computers are better than the sports equipment and the TV is good as well because computers teach you more than a basketball can. And a TV can teach you more than a football can teach you.

In terms of basic exchange value, computers are signifiers of a high value commodity because they are linked to the high status employment of the high-tech industries and because they have a central role in providing entertainment. In this sense, the Coles/Apple computers for dockets competition taps into a well-established set of understandings and values about the links between education and the maximum value zones of the emergent global information-based economy.

Most students recognized the ramifications of the market environment: 'Schools should probably take advantage of it because if they don't they're going to miss out on the stuff and they need it to survive' (13-year-old boy). The notion of scarcity amid abundance is a key concept of consumer culture wherein 'Although an excess of materials is available, consumers must believe that if they don't act quickly and impulsively, the opportunity will pass them by' (Tobin 1997: 16). Our data show that this awareness was mapped onto students' understanding of educational sponsorship and placed pressure on them to participate in competitions and to purchase certain products or to shop at certain stores. This view is supported by a student who commented 'they'll take their sponsorship somewhere else anyway' (13-year-old boy). He obviously felt some pressure to contribute to this opportunity for his school, given the possibility that it might be lost permanently if the activity was not taken up.

These positions suggest that the shift in the marketing site to the domain of education disrupts the generational opposition which consumer culture cultivates in the domains of leisure and entertainment. They echo the adult tendency to regard consumer products in instrumental terms – that is, in terms of teaching and self-improvement. We also found that kids echoed the critical and moral positions of the adult generation.

Kids as critics

When we asked a group of 8- to 11-year-old kids what they would think
if McDonald's, for instance, offered to buy sporting equipment for the
school if the kids wore a McDonald's hat in return, the response was a
unanimous 'No'. The perception of McDonald's which had emerged in
response to an earlier set of questions relating to preferences in takeaway
food was far less critical. In this instance, McDonald's was considered a
'treat' because of its 'really cool playground' and because 'You get toys
out of the Happy Meals'. The shift in context from the domain of leisure
to education clearly made the difference, acting to defamiliarize the familiar. As the following transcript suggests, these 9-year-old students saw
the equation between fast food and athletics as a contradiction in terms:

Boy:	Like, it's not really sporting equipment, sort of McDonald's sporting equipment. And you would like, expect an Adidas hat or something.
Interviewer:	Oh, I see, because McDonald's is not really associated with fitness and sport, you don't think it would be a good idea?
Boy:	Yes, it's sort of junk food.
Girl:	I think it wouldn't be a very good idea because, like, they sell . . . if they give you sports equipment to get you fit, why would they give you junk food that would make you fat and stuff?

A group of 11-year-old students picked up on this same theme but
'cool' was more of a factor, reflecting their greater awareness of – and
susceptibility to – brand advertising:

Girl:	Most hats are advertising things. Like I have a Nike hat, and it's got a little tick on it, and people see a Nike hat, they think, 'Oh Nike'. It's a little tick. So like James has got a hat, and it's got . . . What's it got written on it?
Boy:	Oh, just a basketball team.
Girl:	Yes, so that's sort of like . . .
Interviewer:	Advertising too, isn't it? In a way? Yes?
Boy:	Except they are the cool things to advertise, so like . . .
Interviewer:	So, it's better to advertise Nike than McDonald's?
All:	Yes.
Boy:	Nike makes clothes and things, and McDonald's makes food, so McDonald's should stay making food.

Clearly, the students were able to decode relatively transparent attempts
to promote corporate products which lack an inherent or logical
educational/extracurricular dimension or connection. Would these same

students be as critical of, say, Nike Australia's sponsorship of 'Pitch, Hit and Run', a primary school baseball and teeball programme or of Kelloggs' low-key sponsorship of 'Hands on Food', a nutritional education programme, which blur the boundaries between advertising and education?

As the following comments suggest, children are aware of the purpose of promotions and competitions:

> *Girl (11 years):* Mainly all the businesses do it just so people will go there . . . advertisement . . . just by their name being on a blackboard or something they're getting more out of it.
>
> *Girl (11 years):* They do that so you go there and buy their things . . . they just have to buy a few computers but they're making money really . . . more people want to raise money to get the computers but while they're doing that they're giving Coles money.
>
> *Girl (13 years):* Not really for our advantage because they're just publicizing their product on the children. If they walk around wearing a McDonald's cap or a Pizza Hut T-shirt, well, it's just really walking advertising.

A significant number of students feel that businesses are getting more out of running competitions in schools than the schools are for the amount of work they do.

Kids' ambivalence about who benefits from competitions and in-school events like McDonald's or Pizza Hut Day where schools receive a percentage of sales reveals a degree of self-interest. Clearly, the pay-off for schools from educational philanthropy, sponsorship and competitions is not the same for all kids and varies greatly with age group. If, according to market research, cause-related marketing strategies appeal to older kids, it is clear that they are not motivated in the same way when the beneficiary is the school. Our research undertaken during the Coles/ Apple computer promotion in Australia suggests that older kids were more likely to participate when individual prizes were offered. As one 12-year-old boy put it, 'You don't get anything for bringing your docket or being in the competitions, most of the prizes are for the school and sometimes you don't even get to use them'.

Unlike younger students who were often enticed by the perceived value of the prizes, we found that the older students were tired of computers as prizes. They were generally not as interested in being involved in competitions – unless they were fun in themselves or if they were to pay off in other ways. If they were to participate, like the younger students, they also wanted something more personal, such as CDs. It was no doubt for this sort of reason that, in its second year of operation, the Coles/Apple promotion offered a trip to Hollywood for the prize-winning class. Ultimately, however, the competition was cancelled. As this suggests, in-school advertisers are constantly adapting in their bid to target the needs and desires of their consumer market although, as yet, few openly exploit the marketing strategies which they have used to capture the kids' commercial segment. However, we argue that certain existing and emerging forms of in-school marketing suggest that this will not always be the case.

Edutainment

In some respects, the fact that kids' understandings of the critical and moral issues of in-school marketing echo the views of adults is hardly surprising. They are responding to marketing strategies designed principally to counteract adult opposition to in-school commercialism. However, given the social, economic and structural pressures on schools to succumb to the commercial push, the capacity of schools, teachers and parents to act as 'gatekeepers' is weakening. This opens the way for commerce to woo kids directly by tapping into their desires, pleasures and processes of identity-building. Currently, few commercial educators seek to entertain kids in schools – competitions are the closest they seem to get to the pleasure principle. Fewer still operate at the level of utopias. Our research yielded one significant exception to this rule but, we suggest, it anticipates the emergent trend in in-school marketing.

'The Rock Eisteddfod Challenge' is a performing arts competition for secondary schools which originated in Australia in 1980 and now operates internationally. In its original dance/drama competition format, participating schools choreographed an 8-minute production on a theme of choice set to contemporary, commercially available music. From its inception, 'The Rock Eisteddfod Challenge' has been a tobacco, alcohol and other drug prevention vehicle sponsored by the federal government, notably The National Drug Offensive and its state counterparts, and the Department of Education, Employment and Training. It thus has links to the health education curriculum as well as music and drama. As the concept has expanded, so too has the sponsorship arrangement which now includes corporate and print and broadcast media sponsors.

Unlike much school activity, 'The Rock Eisteddfod' inspires enthusiastic support among participants and many other school students. In so doing, it offers educators and policy makers some lessons on pedagogy and curriculum development and, for this reason, we will return to evaluate 'The Rock Eisteddfod' in relation to pedagogies in the final chapter. However, 'The Rock Eisteddfod' not only offers a pedagogical model for teachers which brings together education and pleasure, it also points to an emerging trend in in-school marketing.

As we indicated in the introduction to this chapter, advertisers are becoming more sophisticated in their approaches to in-school marketing. According to the promotional material for the Westpac Olympic Ideals campaign described above, the Sydney Organizing Committee of the Olympic Games 2000 National Olympic Education Program would reach Australia's 3.1 million school children through a student newspaper and kids' Internet pages, as well as the competition. It also provided a teachers' multimedia pack including CD-ROM, posters and video. The appropriation of multimedia and interactive technology, in particular, are examples of how the in-school marketing industry is finding ways of reaching kids which map onto the pleasures they derive from home entertainment media.

While home sales continue to remain the strongest market segment, McLester (1996) suggests that the latest 'edutainment' packages are designed to target the in-school market and kids as well as parents. They offer direct tie-ins with curriculum or educational resources and 'teacher pleasing' features like 'options to turn off the sound, the ability to save for a large group of users, and a choice of structured or open-ended approaches to activities' (McLester 1996: 54). Virgin Interactive and Discovery Channel offer online scrapbooks and journals so that students can take notes or respond to the material.

More insidiously, education software companies are now employing mainstream marketing strategies and linking edutainment packages with children's mass culture. These strategies include licensed merchandising, cross-selling and programme-length commercials and, thus, the use of familiar characters, TV programmes and toys to attract kids. Recognizable brands like Disney are entering the market as a further means to reach them. The Scholastic Software Club now offers titles like *Madeline 1st and 2nd Grade Math*, *Art Attack*, *Sabrina the Teenage Witch*, *Brat Attack Knowledge Adventure* and the *Rugrats Print Shop*.

Another emergent trend in in-school marketing which combines advertising with pleasure and identity building is the use of kids' cultural icons. In 1999, Save the Children Victoria reissued the society's child-shaped pins clad in Australian Football League (AFL) team colours. They issued four pins, two of what they call 'dark' children and two of white, for each of the eighteen AFL teams and put them in primary and secondary schools. This is one example of how celebrity endorsement by sporting icons has been used in schools in order to tap into the desires and fantasies produced by popular children's and youth-cultural forms. Nike exploits young people's passion for sport and esteem for sporting stars and links them with programmes designed exclusively for racial groups and 'underserved' communities. The Nike Premier Cup Pre-Qualifying Tournament in California is exclusively for Latino teams. As a news story at Nikebiz.com puts it, 'The Nike Premier Cup is the beginning of a dream come true for many of the players'. Nike also sponsors the Play Zone project which has markets in Singapore, Indonesia, Thailand, the Philippines, Malaysia and India. The advertising campaign features inspiring and aspiring young Asian athletes with the aim of building Asian role models.

As this suggests, national, racial, ethnic and cultural identities are providing the basis for child and youth-focused cause-related marketing in the classroom and schoolyard. This final example of the trend towards the importation of mainstream marketing strategies commodifies kids' concepts of 'political correctness'. Some companies use sponsorship and donations to demonstrate their ideological allegiance to young people's causes. Others 'simply appropriate the language or imagery of social-change movements such as environmentalism or feminism' (Jacobson and Mazur 1995: 91). We take the commercial exploitation of Black History Month in the USA as our case in point.

Black History Month has strong links with education but is not yet fully integrated into the curriculum (Christensen 1999). This is where commerce has stepped in. Pacific Bell Education First offers video-conferencing events for the classroom 'in honor of Black History Month'. A company now produces Black History Month book covers, having responded to consumer information gathered by Cover Concepts (Mormon 1997). Nike has its own African-American Network. In 1999, the network named vice-president of marketing of the JORDAN brand, Howard White, African-American History Month honoree for his contribution to Nike's 'Believe to Achieve' seminars. These seminars, which are held in schools, emphasize vision, faith and commitment as the key to success and empowerment for 'at-risk' and 'troubled' young people and, thus, disadvantaged minorities. Past speakers have included Spike Lee, rap star Kid of the duo Kid'N'Play, prominent coaches and sporting stars, and Nike executives.

In the above examples, class, racial or cultural differences are emphasized and affirmed. However, this is only one pole of the 'seriality of commodification' we described in the introductory chapter. At the other pole, difference is levelled or homogenized. The 'American Girl Collection' of dolls and curriculum materials which we mentioned earlier in this chapter is representative of this opposing tendency. In fact, the 'American Girl Today' collection of dolls attempts to go against homogenization. These dolls are available in 20 combinations of eye, hair and skin colour. They also incorporate some subtle racial variations like eye and nose shape and hair texture. Yet the dolls are otherwise replicas of one another. Like the multicultural range of Barbies and Mattel's 'Dolls of the World Collection', regardless of the race or ethnicity they claim to represent, they 'are just like us, dye-dipped versions of the archetypal white American beauty' (Ducille 1994: 49). Indeed, Brady (1997) argues in her deconstruction of the 'American Girl Collection' that this homogenization occurs even more insidiously.

As we indicated earlier, the 'American Girl Collection' now incorporates African-American and Hispanic dolls to offer a more 'inclusive' representation of the various periods in American history. However, in spite of their good intentions, the manufacturers of the 'American Girl Collection' offer a very narrow view of history which: 'fail[s] to connect their readers with a critically interrogated past by providing dominant forms of representation and making claims on history and their targeted audience that serve to delete and reduce oppositional historical narratives and knowledge' (Brady 1997: 222). These narratives ignore 'Issues of struggle, conflict, imperialism and repression' and, instead, reflect the 'class, racial and gender stereotypes and inequalities which characterize the present' (Brady 1997: 222). Here history is 'disguised in the image of nostalgia, innocence, and simplicity'.

This points to a fundamental oversight in the attitudes of the principals we interviewed. Whether expressing concern about students being manipulated and exploited or embracing the potential benefits of commercialization, many principals failed to appreciate the hidden curriculum associated with it – the 'subliminal' messages children receive when, for example, Kellogg's funds nutrition kits. More critically, their positions clearly ignore the role of consumption in the construction of both young people and their different cultures and, indeed, the role of consumption in the life of the parent. Only one of the principals we interviewed made any reference to ensuring that the school curriculum develops students' critical understanding and knowledge of the market environment.

◯ Conclusion

The Australian students we spoke to sometimes proved to be more adroit at recognizing advertising intent, and less likely to be persuaded by in-school marketing, than the adults. This suggests that there are some highly critical consumers in Australian schools. However, the market presence in Australian schools is a mere fraction of that in US schools. Still a relative novelty, it is infrequent enough for students to be in a position to make wise, critical judgements. At the same time, these students were accepting of the presence of market culture in schools and their views often resonated with opinions expressed by adults.

However, if students are sophisticated consumers drawing on a knowledge base which comes from their location in consumer–media culture, they also lack critical capacity for a sociocultural reading of how they and their social relationships are constructed within this semiosis. While critical of aspects of consumer culture, they are not critical of consumption as a way of life. We found them to be intense consumers, prepared to and/or wanting to spend large amounts of money on brand names and fashionable or popular items. It is predictable that as mainstream advertising strategy becomes more commonplace in schools, child and youth consumers will become less astute in their understanding of the position consumer culture asks them to occupy.

This suggests that consumer–media education is an imperative both for students in locations where in-school advertising remains a novelty and where it has become normalized. There is no doubt that cultural markets will increasingly overlap with educational markets in the future. This means that an understanding about the relationship between schooling and commercial markets – indeed, of the commercialization of schooling – will become increasingly important for educators and parents. It is to the matter of the commercialization of schooling itself that we will turn in the next chapter.

⑤ Designer schools, packaged students

Compulsory education is one of the defining characteristics of modern childhood; to a degree, therefore, any politics of schooling is also a politics of childhood, with inevitable implications for the lives that children lead and for the way that childhood itself is understood.

(Wagg 1996: 8)

◯ Introduction

This chapter is concerned with the marketization of schools in Australia and has implications for other countries where schools have taken up a market identity. It focuses on the semiotic work involved in schools' marketing practices, the identities offered to students and others, and the different desires, fears and fantasies which such marketing practices produce and ignore. In considering the standpoint of students and to a lesser extent parents, we go beyond well-known accounts of 'choice'. We point both to the manner in which schools construct students as educational commodities and to the manner in which students construct themselves as consumers and producers of the semiotic value of schools, drawing on the 'worldliness' they have developed through their engagements with consumer–media culture. As we have explained throughout, this culture has created a cohort of semi-sophisticates, prompting Guber and Berry (1993: 14) to assert that 'kids are worldly'. As indicated, their worldliness comes from access to consumer–media culture and its reconstructions of children as active consumers with, as Baudrillard would say, a certain expertise in the 'consumption of signs'.

Two main themes run through this chapter. The first concerns intergenerational relations between parents, teachers and students and the manner in which these are implicated in the relationships between school education and the promotional culture it has now adopted. We will contrast this sphere with that of its 'other' – children's culture in the form of entertainment and advertising, as discussed in earlier chapters. In so doing, we will point to the identity dilemmas that arise for young people in the marketized school. The second theme also addresses identity dilemmas but focuses specifically on the ways in which a group of working-class/'under-class' students in their local primary and secondary schools read their schools' commodification practices and write themselves within and around them. Most of the students whose voices emerge here are aged between 8 and 17 years and come from three schools (Willis Primary, Hall Middle Secondary High School and Willis Senior College). They live in Willis, a suburb of the Australian provincial city of Geelong. This suburb is part of an area surrounded by heavy industry and subject to intense industrial restructuring over the last few years, with several of the major industries closing down while several smaller industries have been set up there. The overall unemployment rates are high on a local and regional basis and the suburb is stigmatized by those outside it. By way of contrast, we have also included the voices of some students from Morely High, a more prestigious State school in a more esteemed suburb and catering for a much more privileged class grouping.

The first section of the chapter provides some brief information on the main features of the marketization of Australian schools, pointing to some gaps in the literature on the marketization of schooling more generally. The remainder of the chapter draws on ideas from the advertising industry and from cultural theorists' discussions of advertising and commodification to interpret the marketization of schooling and its implications for students' identities and for adult/child and social class relationships. Overall, the chapter will point to the ways in which the marketization of education has involved a reorganization of the symbolic production and everyday experiences and practices of schooling.

◯ Simulating schooling?

Like many of their counterparts in the UK, Canada, New Zealand and the USA, Australian governments have spent the last decade redesigning educational institutions along market lines. As a result, the everyday life of education systems and schools has been altered in very deep but apparently unspectacular ways. They have been steered towards 'free' market mores, manners and morals but within the tight rein of State and Commonwealth government curriculum and management policies. These imply that school systems are primarily investments in human and political capital and national and state identity. Schools are now expected to operate within the tight and narrow curriculum frameworks developed by State and national governments but also to operate as 'free' agents within such frameworks. At the same time, schools and school systems have been stripped of finance, staff, assets and previous educational ethics. A range of practices associated with such 'devolution' and with deregulation, de-zoning and deliberate disaggregation have encouraged schools to see themselves as free-standing entrepreneurial small businesses (Kenway 1995).

Over the last decade schools have come increasingly to compete with each other for 'clients' – namely, parents, industry partners and sponsors – and the money which flows from them. Parents and students have been encouraged to adopt a consumerist stance to schools and to know-ledge. In their governance, schools are expected to (and often do) draw inspiration from industry management models. Such a standpoint is exemplified in the following press coverage of another state school in Geelong, Australia:

> Allan White is the general manager of a $4.5 million business with 1000 teenage clients all wanting to buy a bright future. In short he runs a high school.
>
> Business, budgets and clients are not the traditional bywords of a school, but under Schools of the Future, they have become as much a part of school as chalk and dusters.
>
> Mr White's Belmont High School, in Geelong, was among the pioneer Schools of the Future in 1993, and now boasts a management team, which includes the executive officer (principal), and line man-agers (two assistant principals and a pivotal business manager).
>
> ... What distinguishes this school is not the building, but what happens inside. It no longer relies on a central bureaucracy to hire and pay staff, fund educational goals, maintain the buildings and grounds, and refurbish.
>
> 'Now they give us a bucket of money and we determine how we spend it,' says Mr White. But grabbing the purse strings has meant working out how to manage the purse. During the 12-month tran-sition, money was spent on refurbishing the school's business office (formerly administration), getting new management software, train-ing staff, formalising management structures and, critically, hiring a professional manager.
>
> (Messina 1995: 6)

Further, many schools are importing expertise from marketing and fundraising experts, developing marketing plans, establishing sponsorship/fundraising committees and undertaking advertising programmes. As we showed in the previous chapter, many businesses are now advertising in schools, using them for the production of such things as brand loyalty

Table 5.1 The lexicon of the market in education

Market language	Educational language
Client	Parent/business partner, sponsor
Consumer/customer	Parent
Product	Student
Enterprise	School
Total quality management	School improvement plan
Manager	Principal
Line manager	Principal who does what he/she is told by those 'up the line'
Choice	Something exercised by those with the best resources
'Value-adding' to the school	School improvement
User pays	Passing on educational costs to private individuals or groups
Downsize	Sack teachers and close facilities and schools
Outsource	Pass on educational activities to those outside schools and educational systems
Image	School profile
Image audit	Assessment of how the school is viewed by those outside it
Benchmark	Compare your school profile with that of another school
Performance indicators	Assessment and evaluation
Performance pay	Payment by results

and reputation. This broad set of changes is now commonly referred to as marketization. Although with somewhat different manifestations, marketization is now a feature of public schooling systems in the USA, UK, New Zealand and much of Canada.

Educational language in all these locations is being subsumed by marketing language as many articles addressed to educational leaders make very clear (for example, Chambers 1998). Table 5.1 shows the new lexicon which bears a strong relationship to the features of post-Fordism that we identified in Chapter 1.

New ICTs have been a key feature in the emergence of post-Fordist economies and they are also implicated in the expansion of the marketized economy of schooling, as we indicated in the previous chapter and elsewhere. Broadcasting, publishing, computing and telecommunications are becoming integral to the process of marketization. They have become part of more traditional market and quasi-market forms and orientations and they have made possible a multiplicity of new market genres. More traditionally, for example, because of their increasing use of 'new' technologies, state and private educational institutions are regarded by commercial marketers as an expanding market. Also, educational institutions are using their relationship to information technologies in their own promotional activities.

Some are seeking to promote themselves on the basis of their use of such technologies in the curriculum. Methodist Ladies College, Melbourne, with its laptop computers is the best-publicized example, but many schools highlight their 'state of the art' technology centres in their publicity materials. Interestingly, a number of girls' private schools have been quick to tie such developments to feminist discourses about girls' empowerment through their use and control of technology. Other institutions are reshaping their identities in order to concentrate on preparing their students for employment in 'high tech' labour markets. Former public technical high schools and specialist technology high schools are the most obvious examples here. However, some private schools have also sought to move to the front of the pack in this new educational race by blending technology with corporate logic. For example, in 1993, Ormiston College in Brisbane promoted itself on the basis of its ambition to 'move to the forefront of computer/technology education' in the context of its development of a corporate culture which involves strong links with 'highly prominent entrepreneurs, marketers and successful small business operators'. It has a school foyer which is 'more akin to that experienced in the corporate world', an annual trade and commerce fair and 'annual trips for groups of students to South-East Asia to examine innovative business and technological practices' (Holmes n.d.).

Further, some educational institutions are using ICTs to enhance old pedagogies and to give an impression of cutting-edge curriculum innovation. For example, schools in Victoria responded eagerly to SOLAS, the student online academic service. For a substantial fee per hour, this service assists Victorian Certificate of Education students in the senior levels of their schooling to respond easily to the demands of research-based pedagogy. Schools are provided with various levels of incentive to sign up as many students as they can. More broadly, many governmental and non-governmental agencies are currently exploring a range of ways in which education, markets and IT can come together efficiently and profitably. Another example is the CD-ROM for primary school science produced jointly by the New South Wales Board of Studies and IBM (see Bigum *et al.* 1993). Successmaker, a multimedia integrated learning system, developed in the USA by the Computer Curriculum Corporation, now owned by Paramount Communications, has established itself in a number of schools (at considerable cost) with the support of the government education systems of the eastern States of Australia.

The claim is made that new technologies will eventually 'liberate' educational consumption from certain time and space restrictions. But this can also be seen as part of the overall process whereby market expansion into previously 'commercial-free zones' is assisted by new IT.

Market research

The marketization of schools in the western countries noted above has attracted a great deal of critical research. The focus has largely been on government policy, principals and parents and on associated issues of school choice, school management and, more broadly, economic and philosophical imperatives and implications. These studies privilege the role of the economy, governments and educational systems and institutions, and rely heavily on political, institutional and economic theories in their analyses. In relative terms, remarkably little attention has been paid to students and to the ways in which they participate in the market culture of schooling. Equally little attention has been given to the consumer contexts of marketization and their implications for the construction of young people as consumers. This chapter is in broad sympathy with these critical perspectives but seeks to move away from the rather masculinist focus on the economy and the State, and from the heavy emphasis on hyperrationalistic critique which has largely characterized critical analysis.

It is our view that such perspectives insufficiently recognize the power and importance of the psyche and of people's everyday lives in all their spectacular ordinariness and complexity. To ask about the role of educational consumption in people's identities and lives involves seeking to understand how differently located people come to 'want what they want' (Walkerdine 1991: 89) regarding education and what they believe they gain and lose from its commodification. What aspects of their psyche does it appeal to? How do they experience and cope with the disjunction between the appeal and the real? Is there something about the ways in which commodities work which means that this disjuncture can be written off and thus depoliticized?

Such understandings are enhanced by insights from studies of consumer culture generally and young people and consumer culture specifically. Such studies help to expose the ways in which schools' marketing practices map onto other marketing practices and how educational consumerism maps onto broader patterns of consumption. For example, it could be argued that the marketization of education is an indicator of the rapid growth of 'experiential commodities' which are part of the more general move 'to make more flexible and fluid the various opportunities and moments of consumption' (Lee 1993: 135, 137).

Studies of consumer culture also draw our attention to the semiotic and identity aspects of schools' marketing practices and to the manner in which social relationships are formed, in part at least, in the sphere of educational consumption. For instance, such studies alert us to the ways that children/students are constructed within the discourses of market-ization and how adult/child relations and the family are implicated. As Oppenheim and Lister (1996) point out, on such family/market matters there is a dual and somewhat contradictory emphasis within the neo-liberal thinking that informs government policy in the UK. On the one hand, we see the individual 'consumer and economic actor' involved in maximizing self-interest and, on the other, we see the family unit with all its incumbent gendered traditions of male/female, adult/child respons-ibility and obligation. Social conservatism is in strange juxtaposition to neo-liberalism. Further, with regard to the UK, Wagg (1996: 9) observes that 'although one of the central axioms of the contemporary politics of British schooling is that providers of education are now beholden to "consumers", these consumers are taken to be, not the children con-cerned, but their parents'. This reflects the more general marginalization of children in both recent education policy and in research on policy. There exists very little research on the implications of the construction of young people as educational consumers – the ways in which students' educational consumption connects with the specificity of their other consumption patterns. And, strikingly, there are few explorations of the consequences and implications of such matters for schools' educational purposes as opposed to their management practices.

So, what are the marketing practices of schools, what are their implica-tions for the students and how are both best understood?

◯ Advertising

Direct advertising is now considered a normal and uncontroversial prac-tice through which schools seek to attract students and, thus, finance and reputation. They mount billboards in school grounds, sometimes supported by sponsors. They advertise in newspapers, on the radio, in increasingly glossy brochures/prospectuses and at education fairs (Symes 1998).

A deeper understanding of the logic of the educational commodity can be gained by drawing on cultural analyses of advertising. There are several points to be made. First, advertising is central to the process of market exchange, so as soon as schools entered market relationships with each other it was inevitable that they would advertise. Second, advertising is not only a key element of a market culture, it is also pivotal to the growth of such cultures and, at the same time, it establishes its own momentum – it feeds on itself and takes on a life of its own. Thus, the more schools advertise, the more they become absorbed within a market culture and the more they have to advertise. As a consequence, an increasing proportion of school budgets has been diverted to advertising and away from educational matters. Clearly then, advertising is a key element in institutional redesign. Of interest here is the increasing role of 'cultural intermediaries' in school education and schools' increasing dependence upon such people (Cervini 2000). Clearly, new power relationships are emerging between such cultural specialists and educational and administrative specialists. The latters' capacity to monopolize the ways in which schooling is understood and practised is gradually being erased as a function of the ever-growing centrality of design in the development of schooling's 'second skin' – as Haug (1986) calls the packaging that sells schooling and which is often more attractive than what it contains.

Third, as we explained in Chapter 1, advertising is selective and seeks to persuade. As Young (1990: 291) says, it is about *face value* and *best face*. It thus stands in direct opposition to education in the sense that education, in its best forms, encourages students to consider issues from many angles and to look beneath the surface, to examine assumptions. Fourth, advertisements and the commodities they promote carry the values associated with their production and their exchange. In this sense school advertisements set certain educational agendas, establish priorities and seek symbolic closure around them. Fifth, advertising's 'art of social influence' involves an understanding of the 'sign value' of goods and services to the consumer. As Lee (1993) argues, goods and services are used as a form of cultural expression by the consumer. But as we have also observed, advertisements 'produce dream-scapes, collective fantasies and facades' (Zukin 1991: 219). Through their advertisements, schools are constructing educational dreams which tap into a whole range of fantasies, some of which are only indirectly connected to education.

A large number of schools now distribute professionally produced, multi-coloured, usually glossy brochures, booklets or folders complete with numerous colour photos. These usually depict attractive, happy, busy, often multicultural groups of children actively engaged in learning, play, sport and cultural activities and almost invariably in school uniform. However, these promotional materials differ greatly in their aesthetics. The more expensive and private the school, the more minimalist, 'tasteful', exquisitely photographed and artistically designed the brochure.

Enrolment times in Geelong result in a rash of advertisements in the local press. Schools are now constantly on the lookout to identify the best value to add. Hence, their advertising is not just about the matters noted above or the communication of information, it is also about product differentiation. Schools are now searching for their differences rather than their commonalities and thinking in terms of market share. They are searching for the right commodity sign or market signal – the key word, image or slogan that will mark them out as distinctive and attractive.

The schools' slogans published in local newspapers during the first period of our research in 1994 included: 'Quality education', 'Latest techno-logy', 'Caring community', 'Securing the future', 'New VCE [Victorian Certificate of Education] campus', 'International reputation', 'Girls set for future', 'A career pathway', and 'Preparing for life'.

When reading such advertisements, these students responded in two ways, both of them worldly. First, they commented on the quality of the advertisements' semiosis, on the pictures, on the size and the structure of the message, and the amount and type of information. The following remark made by an 11-year-old boy was typical: 'That one is the best. Geelong College, because it tells you about it and it has got a photo and it has got some information here and the heading stands out' (Willis Primary).

Second, students remarked on the slogans which attracted them and why. Like the 11- and 12-year-old girls at Willis Primary below, they preferred the following:

Girl: 'Latest technology', 'New VCE campus' and 'Securing the future'.

Girl: I reckon 'Career pathway', 'Latest technology' and 'Preparing for life' because you have to always pass VCE to get a job.

Girl: 'Caring community'. That if you can't cope with that school they care for you, like they understand what you are going through.

Advertising depends on touching something deep in the consumer's psyche. In Chapter 1 we noted Williams's (1980) observation that advertising inscribes goods with a 'narrative capacity'. It tells fictional tales but implies that the purchase of goods will fulfil the story's pro-mise. However, the exquisite irony is that advertisements are not expected to fulfil their promises or to connect to reality but, rather, to connect to their readers' fantasies about themselves and their futures. As we observed, advertisements are judged by the spectator/viewer ac-cording to their relevance to fantasies or yearnings: 'seductive illusion' is what sells. Successful advertisements also provoke *plaisir*, which can be understood to apply to the pleasure which is derived from a recognition that 'the text' acknowledges a group's distinctive values and aspirations (Barthes 1975). All three matters can be seen in the students' responses.

Recurring themes emerge from discussions with children about the desirable features of school life. Students of all ages were most respons-ive to themes about social dynamics, the new and the future. They also showed a marked preference for advertisements which stressed caring relationships. Such foci are no surprise. They are consistent with the findings outlined by David *et al.* (1994) in their UK study titled *Mother's Intuition?: Choosing Secondary Schools*. In this study, the authors assert that there are three significant factors important in school choice. They dub these factors the '3 Ps': performance, pleasant feel (atmosphere/ethos) and proximity (p. 78). Further, the anxiety generated by social and political change is registered in the students' concerns that schools are secure and safe environments. Accordingly, how schools 'appear' (friendly/safe/pleasant compared to hostile/unsafe/alien) is fundamental. As Mackay (1993) and others make clear, young people are being educated during a period of massive social uncertainty and redefinition. Schools are supposed to be integral to their search for identity and security. At the same time, the students indicated preferences about matters that were deemed to be technological. These students are, as we have explained, frequently referred to as the 'Nintendo' or 'Sega' generation. Growing up with computers and video games sets new parameters of expectation and hope.

Identifying problems and anxieties and solving them through consumption is a standard advertising ploy and school advertisements are no different. They tap into parents' and students' fears of the present and the future (matters of employment and unemployment) and promise them a consumerist solution – that is, 'success, happiness and well-being' through the right choice of school. Students implicitly understand that advertising works in this manner as the following response from a boy at Hall High demonstrates:

Interviewer: If you made an advertisement for this school what pictures would you use?

Boy (13 years): The new bike shed, the library, sporting facilities, artwork display, computer room, with kids playing football and netball. They would be having fun. People reading the books in the library. Cooking. The kids would be in uniform or their sport's uniform. A display of teachers reading books to the kids. The words they would use would be 'good education'. Lost property box, the stuff in the canteen. They want to hear that you have good discipline, a good range of subjects, happy students, safe . . . secure.

Gender is a feature of the markets in schooling for students as well as for parents and again, hope and anxiety are not far apart. Girls' schools are selling themselves as specialists in girls' education – some emulating the status aspects of private schools for girls and others drawing from liberal and cultural feminist agendas. Many girls find the prospect of a girl-only school attractive, echoing this type of remark: 'I would like an all-girl school because that way boys aren't teasing you and not lifting up your dresses and all that. They do at this school'. Boys' schools do not have a similar niche market – the reverse in fact:

Interviewer: What about you, what would you think about an all boys' school?

(*All talking at once*)

Boy (13 years): It would be boring.

Boy (13 years): The boys would be throwing paper planes.

Boy (13 years): Because it would be all boy teachers.

Girl (13 years): Trouble.

This was a common view. With the stress on style and tone as market-able commodities, girls have come to be regarded as good value to add – particularly to schools with a high percentage of boys. These now seek to attract girls for their 'civilizing' capacities. Of course 'trouble' can be interpreted in many ways and for some boys, boys-only schooling was interpreted as 'poofter paradise'. They didn't want it because of their fear of being seen as gay, even of becoming gay. Homophobia as a factor in choice does not appear in the 'choice' literature. Indeed, as the special issue of *Discourse* (1996) indicates, the marketization of education has a strong gendered dynamic.

◯ Impression management

Marketing, as opposed to advertising, involves a wide range of contrived semiotic practices or what Gewirtz *et al.* (1995: 121) call 'symbolic pro-duction'. These include such things as product design – packaging and imagery, product differentiation or positioning and repositioning when necessary, and product renewal involving redesign and redefinition. It may involve market segmentation and associated population targeting and impression management associated with such concrete matters as location, architectural design, floor layout and display.

All schools promote themselves through a variety of impression management activities and techniques. These include open days for pro-spective students, open nights for parents, good-news stories in the local press, the 'glossification' (Gewirtz *et al.* 1995: 127) of foyer/school en-trances, the 'look' of the school and logos on stationery. Modern times also require many schools to redesign themselves.

In the context of inter-school competition, those schools with his-torically poor reputations usually employ the 'tactics' of image redesign and repositioning. This is the case with Willis Senior College, the senior school of the set of schools which are the focus of this chapter. It was previously a trades-orientated technical school and attracted all the usual stigma of such schools. It now has a programme catering specifically for Year 11 and 12 students, with a dual focus on professional and trade subjects. The school is part of an amalgamated multi-site campus which combines three schools including two middle-level feeder schools. Hall Middle School is one of these feeder schools. Features of Willis Senior College connect strongly with the needs of the local area and include a wide subject range, a focus on IT, no uniform and free movement for students. The school is making a concerted effort to change public awareness through such activities as advertisements in local newspapers, newsletters, students on radio talking about different programmes offered at the school and displays in the local shopping centre about courses and classes. It has identified its market niche and now seeks to persuade both insiders and outsiders of its merits. This is no easy matter given the suburb's bad reputation even among some who live there.

The emerging quasi-corporate style of schools is not addressed to students so much as to parents and potential sponsors. None the less, students understand the importance of 'the look'. They explained teachers' apparent obsession with tidiness in terms of the school image and agreed that such material factors are important. At Hall they said, 'They want to sell the place by making it look swish', and 'The school needs painting and dressing up a bit'. They were disgusted that 'Some of the schools around don't even have grass' and observed that 'Having gardens is important'. The older students at Willis Senior College were particularly aware of the connections between a school's physical appearance and its reputation, and felt aggrieved at the way their school looked. They commented forcefully on the need to improve the grounds. In contrast, Morely High looked 'smart' and, interestingly, smart appearance is equated with smart kids: 'This is a smart school. The kids from Year 12 get good jobs and scholarships. The uniform is very strict. The way the kids look, the appearance of the school is important. If there is any graffiti it is fixed straight away' (16-year-old boy).

For the students in their final years of schooling, school visits and information nights had not figured prominently in their educational histories. Times have changed greatly in the intervening years and the reverse is true for the younger students. As Gewirtz *et al.* (1995: 128) say of similar events in the UK, such events 'are becoming slicker and are geared towards selling the school in a far more thrusting way'. When asked about the impact of school visits on them, students from Willis Primary were articulate and thoughtful:

Interviewer: When you visit the schools on open day what would make you think 'I would like to come here'?

Boy (11 years): I am going to Hall because we went there with the school . . . they had some good stuff there. The darkroom where they do the video, and the cooking and they have got a big library – for when you do projects. And the cooking and the computer groups. And they have got this room where, when you want a job you can go and ask . . . and they can look for a job for you.

Girl (12 years): I decided to go to Brunsdon Heights because they have got everything set out, like there is a big hallway and they have got what is down that hallway, like it says technology and maths. It's a smaller school and you won't get lost. And they've got tennis courts and basketball courts and they have got a big gym and they've got good stuff. At the other end of the school they have got a primary school and they use their oval as well.

The school visits are geared directly to students in various ways. Some schools seek to establish strict standards right from the outset. Others seek to create an attractive atmosphere while others again seek to blend both. Our students enjoyed visits to schools which offered them hands-on activities, where obvious care was given to planning the day, where the teachers were friendly and, in particular, where they were given food and drink. Their comments make it clear that such brief encounters count to some extent, although they are not necessarily the deciding factor in choice of school. The older students emphasized friendly relationships with peers and teachers. However, as the following remarks made at Hall High indicate, they usually wanted a friendly controlled environment, not one where kids were out of control:

Boy (15 years): I went to the Johnston Park open day . . . you looked sideways and you'd get into trouble. You come here and can be chatting away and it seemed like a breeze. I wanted to come here.

Girl (15 years): I didn't like the teachers at the other schools and the classes were out of control. I expected to see the teachers in control.

Students were also aware, however, that the school was trying to make a good impression and commented with some bitterness about being 'sold out' when the school did not live up to its image in the following years.

Other school image work includes making success visible and concealing 'failure' and 'failures'. As Deem *et al.*'s (1995) research in the UK shows, this has curriculum implications. For example, it often means moving away from accepting school-wide responsibility for matters of racism and sexism – after all, they imply to the market that the school has a problem. Of course, as schools become more caught up in partnerships with industry and as they become more dependent on sponsorship, the socially critical dimensions of their curriculum suffer as well.

Knowledge increasingly becomes understood as a commodity both for individual students to invest in and also for schools. 'What knowledge can we niche to "add value" to the school?' is a question that schools now regularly ask themselves. Almost invariably this means that the expressive and creative aspects of the curriculum give way to instrumental cognitive-based regimes, particularly those with strong vocational and technological linkages. The exceptions here tend to be associated with the extent to which the expressive and creative can be reinscribed within vocational discourses or whether the school understands or constructs itself as culturally élite, as do many of the expensive private schools.

Best face involves publicizing successes in sporting and cultural competitions and in public exams, and making visible high-achieving students. While schools like to emphasize academic achievements, the students notice sport and culture most. 'The Rock Eisteddfod', the annual national performing arts edutainment competition we referred to in the previous chapter, has a particular impact. It performs a powerful marketing function for the winning school and is remembered by students from a range of schools long after the competition is over for the year. Students equated winning with being a good school, even when it was understood that resources were implicated. Indeed, good education was implicitly associated with plentiful resources in the students' minds.

◯ Working for the image

The fetishism of commodities, according to Lee (1993: 15), involves the total and necessary effacement of the concrete social relations of their production from the surface of commodities. Lee elaborates:

> The ways in which commodities converge and collect in the market, their untarnished appearance as they emerge butterfly-like from the grubby chrysalis of production, the fact that they appear to speak only about themselves as objects and not about the social labour of their production is ultimately what constitutes the fetishism of commodities. The sphere of production is thus the night-time of the commodity: the mysterious economic dark side of social exploitation which is so effectively concealed in the dazzling glare of the market-place.
>
> (1993: 15)

So, what of the 'social labour' which goes into the production of the image of the school but which is so frequently concealed beneath the smoothness of the school's surface – its uniforms, its conformist behaviour? According to the edicts of the education market, all members of the school community are to play their part in the school's image work.

Principals are expected to hustle for customers, reputation and resources. Encouraged to cultivate clients and the media, and to seek
sponsors, they have become educational entrepreneurs. School councils
are expected to accept the responsibility for favourably positioning the
school so it can gain a competitive edge over other schools. School
charters and image audits help them to fulfil this function and their
audience is external not internal. Teachers are expected to do their share
of image work by devoting extra time and effort to those things which
count in the educational marketplace – teaching to the market, which
may mean 'teaching to the test', particularly in the context of league
tables such as those in the UK. Again, this means teaching to the outside
rather than the inside – to the image.

In the educational marketplace teachers play many roles. They are
rather paradoxical figures for students. While students' long-term and
most heart-felt comments on their schooling are tied up with the quality
of teachers, school advertisements almost never mention teachers. Until
their senior years, most students believe that 'strict teachers' enhance
the image of the school.

Common assumptions about what gives a school a good name include
strict teachers, good students and tidy grounds. Teachers who are not
strict are seen as uncaring. Lifting the image is associated with teachers
becoming stricter. Interestingly, this is not necessarily what the students
value and enjoy. As the Year 12 students said of Willis Senior College:

Girl (17 years): We have better rapport with teachers here. There are
                   not two levels.
Boy (17 years): There is not so much discipline so we can all relax.

While at one level students say they prefer their teachers to be 'loving
and caring', they know that most adults value discipline and that it pays
off in enhancing the name of the school, which has flow-on benefits to
them. It is ironic, however, that the schools in Geelong with the worst
reputations were those where the senior students spoke most favourably
about their teachers, their relationships with them and their enjoyment
of the atmosphere of the school. The better the reputation, the more
critical were the students of the teachers and the atmosphere. Witness
the comments of 15- and 16-year-old students at Morely High:

Boy: Here it's just discipline. 'Do this, don't do that.' There's no
     atmosphere to encourage educational learning.
Boy: I wouldn't recommend it. This school is somewhat old-
     fashioned in its ideas. The principal is just too concerned that
     he is going to offend someone by having progress.
Girl: I don't think this school sort of sticks together. It's all secret
     and everyone competes against one another.

Marketing provides the vital link between production and consumption. Thus, it facilitates, mediates and arbitrates culture. As Kline (1993: 30) argues, advertising 'forcefully communicates about the nature of social relations and ultimately asserts its place in shaping those relations'. He continues: 'By amplifying, augmenting, recycling and reinterpreting established social mores, values, attitudes and customs, marketing communication legitimates, guides and sets priorities for particular relations of consumption – and, of course, overlooks many others' (p. 31).

The question is, what social relations do school advertisements help to shape and whose fantasies do they tap into? Our research suggests that an adult fantasy here involves a return to particular educational traditions invoking respect for elders and clear discipline – a form of educational fundamentalism. We see an attempt to create some certainty in the 'manufactured uncertainty' which characterizes current school education and adult–child relations. Clearly, the education market reflects and refracts the power relations between adults (teachers, parents) and children (students). It also has important implications for the ways in which children construct themselves as learners.

If students are to 'add value' to their school they must be a particular sort of learner. The conventional marketized school, such as Morely High, is about discipline, seriousness, intellectual achievement, respect for authority, planning for the future and delayed gratification. It divorces education from entertainment. In other words, it stands for many of the things which are marginalized and stigmatized in children's and young people's consumer culture. It has its own 'aesthetic' but this is a far cry from the 'magic system of inducements' which characterizes children's consumer culture. It has little or no place for detraditionalized students who are autonomous and pleasure seeking, who switch, test and taste various codes, and who transgress strict adult codes. Such a school is no place for students who call teachers to account and require them to justify themselves. Students who work for the image are expected to adopt a subservient long-term view and to subscribe to the adult fiction and fantasy that education can get them jobs and automatically stave off economic insecurity. Students who adopt short-term goals and temporary solutions are not appreciated. While current generations of young people are capable of living comfortably with hybridity and fluidity, this none the less poses certain 'dilemmas of the self' for school students. How are they to mediate their different commodified experiences of children's, youth and school culture?

For Stress Generation teachers who are frustrated and unnerved by the young people of today, the marketized school with its clear intergenerational codes and values offers a consumerist 'solution' to the problems of school order and discipline. It wards off the vulnerabilities that teachers feel as a function of educational and generational change.

These problems are seen to have arisen from 'stress generation' parents being too permissive and overindulgent with their children. They are also seen to arise from children's and young people's consumer–media cultures which generate in students a lack of respect, a ready propensity for boredom and a need to be entertained. By divorcing education from entertainment, the marketized school relieves the teacher from the expectation to be entertaining.

Freeing teachers from any obligation to entertain students has implications for the promiscuous corporations we discussed in the previous chapter. For advertisers from the world of children's consumer culture, the pleasure-free school is just as attractive as the ad glut-free school. As kids in de- and retraditionalized schools are plodding their way through the pleasure-free curriculum, the commodity can again come to the rescue and save kids from boredom with its 'magic system of inducements'. With logos attached, it can bring into the school the pleasures of children's and youth consumer culture – computers, CD-ROMS, competitions, prizes, 'The Rock Eisteddfod' and so on. This is a powerful way to gain additional brand loyalty, to further discredit traditional formal education. Paradoxically, it also earns advertisers teachers' reluctant gratitude and helps to defuse teachers' 'othering' practice towards children's consumer culture. Ultimately, children are reminded that consumer culture 'knows what kids like' and that teachers and schools do not.

◯ Parents and students as educational commodities

In the market context of schooling, parents and students have become commodities. They are both consumers of the school's use value and producers of its exchange value. They have a double role, the second aspect of which is usually overlooked in the literature. Parents (usually mothers) are told to 'shop around'. In this process there are complex psychological forces at work. At one level, the task of choosing a school operates through the conventional discourse of education including a focus on such issues as school facilities, appearance and 'performance ratings'. On the other hand, however, this task activates a non-rational sphere of desires, fears and fantasies, commensurate with everyday shopping practices (see, for example, David *et al.* 1994).

As we discussed in Chapters 1 and 2, within consumer culture people's lives are saturated with commodities and images which have the potential to generate dreams and desires, fears and fantasies, repressions and displacements. In this context, not only do advertisers seek to ensure that consumption becomes a primary source of identity, but that desire to consume becomes a primary motivating force. According to Lasch (1979), it involves a restless narcissistic pursuit of pleasure, of self-indulgence – it promotes the id of society. Therefore, as Seiter (1995: 40) explains, because women and children are cast as the main consumers, they are also cast as the irresponsible id.

Educational marketing takes such levels of consciousness into account but, at the same time, implies that it does not. Having assessed all the market indicators, parents (mothers) and, by implication, students are to make an informed rational 'choice'. They are implicitly told that they are 'sovereign consumers'. Promoters of educational markets imply that such 'choices' are made on educational grounds alone, and that they thus represent a statement about the quality of the school. However, there are many non-educational reasons for school selection and, indeed, many intuitive and non-rational reasons.

Students at Willis Senior College point out that usually the decision about the school they will attend is either predetermined by the range of schools within the immediate locality, by finance or friends. The students also point out that 'information evenings' will thus not necessarily have a major influence on their parents. Many reported that their parents did not attend them. However, they indicated that when there was a possibility of 'choice', such occasions might hold sway, but again for reasons not necessarily educational. Take an example: 'My parents didn't want me to go to McRobbie because when they went there they saw girls spitting on the table and rubbing it in' (15-year-old girl, Hall High).

The following example, from a 15-year-old boy at Morely High, also indicates that an arbitrary approach to 'choice' is not limited to Willis:

> We had two schools to choose from and I was the oldest and we decided this school for pretty silly reasons when you come to think of it. Like at the other school (School Y) they had the heating too high at the information night and the principal talked for too long . . . and there was graffiti on the wall . . . Our first impressions were pretty incorrect really. My sister, who came to this school two years later, just had a horrible year and she's at School Y now and I'm still at Morely. We just decided on this school because the principal could talk very well and come to think of it we didn't really base our decision on good things . . . just impressions, sort of.

Having made their choice/investment, parents are then expected to protect it by adding to their school's resources and by advancing its reputation. Parents are expected to work hard at making their children work hard. At the very least, they are expected to invest time and/or money in their child's schooling and, at most, to invest time and money in the school itself. Despite their limited funds, Willis parents pour many additional resources into the education of their children. It is not unusual for students to have tutors, encyclopaedias, desks and computers at home or for them to attend dance, gymnastics, music, drama and tennis classes. In contrast with schools on the other side (the up side) of town, few have extra tutoring, pointing out that their teachers give them extra help if they need it.

Those parents who do not invest in these ways are increasingly regarded by all our research schools as negligent. All participants tend to believe that 'best value' parents (usually fathers) are those who deliver networks into sponsorship circles, financial and other capital, including the appropriate intellectual capital for school governance. Legal, accountancy and management skills are highly prized. This pattern is also evident in schools in the UK, as Deem *et al.* (1995) in their book *Active Citizenship and the Governing of Schools* show. Those who are prepared to offer other unpaid labour (for example, mothers in school canteens) are also 'appreciated' but not necessarily prized. By implication, single parents, parents in poverty or, indeed, any parents who do not fit the middle-class 'white' norm or who expect something different from the norm are seen to add *negative* value. This suggests that critical analyses of education markets must account for power relations as constituted across a range of different axes. Let us elaborate.

It is widely recognized that advertisements and commodities are used by both producers and consumers to 'construct and articulate' (Kline 1993: 12) the social relationships between social classes, races and the sexes. For example, as we have indicated throughout this book, gender identities and relationships are a central feature of consumer culture and of educational markets. Research has pointed to the ways in which school shopping adds to mothers' consumption work and confirms the domestic and familial ideologies in households (David *et al.* 1994; Kenway and Epstein 1996a). However, the further point needs to be made that it also confirms the idea of the household as a consumption unit. It is clear from this literature that markets in schooling 'construct and articulate' the gendered power relationships within families. What is less evident in this literature is the ways in which such markets 'construct and articulate' the social power relationships between adults (parents and teachers) and children. We suggest that while it does involve a certain level of negotiated reading, ultimately it does not involve much 'semiotic democracy' (Fiske 1994).

An understanding of broader marketing practices with regard to children is useful in coming to grips with the commodification of school education. As we showed in Chapters 2 and 3, the commodity and the media have been central in the social construction of the child consumer, changing family forms, gender and age relations, and the connections between them. Advertising and new media forms have increasingly detached children from adults and from each other, offering them new identities and relationships. Consumer–media culture has encouraged children to construct their fantasies, rank their preferences and resolve their difficulties though consumption. Further, it has taught them to produce identities, weave social bonds and display and sustain differences through consumption. All of this has implications for the commodification of schooling and for students' perceptions of it.

In school education, childhood is implicitly defined as a powerless and dependent state and the commercialization of schooling reinforces this. Selling children's school education to parents offers a strong message to children about who is in control and what matters. Advertising in children's consumer–media culture promotes 'informality, impulsiveness and lack of deference to authority' (Holland 1996: 164). It offers autonomy and pleasure. In contrast with the child of consumer–media culture, the child of school advertising is compliant and serious – attending constantly to the needs of the school and implicitly to those of adults. We do not know of anyone in the literature who has considered this, yet even students as young as 8 or 9 know what parents want in a school. They do not want a children's space but one like the unattractive world of education constructed on the screen in TV and films – serious, controlled, old-fashioned, puritanical and disciplined – a place where children must be restrained for their own good:

> *Interviewer:*   What do you think parents would look for in a school? What do you think they would see as important?
> *Girl (11 years):* What type of people you will be mixing with. Like if they are nice.
> *Girl (10 years):* Discipline system, whatever that is.
> *Girl (10 years):* The behaviour.

Value-added students, those with *face value*, are those who lift the school's academic, sporting or cultural performance and image and who conform to the school's and the teachers' educational norms – only the good are good for the school. As a 15-year-old Year 10 girl at Hall says, 'Our school stresses on getting high marks. If you don't get high marks you are gone and you are just a person that sits up the back'. All students have similar perceptions and invariably the smart/dumb category is mobilized. Clearly this is an old story but with a market gloss.

Low performing and/or badly behaved students or those who place extra demands on the school are also seen to add negative value. This is something that the students understand very well indeed. Again we see the students' terms and the likely school's terms alongside each other but we also see that the students believe that they, too, have a vested interest in closing the gates on certain students. Witness the following conversation between 10- and 11-year-olds at Willis Primary about students who give schools a poor reputation:

> *Girl:* Bad students, they kick people.
> *Girl:* They tease people.

Girl:	Punch you.
Girl:	Without them it would be better because everyone would be up to the same standard and then they wouldn't have to slow down that much. They could go at their own speed.
Girl:	And learn more things because if they don't know how to do one thing they can't learn to do other things.
Interviewer:	So you think the less bright would hold the others back a bit?
Girl:	Yes. And all the naughty kids would make their grade miss out on all the good stuff.

Sociological and cultural, as opposed to economic, analyses of markets point to the various social and cultural uses to which all sorts of consumer goods and services are put. The commodity is 'consumed symbolically, as a social meaning or as a cultural good, as well as in its material substance as a functional utility' (Lee 1993: 17). They point to the dual nature of such commodities as both objects and symbols. For consumers, consumption performs a number of purposes above and beyond necessity. It plays an important role in group formation, identity, distinctions, differentiation and relationships. Consumption also works as a form of displacement and social control and, as indicated with regard to adults and children, relationships of power are refracted through practices and patterns of consumption. While there may not be a perfect fit between production/representation and consumption, unruly patterns do emerge and change, although less often.

◯ Style, behaviour, bodies

As we explained in Chapter 1, style is a central aspect of consumption. In these image conscious 'designer decades' (Lee 1993: 115) it is arguable that style has assumed an increased importance as we see 'a shift away from notions of substance and content and towards packaging, aesthetic form and "the look"' (Lee 1993: ix). Style provides the impetus for markets in appearances, surfaces and mystification as designer schools well know. But style can also be a statement about who one is and wishes to be. Style allows people and schools to imagine themselves differently, providing an opportunity to define and redefine themselves. To quote Barthes (1975), it can be 'a dream of identity'.

Even if they are not the school's most valued students, all students are expected to perform their part in the school's circuit of exchange by being well behaved, 'doing their best', showing 'pride in the school' and not holding others back. They are to contribute to its semiotics, its style or tone. Indeed, school style has become a major marketing tool, another product that is implicated in the school's system of communications. While, as noted, style can be seen as providing a tool for 'constructing personhood' it can also be seen as a tool for constructing the identity of the school and for constructing marketable power relations between adult and child. It often means an emphasis on the school's appearance, its surfaces, and involves a form of mystification or mythification.

Students' behaviour is a major feature of school style and functions as a sign to adults. On matters of style 'hope and anxiety are never too far apart' (Ewen 1988: 159). The marketized school attends to Stress Generation (Mackay 1997) parents' concerns about their children's 'welfare, whereabouts and well-being' by copying adult/child relations from the schools of their childhood. Good behaviour points to order, discipline and adult authority over children, as distinct from the more permissive and unruly behaviour often associated with popular culture. In the repressive environment of the marketized school, the underground economy of peer pleasure flourishes in all its shades of light and dark. The teachers' job is to keep the lid on kids' libidinous energy. It is also their job to ensure that the repressed does not return to destroy the 'face value' of the school. Take this student's remarks about the assembly at Morely High:

> The girls go to one side and the boys to the other and you have to walk in quietly or you get taken to the side. You file in, one by one down the rows and take a seat waiting for the right teacher to come up to talk to you. Then you stand quietly and wait for the official party to walk onto the stage. Then you sit when they sit. Then you wait for the vice-principal to nag at you for the bad things you have done that week, then the principal comes up and nags a bit more. Then all the good things come, all the certificates, and the competition certificates. Then the principal nags again. Then you have to stand again for the official party to leave. Then you sit down again. Then you have to wait for the teachers to quietly file you out of the hall in an orderly manner.

In the interests of the image, adults are expected to be in control and students are to be under control – the teachers 'file you out'. Compliant and docile behaviour is taken as a sign that a school is functioning in a manner that fosters traditional and stable values and is producing 'good' students who, according to these girls from Willis Primary:

Girl (10 years): Finish their work on time . . . listen to the teacher.
Girl (10 years): Don't do stupid things.
Girl (11 years): Have manners.

In contrast, behaviour such as 'backchatting the teacher' is what characterizes a 'bad student'.

Most schools are obsessed with students' appearance and the uniform is a central feature of this obsession. Many students' comments on the uniform show good cost sense and an understanding of its symbolic value. For example, girls at Willis Primary commented:

Girl (11 years): I prefer a uniform because the other kids think that a uniform is pretty good and they might count that as a thing that they are looking for.

Girl (12 years): I would prefer not to have a uniform so your parents don't have to pay more money with all the books and that.

Girl (11 years): We didn't used to have a uniform but we got one this year because Mrs S. said that people were putting people's clothes down.

Girl (12 years): The bad part about having a uniform is that if you lose it people can just take it home and if you bring your own clothes then you know whose is whose.

But school style is also about disciplining and designing students' bodies. Witness the comments of these boys from Morely High:

Boy (15 years): They focus on the uniform. You have to look a certain way and no thought is given to comfort – you are not allowed to have your shirt out. Little things like that – they put the image of the school before the individuals – like today it is going to be really hot and you can't let your shirt out of your pants.

Boy (16 years): I got my nose pierced last year and they went berserk and had a meeting to make rules about nose piercing. All these rules about the principal deciding if your hair is too long or if you dye it.

Boy (16 years): I got told to have a shave today. I don't think they should tell you what to do in these matters.

Boy (15 years): They think if you dye your hair you are going to turn unruly and disregard your studies. One girl was asked to leave because of her hairstyle. Another guy was asked to leave because of a Mohawk cut.

This sort of intrusion into students' construction of personhood has intensified along with marketization. The marketized school cannot readily accommodate young people who use the 'guileful ruse' (de Certeau 1984) of unorthodox style as a means of 'becoming somebody'.

Going against the trend, Willis Senior College treats its students as adults when it comes to their choice of self-presentation and has no uniform. Some of the students think this would be a positive feature of the school were it not for the following problem:

Girl (16 years): Parents don't like a school with no uniform.
Boy (17 years): They think no uniform, no discipline.
Girl (17 years): I'd rather have the uniform. We seem too scruffy when we're out and about; it's feeding the reputation.

◯ Down-market reputations

Reputation is an elusive thing but everyone seems to know when a school has a bad reputation and the fallout for the school is significant.

Girl (13 years): I didn't want to go to Willis Tech because it is not a good school and has a bad reputation.
Girl (15 years): It had a bad reputation when I was in Grade 6 and Hall High had a better reputation so mum wanted me to come here. I didn't have any say.
Boy (13 years): I was going to go to Willis Tech but it had a bad name, drugs and all that. It was up to me and I chose here.
Boy (13 years): I was going to go to Willis Tech but it had a bad name so I came here. It was up to me to choose.

It is not easy to separate matters of style and reputation from students' subcultures and information networks. Schools' advertising and image management practices have difficulty in dealing with the informal in-formation systems about schools – the talk among parents and particu-larly among students, the rumours and gossip, the exaggerations and the innuendo which can make or break a reputation. Reputation is not easy to manipulate and control and, whether negative or positive, it has a tendency to feed on itself and beome self-fulfilling. The students' impressions and information networks are formed everywhere – in the cracks and crevices of the social and sporting life of the city and in the stories that family members tell each other. Here are the thoughts of girls at Hall High:

Interviewer: How do schools get good and bad names?
Girl (15 years): If you meet a friend in town that goes to another school they tell you about it and you tell your friends and it gets around.
Girl (15 years): We get these ideas from other students and friends that go to different schools. We talk to them at week-ends, holidays and after school. We see them at sport and youth groups. We also hear from our brothers and sisters.

Sadly for Willis Senior College, many younger residents within the suburb of Willis have accepted the view that the College is 'a bad place for bad people'. The following comments were made by 8- and 9-year-old students about the school that they would be most likely to attend in their final years of schooling. The implications of these views for the ways in which these children will anticipate and participate in their schools in the future look bleak:

Girl: The Willis Secondary College, that hasn't got a very good name because all these people, they walk past our school and they throw chips and call people swear words and that.

Girl: That one over the hill hasn't got a very good reputation because of the type of children that go there and the teachers aren't that strict.

Interviewer: What type of students go there?

Girl: There used to be people from our school and they were real naughty and they have all gone there.

Interviewer: What other sort of students go there?

Girl: Maybe a few good ones might be there but . . .

Girl: They are all bad people there.

For students, a school's bad reputation often centres on drugs, alcohol, troublemakers, fighting and knives. Aware of this sort of thing, some students point to the safety of Hall as a selling point: 'It is pretty safe. There is no one carrying knives and you don't feel threatened walking around'. Students also point out that girls' styles of dress and sexual behaviour also affect the reputation of a school – 'young girls getting pregnant' or 'girls in short skirts', for instance. In the light of this, it is interesting to reflect on Bourdieu's (1984: 32) claims that good taste is what separates the cultured élite from the masses whose tastes are seen as cheap, undemanding, unimportant, uncivilized and possibly even vulgar. As he says, they are seen to be 'too closely linked to . . . palpable pleasures and sensual desire'.

Educational reputation is also intimately connected with the suburb and the habits and styles of consumption associated with a particular school and its student population. The following comments from Featherstone (1992: 63) are apt here:

the tendency is for social groups to seek to classify and order their social circumstances and use cultural goods as means of demarcation, as communicators which establish boundaries between some people and build bridges with others. Such a focus on the social usages of cultural goods firmly directs our attention to the practices of embodied persons who read off and necessarily have to make judgements about others by decoding the cultural signs which others practice, display and consume.

Suburbs and their schools have 'sign value' and students are adept at 'decoding the cultural signs' and constructing prestige economies, as these comments from boys at Willis Senior College demonstrate:

Boy (17 years): Schools are relative to the area. The schools in Highton are termed snobby. Willis is not the best place to live and the schools are judged accordingly.

Boy (17 years): From what I have seen there appears to be three classes of schools. Morely High is in the middle, the lowest is McRobbie. I say that from being on a bus with McRobbie kids and that is the only time I have been proud of this school, they were so rough and so below us . . . The other class is the private colleges. If you know someone from college and say you go to Morely High you feel inferior.

Particular and general identities are sometimes linked to the ownership of different commodities. Therefore 'nice' suburbs go with 'nice' people. This logic extends to the impressions about schools in different districts. For instance, students from other schools and suburbs refer to Willis as tough and feral. Students from Willis Senior College are aware of this type of stigmatization and labelling:

Girl (17 years): We know that other kids say we are bad.
Boy (16 years): My friend at another school in town says that people there bag Willis.
Girl (16 years): Even people at Hall look down on us because of the area – Willis.

Most Year 10 students from Hall understand the connections between their school, consumption and social class:

Interviewer: What type of a store would you suggest to represent this school?
Girl (14 years): A clothes shop selling clothes. A casual style of clothing like jeans. A good quality basic.
Girl (15 years): A Reject Shop.
Girl (15 years): Something cheap like Target, a department store like K-Mart, nothing too flash.

Lifestyle and consumer goods are a representation of the personal and social characteristics of the owner:

Boy (15 years): To be a hero, they've got to be like the middle class. Like you don't see really poor kids as big heroes, not usually.

Boy (15 years): Definitely sporty.

Boy (16 years): Like got all the brand names and that. Yeah, good clothes like Rip Curl.

Boy (15 years): I've got good fashion sense and get the Family Allowance Supplement, so that goes into my pocket money. I buy all my own clothes. Yeah, 'cause I live on a farm and there's no money coming in from dad. My mum lets me have, like I get twenty bucks a week, 'cause we get Family Allowance Supplement, so she can have some left over.

Boy (16 years): I didn't used to wear my uniform in Year 8 – not much, 'cause I really hated it. But I've got to be in uniform now because I wear these shoes, they're black and you're allowed to wear black sneakers now – and I wear Stussy grey pants instead of grey jeans, 'cause my grey jeans are too tight.

Boy (15 years): You've just got to be sporting and have good clothing. You don't see people that are really cool wearing K-Mart clothes, you know, they're not really the most popular kids.

One of the reasons students at Willis Senior College actually do not mind uniforms is that 'You don't get comments on whether your shoes are Nike or Adidas'. 'Choice classifies, and classifies the classifier', argues Bourdieu in *Distinction* (1984: 6). It is not possible to keep aesthetics, style and socially constructed meanings out of a consideration of the exchange process of schooling. Neither is it possible to ignore the connections between educational consumption and matrices of social power relations.

The literature about the role that education markets play in class formation, differentiation, distinction and mobility shows that those with few financial resources make the 'choices of necessity' to which Bourdieu (1984) refers. In contrast, parents in a position to exercise 'choice' use schools as positional goods in the class interests of their children and themselves (see, for example, Kenway 1991; Gewirtz *et al.* 1995). This implies that choice of school is more about parental ambitions, hopes and anxieties than those of their children. School change in the interests of marketing is implicitly built on this understanding and is often characterized by a process of *emulation*. Seiter (1995: 48) points out that emulation involves a double movement: an imitation of those richer as well as differentiation from those poorer or less refined. Many schools model themselves on those perceived as better – usually those private schools or those State schools serving the 'comfortable' or privileged classes. They commonly distance themselves from the ideas associated with schools of lesser standing – those usually *serving* those of lesser standing, for example, vocationally-orientated schools. In the words of the principal at Willis Primary: 'My entrepreneurial dream is that some day somebody from the "other side of the river" is going to walk in here and say, "I want to send my child to your school"'.

Further, the following comments from pupils at Hall are typical of the views expressed by students about private schools:

> *Girl (15 years):* The private schools are really snobby and the rich people go there, the upper-class people, so we are just, like, the Hall scum. I suppose we are the poor people that can only afford the uniforms.
>
> *Boy (15 years):* You get a better education and the school looks better and you get a job easier if you have been to Geelong Grammar. You get preference over someone that had been to Hall.

These students did not even consider going to a private school – financially such schools are too far out of their league. Most Hall students were very positive about their own school yet, if given the money, over half of them said they would move to a private school.

A second feature of emulation is a process of *chase and flight* (Seiter 1995: 46, based on Simmel 1971). In a socially mobile endeavour, the 'lower orders' copy, and are expected to copy, the 'higher orders' but, in order to maintain their distinctiveness and superiority, the higher orders move to establish new benchmarks for consumption practices. This results in an unending cycle of consumer desire. It is a brave school that seeks to break this emulation cycle and Willis Senior College is one such school. It is too early to tell if the 'tactics' it is employing to respond creatively to dominant cultural 'strategies' (de Certeau 1984) of a class-segmented educational market will be successful.

Generally, in putting themselves on the market, schools seem to make little attempt to connect to the dreamworlds, interests, pleasures and yearnings of all students. It seems that the dreamworlds of the many are put to the service of the few 'smart people' and 'rich people'. Students clearly have difficulty articulating their desires in a market context that promises them reputation and advancement in exchange for their conformity. And, as they go through school they learn that schools can best deliver their promises to certain students, certain schools and certain suburbs. The students are informed and agential in this context, partly because they draw on the consumption skills learned outside schools. They know how to put on *best face*, they know what the education market values and that it does not value difference (particularly social class difference) and genuine student agency. They know it is two-faced.

They know what they have to sell and give away in exchange for the image and reputation necessary for school success; they know how to *comply with illusion*. However, they learn as they go up through school and become more sophisticated, disenchanted and cynical that more things are lost than gained in this schizophrenic process. In particular, cruel dilemmas are posed for schools like those in Willis and the students who attend them. Such students are generally likely to accept that the education market rules in order to survive in a system which makes their success difficult.

◯ Conclusion

The pincer movement of the market and the corporate State squeezes the liveliness from schools. It is evident in the above scenario that the de- and retraditionalization of schools leaves them little room to move, and in only one direction – towards the commodity form. We have shown that when schools put themselves on the market they are pitching to anxious Stress Generation parents who want to protect their young from the present, the future and themselves. They are also pitching to Stress Generation teachers who are nostalgic for traditional authority relations between teacher and student. Educational fundamentalism is comforting. It provides apparent certainty in an age of uncertainty. It talks of the future in terms of the past and offers adults a sense of control when they feel their lives and their young are out of control.

As we elaborated, putting schools on the market and divorcing school education from entertainment allows schools to further distance themselves from the 'dangers' of children's consumer pleasures. It also assists school advertisers to develop a 'social narrative' about security and certainty through schooling. But this divorce has other effects for kids. It confirms school culture's bad reputation which has been generated in consumer–media culture. However, our research also suggests that many children turn elsewhere to construct their personhood. Schools are on the margins of their identities.

Students, as we have shown, are constrained but discerning, sophisticated but cynical participants caught on the horns of many dilemmas in the Janus-faced world of school marketing. This world celebrates surfaces, encourages conformity, hypocrisy and repression and encourages a view of education which favours the interests of adults over children. Redefining the student as a consumer of schooling maps onto and capitalizes on some of the wider redefinitions of childhood introduced by consumer–media culture. However, it ignores those aspects which celebrate childhood and which challenge asymmetrical adult/child power relations. Indeed, as we have demonstrated, consumerism in schooling

can be used to reinstate traditional and oppressive educational practices. We have shown that educational consumption works as a form of
displacement and social control, and relationships of power are refracted
through it. All of this leaves educators with some urgent questions which
we will address in Chapters 6 and 7.

6 Popular and profane pedagogies

◯ Introduction

As the distinctions between education, entertainment and advertising diminish, we increasingly hear talk of popular culture as popular pedagogy, corporate cultural pedagogy, and the corporate curriculum. Steinberg and Kincheloe (1997: 3) observe that 'education takes place in a variety of social sites including but not limited to schooling'. In children's consumer culture, identities are formed and knowledge is produced and legitimated. In many ways, corporate pedagogues have become postmodern society's most successful teachers (Steinberg and Kincheloe 1997).

They have been able to engage and hold their students' attention. What is more, the children and youth of today have learned their lessons well. At the same time as they are increasingly inscribed within consumer culture, many young people now relegate school education to the margins of their identities. This is a result of the uneven hybridization of education, entertainment and advertising and, by and large, the polarization of adults from the young, and of youthful pleasure from school education and from adults. It seems that many young people expect and get little gratification from school. Indeed, we suggest that in comparison with consumer–media culture, schools generally *lack enchantment* for students. What lessons might there be in this for schools and teachers who are finding it increasingly difficult to persuade young people that the knowledge they have to offer is worthwhile?

To answer this question, we must first return to some earlier points from Chapter 1 where we made the case that a political engagement with consumer culture is vital for young people in schools. There, drawing on Featherstone (1992: 84) and Lee (1993), we noted that several aspects of consumer culture need to be recognized as integral to such a political engagement. These are: the cultural dimensions of the economy (the use of material goods as communicators); the economy of cultural goods (the market principles of supply, demand, capital accumulation, competition and monopolization); and the 'night-time of the commodity' (the concrete social relations involved in the production of commodities). We also indicated that such political engagement would recognize both popular participation and 'everyday outsidedness', and appreciate the wide human motivational range that consumer culture invokes. These different 'angles of scrutiny' (Harwood 2000) allow for a comprehensive 'take' on the complex phenomenon that is consumer–media culture. We further insisted that students do need to understand how consumer culture works with and against them, when and how to oppose it; to comprehend what else is possible and how these possibilities may be made real.

Can corporate pedagogies and anti-corporate activism be mobilized in the classroom as a means to these ends?

In this chapter, we begin by making a case for the appropriation of corporate pedagogies and anti-corporate activism in the classroom. Our arguments are based on the various 'angles of scrutiny' taken in this book. On such bases, we also theorize a pedagogy of the popular and the profane. We conclude the chapter with some examples of popular pedagogies that involve 'unholy' but seriously playful educational alliances.

◯ Capturing corporate pedagogies and anti-corporate activism for schools

Can schools learn about good pedagogy from their 'pedagogical peers' in the corporate and anti-corporate world? We think that there are many lessons to be learnt. Consumer–media culture suggests a number of new educational modalities with the potential to both delight and educate. Inspired by many of the ideas in Brown (1995), Grace and Tobin (1997), Buckingham (1998c) and Klein (2000), we will shortly outline the contours of some of these modalities. We will make the case that education and entertainment need not and should not be polarized. However, the obvious next questions are, 'Should teachers' role differ from the role of the popular pedagogues who teach the corporate curriculum? If so, why and how?' It is at this point that we must turn to the different 'angles of scrutiny' noted above and developed more fully throughout the book.

In its current manifestations, consumer–media culture is multi-faceted in its politics, in the positions, identities and relationships it offers young consumers, and in the emotions it provokes. It bites and delights, gives and takes away. In terms of young people's identities and relationships, it mobilizes feelings of connectedness, gratification, pleasure, excitement and passion. But it can also provoke a sense of inadequacy, anxiety, shame, yearning, envy and contempt for the self or the other. It empowers and disempowers, legitimates and delegitimates, reveals and conceals. Indeed, it could be argued that, in the latter instance, it conceals much more than it reveals at the same time, paradoxically, as it visually and ideologically dominates public and civic space. Clearly then, it is not just harmful as critical theorists suggest or just benign as semiotic democracy theorists imply – but both at once. Consumer–media culture does have a 'menu of meaning' but some have more choice to dine à la carte than others. Further, many 'choices' are forced in the processes of production and consumption. Indeed, as Klein (2000) makes clear, the commodity form is so dominant that it appears as if we have 'no choice' about it as a way of organizing our worlds and our lives.

Students who have grown up in consumer–media culture are positioned in particular ways as educational subjects, as we have shown throughout this book. Green *et al.* (1998: 22) put the point succinctly when they say that schools and teachers 'need to take account of emerging synergies among cultural formations and practices, new technological initiatives, and emerging populations and markets'. More than this, they must *'engage with the popular as the background that informs students' engagement with any pedagogical encounter'* (Sholle and Denski 1995: 19, original emphasis). To do so, schools and teachers must recognize the ways that consumer–media culture exists as a competing pedagogy – in a sense. But this is no straightforward matter.

To argue that teachers 'engage with the popular', then, is also to urge them to recognize the complexity of consumer–media culture – its 'multisidedness'. Addressing this adequately means including, but going beyond, questions of culture, identity and communication, to address matters of economics, sociology, geography, history, psychology, art, design and technology. This recognition has enormous implications for curriculum and pedagogy across many learning areas. It requires teachers not only to enter the field from multiple standpoints, but also to weave these together – 'this goes with that'. It requires them to develop an integrated package of pedagogies which help students to recognize and deal with the ambiguities, tensions and contradictions involved. To point to these multiple entry points is to suggest several further things.

First, at the same time as teachers learn from consumer–media culture, they might also adopt a critical distance from it – an 'everyday/every night' outsider stance. This means that consumer–media education must have critical and postcritical dimensions so that the earnestness of the critical is balanced with parody, play and pleasure, but that parody, play and pleasure are understood as political.

The many dimensions of consumer–media culture indicate that it cannot be reduced simply to a topic – for example, consumer education. Neither is it solely the province of one field of study – media education, say, or English, or social studies. Postmodernity has not only disrupted the borders between high and low culture, it has also challenged the boundaries between the disciplines – new knowledge formations and fusions have emerged. Indeed, politics, art, science and technology are now being reconfigured, with implications for youth culture. This reconfiguration is challenging knowledge in ways that are still evolving. Braidotti (1998) explains some of the underlying politics in regard to art and technology:

> If in a conventional humanistic framework the two may appear as opposites, in postmodernity, they are much more inter-connected.
>
> In all fields, but especially in information technology, the strict separation between the technical and the creative has in fact been made redundant by digital images and the skills required by computer-aided design. The new alliance between the previously segregated domains of the technical and the artistic marks a contemporary version of the post-humanistic reconstruction of a techno-culture whose aesthetics is equal to its technological sophistication.

In other words, 'Science becomes the handmaiden of magic' (Schroeder 1994: 526).

This techno-scientific and aesthetic fusion is evident in a range of on- and offline sites and technocultural artefacts. Many recreational computer activities, such as computer games, provide obvious examples which, incidentally, also challenge the boundaries between 'fantasy and science, between high-tech and primitivism, and between play and real life' (Skirrow 1990: 323). ICTs are also brought into close association with various youthful counter-cultural forms. Cyberpunk nightclubs and cafés in such global cities as San Francisco and London draw on a similar fusion, also emphasizing their challenges to the senses. As Schroeder explains, they seek to attract customers with promises of 'Altered images, altered sound, altered minds and altered states' (1994: 522). These are to be achieved through 'VR machines, SEGA computer games, psychoactive cocktails, brain machines, cyber and VR demos, massage, tarot and guest cyber scientists and artists' (Schroeder 1994: 522).

Clearly, the disciplines can no longer so readily discipline and, accordingly, consumer–media education cannot be disciplined by the disciplines. Thus, throughout this chapter we will address those whom we call 'consumer–media culture teachers'. This is an inclusive term – an open invitation to any teacher from any field of knowledge who recognizes the importance of what Giroux calls 'border pedagogy' (1992: 28–36).

All this raises questions about the values by which young people have come to live their image- and commodity-drenched lives. As we have explained, they have come to learn that they can satisfy all their needs through consumption. They have come to 'know' this, despite both the regularity of their cycles of dissatisfaction and desire, and their acknowledgement that commodities both include and exclude – with all the accompanying insults, injuries and injustices. To quote Jacobson and Mazur (1995: 188, 190):

> The late Christopher Lasch, in his book *The Culture of Narcissism*, maintained that advertising 'manufactures a product of its own: the consumer, perpetually unsatisfied, restless, anxious, and bored. Advertising serves not so much to advertise products as to promote consumption as a way of life. It "educates" the masses into an unappeasable appetite not only for goods but also for new experiences and personal fulfillment. It upholds consumption as the answer to the age-old discontents of loneliness, sickness, weariness, lack of sexual satisfaction . . . it creates new forms of unhappiness – personal insecurity, status anxiety'.

This raises the question, 'Can consumer–media education help students to find a satisfying code to live by – one that is in critical tension with consumption as a way of life?' It is a question we will later attempt to answer in the context of a pedagogy of the profane and the popular. To that end, however, we must first consider something of the nature of pedagogy.

Pedagogic intentions are not necessarily matched by students' responses. Indeed, the texts of teaching will always be 'read' by students according to the ways in which relationships of pleasure and power come together in the process of reception by both individuals and groups in and beyond the classroom. In one sense, then, the curriculum is produced by its readers. Viewed in this way, the meaning of consumer–media education is constantly negotiated and selectively appropriated by students. Our arguments throughout this book suggest that the success or otherwise of consumer–media education will hinge on the nature of the positions offered to students in teachers' pedagogical texts and on how students feel with regard to them. Conventionally, as we have indicated, teachers have a propensity to claim a moral high ground built upon the negative critique of children's culture, popular culture and youth culture. They offer their teaching as a non-oppressive, enlightened, enlightening and empowering alternative to popular pedagogy and the corporate curriculum. But this is not necessarily the way it is understood by students who may experience it as *authoritarian*.

If consumer–media teachers were to attend to students' responses to their teaching, in particular their emotional responses, what might this

mean? To put it simply, we suggest that such teachers ask themselves, 'What scripts do my consumer–media education programmes
offer students about themselves, through what lenses do students read
and rewrite them and with what effects, in terms of what I am trying to
teach?'

The danger with consumer–media education is its potential association in kids' minds with negative authority, with adult criticism of kids'
pleasures and fantasies. Deconstruction may appear more like destruction, teaching more like preaching and teachers may be construed as
anti-youth and anti-pleasure. It is possible that teachers unwittingly
offer students the implicit message that somehow or other they are in
the wrong – 'their own worst enemy' in fact. Take the case of certain
feminist approaches to media analysis documented in Kenway *et al.*
(1996).

In the English classes of this study, the things that many girls take
pleasure in – for example, romance novels, soap operas and fashion
magazines – are often the objects of critical analysis. Girls are invited
to identify the restricted portrayals of females, their subordination to
oppressive romance and fashion discourses. Unfortunately, girls are
here offered an image of themselves as passive victims overwhelmed by
negative gender stereotypes or by the unequal relationships between the
sexes. The implicit message is that, as they are, girls are not good enough.
They must stop doing the things they like and do the things that teachers/
adults think are good for them. Needless to say, classes that employ such
logic do not necessarily meet with a positive reception. The students do
not tend to appreciate teachers who make them feel ashamed about
their choices and lifestyles – all in the name of helping them. Indeed, a
number find this insulting and hurtful.

As this example indicates, deconstruction may have an emotional
fallout. It may also mean that students resist resistance. In broad terms,
this resistance can be associated with matters of pleasure, investment
and identity. In helping students to understand the politics of 'why they
want what they want' (Walkerdine 1991: 89), the processes involved
and the various orders of consequence, teachers must work *with* and,
just as importantly, *through* their pleasures, investments and identities.
Of course, gaining an understanding of the politics of consumption does
not necessarily prepare students to re-envisage themselves as agents in
the processes which they have come to recognize as political. Too often,
critique and deconstruction seem only to offer students negative politics.
If students are to become agents of whatever sort, schools must 'position' them as agential and let them take pleasure in it. Unfortunately,
the issues of agency and pleasure in the classroom are a source of ambivalence for many teachers. In fact, in many ways they conflict with the
nature of school and education.

We made the point in Chapter 3 that adult and childhood notions of pleasure polarize according to *plaisir* and *jouissance* respectively. With its associated desires and drives, *jouissance* stands in conflict with the rubric of rationality which typifies dominant conceptions of education. By its very nature, consumer–media culture does not operate at the level of rationality, and hence the pleasures that children derive from it are highly suspect in schools. *Plaisir*, understood as 'making learning fun' through the use of playlike activities, is the most that can be expected in many classrooms (Grace and Tobin 1997). Teachers use play to motivate and reward, but children's concepts of what constitutes playful activities are quite different. Grace and Tobin (1997: 176) quote research by King (1979) and Romero (1989) to argue that 'children consider activities play when they are voluntary and self-directed'. Their own research points to ways in which a pedagogy of the profane and the popular might transcend both of these understandings.

We will now share some lessons about the power of pleasure and the pleasure of power. In what follows, we theorize some critical and postcritical approaches to consumer–media education in order to picture what a pedagogy of the profane and the popular might look like. We draw on some of the critical theory introduced in Chapter 1 and appropriate some postmodern advertising forms and popular culture genres and technologies, as a means of promoting both critical agency and pleasure. The examples we offer are designed to assist in ways of thinking about how students are to become informed and active citizens within the politics of consumption. Let us now proceed by theorizing a pedagogy of the profane and the popular.

◯ The profane and the popular

In schools, the popular is the profane. What do we mean by this? What, indeed, do we mean by the term 'profane'? In the *Merriam-Webster's Collegiate Dictionary*, the profane is defined first by what it is not – an indication that it lies outside or transgresses the dominant order or privileged meaning. There it is defined as 'not holy' (unconsecrated, impure or defiled); 'not concerned with religion' (secular). At best, the profane is irreverent, at worst it is blasphemous to what is held sacred. It is concerned with defilement, impurity, debasement and, thus, the abject. The profane also refers to those who are not among the initiated or do not possess expert or esoteric knowledge, and to the temporal rather than eternal sphere. Our concept of the profane, which we use as a metaphor, also depends on its antithetical relationship to the sacred.

The objects of consumer culture are profane. Product senility makes certain that, like the gods of modernity to which Benjamin (1982) refers, the brittle glittering idols of postmodernity are mortal. Furby succeeds Tamagotchi, only to become yesterday's Beanie Baby. By contrast, the traditions of education are enduring. Consumer culture is an anathema to many schools, parents and educators. Its presence in schools is seen to defile, adulterate and contaminate. It is the excluded other of traditional education. It is inevitable, then, that a pedagogy of the profane will arouse ambivalence, if not horror, since it conflicts with the values of authority, rationality and instrumentality which many schools and educators hold sacred.

This dichotomy is complicated by the fact that the teacher, as the one who possesses knowledge, is aligned with the 'sacred' and the student, as yet uninitiated, is aligned with the 'profane'. This maps onto the polarizing effect of the transgenerational address circulated in consumer–media culture. In contrast, consumer–media culture appears to keep no 'secrets' from children (see Postman 1999). Indeed, in addition to the perspectives on this offered by Postman (1994) and Meyrowitz (1985) mentioned in earlier chapters, much has been written on the effects of exposing children to depictions of violence, sexuality, alcohol and tobacco advertising.

However, as we have already indicated, consumer culture conceals at the same time as it reveals. It, too, has secrets. If we were to ask what is profane to consumer–media culture, we might look for the answer in what disregards or exposes these secrets and, therefore, look at critical inquiry. If we were to say that consumer–media culture cultivates indiscriminate and hedonistic consumption, then we might say that there are values which are profane to this way of life. Postman (1999) makes similar points when he looks to the Age of Enlightenment for a way into the future. He examines ways in which eighteenth-century ideas of a 'proper education', which had 'as one of its goals the cultivation of a sceptical outlook based on reason' (p. 159), might be translated into the contemporary classroom. He also calls for the rejuvenation of the great narratives, of first principles or religion (it does not really matter which, he says). The point is that we find an ethical centre. The problem with this is that little is made of agency except in regard to our choice of narrative or of how these narratives might be accommodated within a sceptical epistemology.

When we raised the question about kids' values earlier, we asked how we might help them to find a satisfying code to live by – one that is in positively critical tension with 'consumption as a way of life'. Singer (1993: 17, 49) argues that the pursuit of self-interest (which, he says, is 'understood largely in terms of material wealth') and 'the ideology of growth' have become a guiding imperative at many levels in western societies. Explaining the 'paradox of hedonism', Singer (1993: 20) shows how consumption is mistakenly equated with fulfilment and how little relationship there actually is between wealth and happiness, growth and a sense of plenty.

'Life politics' (Giddens 1991), on the other hand, involves disputes and struggles about how we should live in our globally interdependent order. It aims for morally justifiable and satisfying ways of living that exclude greed and growth values such as those Singer describes. In Singer's view, 'doing' life politics means making 'the ultimate choice' (1993: 4) to 'live an ethical life'. It involves, he says, understanding the practical implications of one's own attitudes and opinions and following them through. It means applying these values to choices of lifestyle. And, Singer argues, this 'can satisfy our most important human needs'. Life politics also seeks to hold governments and other institutions to account and to place demands upon them. It calls for corporate disclosure and responsibility.

As some schools have discovered, couched in the right way, there is a potentially rich educational agenda associated with life politics and the local and global citizenship activities that go with it. Those who work with young people are well aware that many experience a generalized sense of anxiety, meaninglessness, emotional and moral disquiet, existential isolation and a loss of the moral resources needed to live a full life. They have trouble finding something to live for. Life politics has enormous potential to turn this around, but how are teachers to introduce students to it? How are they to avoid appearing like finger waving moral authoritarians who turn kids off, rather than on, to commodity politics?

Klein's (2000) study of the reasons for the rise in anti-corporate activism points to one answer to this question, an answer which returns us to our earlier question about what might be profane to consumer–media culture. Image may well be all, but as the defendants in the McLibel court trial put it in relation to McDonald's Ronald McDonald, 'Children love a secret, and Ronald's is especially disgusting' (Klein 2000: 359). Beneath the 'second skin' of the commodity lie many 'secret' realities. These include the commercial colonization and privatization of public, civic and linguistic space (corporate censorship); tendencies towards global cultural homogenization; the substitution of lifestyle for living and 'meaningful life'; the exploitation of workers in the West and, in particular, women and child workers in Third World sweatshops; widening gaps between executive and worker, consumer and producer and, overall, the corporate world's contribution to the growing gap between rich and poor. But as Klein (2000) suggests, and the protests against the World Trade Forum in Seattle in 1999, and elsewhere in 2000 indicate, many people from many walks of life are refusing to keep the corporate world's 'secrets'. Anti-corporate activism offers a means of exposing what are, in fact, very unpopular practices associated with popular culture.

The high profile exposure of the chilling exploitation and expansion practices employed by some big brand name companies is an extremely persuasive tool of citizenship. Given the emotionally intense, indeed obsessive, relationship built up between big brands, their celebrity icons and consumers, there is a profound sense of betrayal when that image is tarnished by scandal. This has been intensified by the way certain practices on the Internet have exposed a rhetoric–reality gap, particularly in relation to youth market practices. A case in point is the way the music industry is dealing with the downloading of recordings on the Internet (Ritchie 2000). The heavy-handed legalistic approach adopted by some music industry corporations and performers contradicts their pretence of being 'on side' with young people.

'Ad fatigue', 'logo overload' and 'anti-corporate rage' are some of the terms Klein (2000) uses to describe the growing 'reservoir of resentment' arising from people's increasing awareness of the many negative implications of commerce. She argues that such sensibilities provide some of the impetus for the global growth of 'anti-corporate activism' associated with 'Ethical shareholders, culture jammers, street reclaimers, McUnion organizers, human-rights hacktivists, school-logo fighters and Internet corporate watch dogs' (Klein 2000: 445). Anti-corporate activism involves people calling to account corporations, not just governments. Indeed, it exposes the rather insidious connections between multinationals and governments, particularly in free trade zones. It asks them to change and to make public the manner in which they are cleaning up their acts.

Klein documents a number of ways of achieving this, many of which reinvent new modes of protest rather than repeat the predictable forms of the past. They are frequently playful, often do-it-yourself and some, like the reclaim the streets (RTS) parties in the UK, politicize popular forms of entertainment. Organizers of RTS parties, Klein reports, have described them as 'the realization of "a collective daydream"' (2000: 313). She refers to them as 'travelling carnivals'. Indeed, her description of the music and stunts, elaborate costumes and free food, dancing and games which typify an RTS party is highly evocative of the carnivalesque. RTS parties turn the world upside down by making popular culture political and politics popular. They defy easy categorization. Protesting against corporate colonization of public space and economic globalization, these street parties:

> mix the earnest predictability of politics with the amused irony of pop. For many people in their teens and twenties, this presents the first opportunity to reconcile with being creatures of their Saturday-morning-cartoon childhoods with a genuine political concern for their communities and environments. RTS is just playful and ironic enough to finally make earnestness possible.
>
> (Klein 2000: 316–17)

A pedagogy of the profane and the popular seeks a comparable hybrid blend of the playful and earnest. Like the RTS movement which hijacks busy streets for spontaneous gatherings, it is transgressive. Yet, to bring the profane objects of consumer–media culture into the classroom is to cast 'profane illumination' on the world of the commodity. Paradoxically, this is to rescue childhood from the enchantment of consumer culture by *re-enchanting the classroom*, because it allows the young both to participate in and negate the myths of the metropolis through their play.

As the marketing profiles of children and youth we described in Chapter 2 suggest, advertising and media culture have appropriated and corrupted the transformative power of play. They have offered new resources for children's play – new identities to imitate, new boundaries to transgress and new objects to collect. Kids today are more likely to collect Happy Meal toys or Barbies than pebbles and feathers, and to imitate cartoon superheroes rather than play mothers and fathers. However, one thing remains constant: 'what is prized by the adult brings misery to the child, whereas what the adult despises is precious to the child' (Gilloch 1996: 88). For, in contrast to the adult who seeks to view the world from a position of superiority, the child 'enjoys a privileged proximity' and, as such, a view that continues 'to problematize the habitual, forgetful vision of the adult' (Gilloch 1996: 83).

Bringing the profane into the classroom is to remove it from its 'habitual site' and, we suggest, to do that is to problematize it. It is to allow postmodern children 'to discover the new anew' (Buck-Morss 1991: 274) and to bring together the artefacts of education and consumer culture in an intuitive as well as critical relationship. A pedagogy of the profane and the popular is action-orientated. Of the body and senses, it is a more voluptuous learning that invokes the semiotic and evokes *jouissance*. Such learning is intuitive, playful and pleasurable but not mindless. We see it as complementary to, rather than the antithesis of, the critical. Finally, as Benjamin's assessment of children's dramatic performances suggests, a pedagogy of the profane and the popular is reciprocal. In these performances, 'everything is turned upside down, and just as master served slave during the Roman Saturnalia, so during the performance, children stand on stage and teach and educate their attentive educators' (Buck-Morss 1991: 264). This, of course, evokes Bakhtin's concept of the carnivalesque.

◯ The pleasures of unholy educational alliances

In this final section we discuss the implications of the carnivalesque for pedagogy. Pleasure takes front stage in the pedagogies, as we point to

the benefits of the fusions and *frissons* of some unholy educational alliances. In so doing, we look at Grace and Tobin's study of video production in the classroom and follow this with an evaluation of 'The Rock
Eisteddfod Challenge'. In both cases, the students are actors in, and
producers of, their own performance rather than passive consumers of
images and commodities. Both approaches suggest that the translation
of consumer–media culture into an educational setting is unproblematic
for kids although, in the case of Grace and Tobin's model, not necessarily
so for teachers. With this qualification, then, we foreground how pleasure can be put to good pedagogic effect, and use 'The Rock Eisteddfod
Challenge' as an example of the way in which the pleasures of consumer–
media culture can be productively integrated with the curriculum, as
Fitzclarence explained in lengthy conversations with students and staff
at Deakin University during the 1990s.

Our first exploration of the carnivalesque in the classroom is based on
a three-year research study of a video curriculum developed and evalu-
ated by Grace and Tobin (1997). In this instance, the actual curriculum
is less important than the fact that it acted as a conduit for the entry of
popular culture into the classroom. We are particularly interested in the
conclusions that the authors drew about the pedagogical potential of the
processes of the carnivalesque that it invoked.

In the second stage of the study, students in Grades 1 to 3 were given
the opportunity to choose the genre and content of the scripts they
created. Not surprisingly, they drew heavily on popular culture, bringing
'the unofficial interests of the children . . . from the periphery of classroom life to centre stage' (Grace and Tobin 1997: 164). While this was a
source of ambivalence for teachers, the authors found that 'video production opens up a space where students can play with the boundaries
of language and ideology and enjoy transgressive collective pleasures'
(Grace and Tobin 1997: 161).

As Grace and Tobin point out, there are parallels between video and
creative language curricula. They differ, however, in several crucial ways.
First, video production is a collaborative activity. Second, it incorporates
extralinguistic modes of expression. Third, the video curriculum is more
likely to address peers' interests and expectations than those of their
teachers. Thus, they are more likely to seek to entertain their peers than
meet the perceived requirements of the teachers. In this final respect,
the pleasures aroused are reciprocal. There is pleasure taken in amusing
the audience and pleasure taken in their amusement. In so far as this
curriculum evokes 'laughter, bodily pleasures, hierarchical inversions,
and bad taste' and 'unsettle[s] the existing order of things' (Grace and
Tobin 1997: 168) in the classroom, it invokes the carnivalesque.

The carnivalesque emphasizes pleasure and desire, but it is not un-
political or ahistorical. According to Mary Russo (1986: 218), 'the masks

and voices of carnival resist, exaggerate, and destabilize the distinctions and boundaries that mark and maintain high culture and organized society . . . They suggest a counterproduction of culture, knowledge, and pleasure'. In many ways the video curriculum reproduced this pattern of regulation and deregulation and, thus, reproduced many of the elements of the carnivalesque: parody, scatology, horror, the grotesque and forbidden. Certainly, the carnivalesque has its dark side but curriculum activities which bring popular and consumer culture into the classroom are a form of controlled decontrol which is pleasurable and agential but which also offers the opportunity for critique.

In the case of video production, Grace and Tobin found that the students 'used this medium to play with meanings and messages of [popular] culture rather than absorbing them uncritically' (1997: 165). Understanding becomes an outcome of doing, acting, reflecting, remembering, retelling and reproducing familiar plots, imagery and characterizations from popular culture rather than of critical analysis alone. While some students may not be critical readers of violence, sexism and racism (see Buckingham 1998c), the authors argue that in the process of remaking and imitating these forms and discourses 'there is also, always, an element of newness and thus the potential for transformation' (Grace and Tobin 1997: 180). This coincides with Benjamin's view that the child discovers the new anew.

In Grace and Tobin's analysis, the carnivalesque is used to conceptualize the 'issues and tensions' that arose as a result of their study. As they themselves point out, their intention is not to 'romanticize' transgressive classroom behaviours or 'write them into the curricula'. Rather, it is to 'validate the humour and everyday interests of children' and to create a sense of 'spontaneous communitas' (Grace and Tobin 1997: 185). Marsh (2000) found a similar sense of communal pleasure resulted when she incorporated the Teletubbies into a preschool curriculum, and we suggest that children's media consumer culture icons like the Wiggles in Australia and Sesame Street characters in the USA can be imaginatively appropriated for the classroom. Marsh argues that the presence of popular culture in the classroom affirms kids' 'cultural capital'. It is 'relevant' to their interests, to what they consider 'real' and 'meaningful'. She found that the use of consumer culture icons in the curriculum 'motivated children to make links between different aspects of their experience and their learning', and argues that 'This metacognitive intertextuality, the awareness that can arise as a result of making such links, is important to children's learning' (Marsh 2000: 130, 131).

So far we have concentrated on early childhood learning. 'The Rock Eisteddfod Challenge' is a national performing arts competition for secondary school students which originated in Australia in 1980. It is now held internationally, being known as 'The Global Rock Challenge' in the UK and the USA, and the 'Smokefree Stage Challenge' in New Zealand. It also incorporates a number of other competitions. As we will show, the 'Rock Eisteddfod Challenge' evokes many of the pleasures of the carnivalesque. However, unlike the curricula which Grace and Tobin (1997) and Marsh (2000) evaluate, the 'Challenge' is representative of the marketing equivalent of the carnivalesque – dedifferentiation.

In the terminology of postmodern marketing, dedifferentiation refers to 'the erosion, effacement and elision of established hierarchies – high and low culture, education and training, politics and show business – and the blurring of what were formerly clear-cut entities' (Brown 1995: 106–7). In terms of representation and genre, dedifferentiation is related to the carnivalesque. However, whereas the carnivalesque is a mock inversion of the relational status of these entities, dedifferentiation blurs the difference and now appears in the structural relationships of actual material and historical entities. Moreover, as with the case of the fusion of entertainment and advertising, it is neither temporary nor, for this reason, necessarily liberating. The strategic alliances and collaborations between corporations engaged in cross-selling and licensed merchandising which extend or dissolve traditional product and trade boundaries have resulted in the emergence of 'boundaryless corporations'.

As we have seen, dedifferentiation currently occurs in schools in the form of business and industry partnerships and between education and market culture. While not all alliances between schools and corporations are equally beneficial, there is a need to reconsider the way they are conceptualized and negotiated. In this instance, we do not consider the economic aspects of these collaborations, but how they can be related to a consumer–media education curriculum which combines critical agency with voluptuous learning. Strategic alliances between corporations, government bodies, media and schools can be productive when incorporated into a critical consumer–media education curriculum. We made the point in Chapter 4 that one of the issues underlying ambivalence about in-school marketing concerns which adults control children and for what purposes. In spite of some examples of sophisticated approaches to the marketized schoolyard on the part of schools themselves, we also made the point that schools tend to take a passive role in their dealings with corporations. They take the good (funds and resources) with the bad (advertising).

However, this need not be the case. One of the most long-standing and best examples of a pleasurable and productive fusion of curriculum and entertainment, State and corporate sponsorship is the 'Challenge'. In this instance, popular culture becomes popular pedagogy underwritten in different ways by the school, the State and commercial markets. Broadly, the school is in some senses deschooled and reschooled by different aspects of different markets. The 'Challenge' could probably be regarded as an archetypal unholy alliance. It is sponsored by the State, by various commercial interests and by individual schools, and it performs a marketing function for all. It draws on the full range of educational cultural intermediary expertise and privatized parental support. It is intranational, national and international. It is ultimately orientated towards the disembodied screen, but until then it is certainly no abstraction. It is territorialized and deterritorialized, institutional and non-institutional. It is also a form of anti-corporate advertising, for through it the National Drug Offensive runs a campaign against drug abuse. Let us be less abstract and offer a brief historical overview.

In the original dance/drama competition format of the 'Challenge', participating schools choreograph an eight-minute production on a theme of choice set to contemporary, commercially available music. Students design the costumes and set. Schools proceed through a series of heats at local and State levels. The State finals are televised, and those who win compete in the national final, judged on the basis of the screen performance. Winners are awarded music equipment and also have an opportunity to take a self-funded trip to the USA to perform. In 1999, more than 400 Australian schools and 40,000 students aged between 11 and 18 participated in the 'Challenge'. It culminated in eight TV specials which, in 1998, were viewed by one in three Australian teenagers (Lum *et al.* 1998: iii).

The 'Challenge' has produced a number of spin-offs including the 'National Battle of the Bands' (1998) and the 'National Stage Challenge' (1999) which recognize original writing and live music, and the 'Croc Eisteddfod' (1996) which encourages the involvement of young indigenous Australians from remote regions including Cape York, Kununurra, Alice Springs, Moree and the Torres Strait Islands. Although the 'Croc Eisteddfod' is a festival rather than a competition, it promotes the same drug- and alcohol-free message among indigenous communities. In 1997, a science and technology category, the 'Scitech Eisteddfod', was created by Lindsay Fitzclarence and the Deakin Centre for Education and Change. Entries are judged on their treatment of science and technology themes or issues, and on innovation in technology, engineering and costume design.

Unlike much school activity, the 'Challenge' inspires almost fanatical devotion among participating students and many of their peers. In so doing, it offers educators and policy makers a few lessons on pedagogy and curriculum development. The 'Challenge' taps into the desires and fantasies produced by popular youth–cultural forms and maps these onto the performing arts in schools. In the case of the 'Scitech Eisteddfod' they are mapped onto science and technology and show how science is the 'magic' which creates the 'illusion' of popular culture (Fitzclarence

1999). Indeed, the 'Challenge' hybridizes art and science, affirming young people's imaginations and resourcefulness. Students themselves have noted that it also promotes teamwork, creativity, commitment, an understanding of social issues and the 'communitas' we mentioned earlier. A submission to the National Drug Strategy Evaluation (Carroll 1996: 32) reported that the event is:

> grow[ing] in popularity – both across different schools and within individual schools [and] this popularity appears to spread across the student population of a school over successive years of a school's participation. Consequently, participation in the event extends over time to those outside the 'hard core' of dance performers, and is associated with a certain attractiveness (or 'coolness'). Specific examples of the positive effects which participation in the event provided for 'problem kids' were also cited by teachers . . . Both students and teachers commented on the dramatic positive impact of the Rock Eisteddfod on 'school spirit'.

Clearly, the success of the 'Challenge' demonstrates that its creators have considerable understanding about the subjectivities of today's students – those who have grown up in consumer–media culture and whose identities, as we said earlier, have been formed at the intersection of the commodity and the image. A combination of social commentary, technology and popular culture, the 'Challenge' offers schools the opportunity, as Fitzclarence (1999: 1) points out, 'to engage in a curriculum in keeping with the multi media world'. It also invites them to consider their lifestyle choices and in that sense invokes life politics.

As we explained in Chapter 4, the 'Challenge' is a tobacco, alcohol and other drug prevention vehicle for the National Drug Offensive and is sponsored by several Australian federal government departments. As the concept has expanded, so too have the sponsorship arrangements which now include corporate, print and broadcast media sponsors and the ubiquitous McDonald's. An evaluation found that 'The Drug Offensive was seen to be a credible message source', with the nexus between the 'euphoria associated with participation in the event and the strong promotion of the "drug-free high" nature of this experience' making students receptive to the anti-drug message (Carroll 1996: 33). Such findings suggest that, in the case of the 'Challenge', the dedifferentiation between education and entertainment, and between government, corporate, media and educational sponsors, has brought educational and popular cultures and official and unofficial discourses into fruitful dialogue. The educational euphoria the students experience – *jouissance* – point to the benefits of the carnivalesque challenge to the rational, instrumental, authoritarian norms of schooling.

◯ Conclusion

In so far as the curricula we have described consider students' 'out-of-school cultures', they reflect a 'central emphasis on the (problematic) concept of relevance and on the attempt to validate students' cultures' (Buckingham 1998a: 35). The 'Challenge' curriculum goes further in that it invites young people to reflect on and alter, if necessary, their lifestyle choices. It does not, however, ask them to reconsider corporate practices, the inseparability of advertising from the media, or, indeed, their own inscription in consumer–media culture. As indicated at the outset of this chapter, consumer–media education must include components that address such matters if it is to properly come to grips with the many faces and types of the commodity form. In the final chapter we suggest some pedagogies with a more feisty political edge.

⑦ Pedagogies that bite/byte back

○ Introduction

The pedagogical strategies outlined in this chapter plunder the corporate vernacular and also anti-corporate activist practices. They are more overtly political than those outlined in Chapter 6. They explicitly blend the playful and the earnest and are intended to both delight and bite.

We begin with a consideration of strategies designed to come to grips with students' affective investment in the commodity and consumer form. We have called this section 'Cool hunting and cool criticism'. Whereas the carnivalesque in the classroom turns standard practice on its head, in this section we turn marketing and media production strategies on their heads. Our object is to offer students ways of understanding how they use consumer culture as a resource in identity building and how, at the same time, *they* are used by consumer–media culture. The second pedagogical approach we describe here builds on kids' inscriptions in consumer culture but also encourages them to adopt an insider-outsider standpoint. We call the young activist who adopts this standpoint the *cyberflâneur*. The youthful *cyberflâneur* conducts his or her life politics and accepts his or her global citizenship 'responsibilities' in the interwoven webs of the Internet and the corporate world – the 'branded web' as Klein calls the latter. Both are prime sites for the youthful *cyberflâneur*, as we will explain. We build on the focus on identity and on multimedia technologies when we consider teens and zines and culture jamming in the final section. These strategies once again appropriate popular cultural forms but with more agency and edge. They offer popular paradigms for kids to make their own media, using the same tools as the media uses but promoting their own ideas and policing 'their own desires' (Klein 2000: 293). Culture is understood as a prime site for citizenship and multimedia technologies come to be viewed as machinery for action.

◯ Cool hunting and cool criticism

Consumer–media culture is a *'pedagogical machine'* (Sholle and Denski 1995: 21, original emphasis) and consumer–media education invites students to prise open its covers, peer inside and see how its mechanics work. Ultimately, it invites them to recognize that 'The overwhelming objective of the media is neither to entertain nor to inform but, rather, to deliver audiences to advertisers' (Davies 1996: 177). Such a recognition involves a number of others. As we explained in Chapter 1, the media is used by producers to sell products to consumers and equally, media audiences have become commodities sold by media organizations to producers, thus creating a process of double exchange (Jhally 1990). At the same time, there is a process of exchange between the media and its audience that relates particularly to young people. In discussing 'adolescent consumer socialization' and MTV, Davies (1996) points to the contention of Schultze *et al.* (1991) that: 'To survive economically, the electronic media need a consumer youth market. On the other hand, young people derive guidance and nurturance from the media because other social institutions do not shape youth culture as powerfully as they once did' (Davies 1996: 177–8). This exchange, however, neither provides equal benefits to both parties nor makes transparent its operations. So, looking inside at the workings of the 'pedagogical machine' becomes an important component of consumer–media education. Equally, looking at the 'pedagogical machine' at work producing meaning and identity is another important component.

Students 'need' to see how consumer–media culture produces both meanings and identities. They need to look at how these meanings construct a certain 'version of reality' and at how 'they hook up with emotional (affective) commitments that are historically situated' (Sholle and Denski 1995: 22). For schools and teachers, this means recognizing both students' agency as producers of their own identity *and* their emotional or affective investment in, and consumption of, media culture and advertising images in the process of identity construction. As Sholle and Denski (1995: 25, original emphasis) explain, this investment is best understood, not as rational decision-making, but as *'emotional and bodily* commitments'. The young are 'vulnerably preoccupied with their self-image' and 'issues of social impression management' (Cohen 1998: 165). Consumer–media culture, likewise concerned with impression management, seeks to exploit this vulnerability and in so doing masks or mystifies its marketing intent. All this makes for pedagogical challenges of some magnitude.

As indicated in Chapter 3, there are many aspects to the work and workings of consumer–media culture. For the purposes of this section, though, we take the marketing concept known as 'cool hunting' and the media production strategy which Gow (1993) calls 'pseudo-reflexive impression management' as stepping-off points to theorize a postcritical pedagogy which invites students to call into question their affective investments without devaluing them. The hunted become the hunters and the pseudo-reflexive becomes the authentically reflexive. We call this 'cool criticism by the cool hunted'.

That kids buy image when they buy products, and that brands are inextricably tied to young people's identity-building, is now common knowledge. Along with this, many corporations have identified themselves as cool, alternative and defiantly young. Brand-name fashion, music and magazines are used as instantly recognizable codes of identity. For instance, 'ravers' wear clothing labels like Snug, Fiction and Porn Star, listen to techno music and read magazines like *Vice* and *Tribe*. Hard core (skate) 'boarders' listen to bands like Korn and Offspring; they wear Vans sneakers and punk-band T-shirts (*Maclean's* 1999). Yet it is less well-known that image-based brands create youth cultural style or attitudes partly through tapping into or resonating with those that already exist. According to Klein, when 'the baby boomers dropped their end of the consumer chain' in the early 1990s, 'Advertisers, brand managers, music, film and television producers raced back to high school, sucking up to the in-crowd' in search of street credibility (2000: 67–8). In other words, they went 'cool hunting'. Cool consultants such as Sputnik do not use market research techniques; they infiltrate, they are 'in with the in-crowd' (Klein 2000: 72). Here, too, we see the looting of such identity politics as green, feminist and black, gay and ethnic pride.

Under such circumstances we see the corporate plundering of the vernacular, of any as yet uncommodified styles with marketable possibilities. Just as consumer–media culture helped to disaggregate youth as we showed in Chapter 2, it also contributed to a general notion that the young as a group have many tribes. In turn, this led to the young inventing their own subcultures and subcultural styles, drawing on an eclectic range of resources and blending them in extraordinary ways. Many big brands have zeroed in on the increasing number of youth subcultural groups or tribes which make up the Y Generation. The subcultural styles of the young from poor neighbourhoods have often been creative 'choices of necessity', and it is an irony that such choices are often those most sought by cool hunters.

Explaining that young and often poor urban African-American males have been the market most 'aggressively mined' for cool, Klein (2000: 74) says that in America, 'cool hunting simply means black-culture hunting'. It is a clear example both of how race is reduced to a matter of style and of the 'plagiaristic commerce' between black and white. Nike is pre-eminent among brands that have appropriated the vernacular cultural styles, forms and discourses of African-Americans and Latinos and packaged and sold them back to them. These young consumers have a colossal emotional stake in the identities they have been invited to construct around corporate logos. As we suggested in Chapter 1, the commodification of race as style is complicated by issues of authenticity and its location in 'the long transactional history of white responses to black culture, of black counter-responses, and of further countless and often traceless negotiations, tradings, raids and other compromises' (Ross 1989: 67).

Klein (2000: 370–1) explains that

> Everyone pretty much agrees that brands like Nike are playing a powerful surrogate role in the ghetto, subbing for everything from self-esteem to African-American cultural history to political power. What they are far less sure of is how to fill that need with empowerment and a sense of self-worth that does not necessarily come with a logo attached.

With a huge emotional investment in such products, kids are usually resistant to criticism – until they find that they have been played for suckers. Klein (2000) reports that the discovery that the Nike shoes they had bought for up to $180 a pair had been manufactured in Indonesia for only $5 a pair resulted in a demonstration by African-American and Latino kids outside Nike's Fifth Avenue store in 1997. This example points to the benefits of tracing the history of corporate cool hunting and its theft of identities and identity politics.

The practice of cool hunting reminds us of Appadurai's (1986) notion that things have cultural biographies and social histories. In turn, this points to the possibilities of a pedagogy based on the notion that *things have social lives* (Lury 1996: 19). They move or transform their meanings, acquire and lose value, create social identities and carry interpersonal influence (Lury 1996). According to Appadurai, different kinds of things are commodified at different times and in different contexts or 'commodity situations' in their social lives. He proposes *'the commodity situation in the social life of any "thing" be defined as the situation in which its exchangeability (past, present, or future) for some other thing is its socially relevant feature'* (Appadurai 1986: 13, original emphasis). Studying this historical trajectory, as Lury points out, 'draws attention to the different pathways along which objects travel' in their particular social history (1996: 20). This involves tracing the biography of the commodity and its particular cultural significance or exchange value. Hebdige (1988) provides a methodological model here, his study of the social significance of the scooter being a well-known example. The sequence of the biography begins with the design and production of the object and Hebdige recommends attending to the larger economic and social frames. His methodology also draws attention to the status of objects in terms of their 'gendering' and aestheticization in the context of the consumer market.

We suggest that students undertake a similar cultural and social bio-graphical analysis of the objects of cool in their own consumer culture. Cool hunting of this sort also needs to take into account subcultural, cross-cultural and retro influence, in addition to asking the simple questions of who made the object and where it originated. For instance, the current cult of body piercing might be examined in the light of ethnic cultural rituals and practices and their often highly gendered significance, as well as in relation to the currency it has for the young 'tribes' of today. What significance do we read into a pierced nose, a baseball cap worn backwards or a Winnie the Pooh lunchbox? When does an object lose its coolness and why? What is its exchange value in terms of the identity, solidarity or pleasure the consumer derives and how does this equate with the functional uses of the product? Are there stereotypes involved? Has the use of the product changed over time? Cool hunting aims to disclose both the appropriation of objects as in the case of Nike's plundering of African-American street culture and, conversely, the way consumer–media objects and identities are used by consumer groups – the African-American expropriation of Bart Simpson (Fiske 1996) being already mentioned. This is cool hunting turned into 'urban anthropology' (Klein 2000: 88).

Students may also elect to study the full life cycle of things by choosing objects (in particular objects associated with earlier youth cultures) which are now obsolete. Opportunity shops, garage sales or family memorabilia provide sources of material objects of this kind and, in some cases, opportunities to learn about the social context and significance of these objects by interviewing parents or previous owners. Such objects can be used as props for classroom displays or fashion parades. Tracing the travels of things across time and space, watching to see who uses what and with what effects, the self-conscious adolescent becomes conscious of the self and other. They watch themselves and their friends to see how they use cultural goods to communicate and they identify the 'masquerades' involved. Turnbull (1998: 102) offers a variation on these themes when she suggests students 'engage in a form of practical work which ask[s] them to create an image of *themselves* in the past, present and the future using a variety of already existing or especially created media forms'.

Clearly, the social life of things must also be considered in the light of the way in which objects are represented in film, print and broadcast media texts and in terms of marketing and advertising strategies. Lury argues that the 'methodological "animation" of objects can reveal new aspects of material culture, aspects which remain hidden if only one moment of an object's life is privileged' (1996: 26). However, there is an irony to this, given the current trend in entertainment and advertising towards reality programming or what has come to be known as 'voyeur TV' or V-TV – programmes like *Survivor* or *Shipwrecked* which do not use professional actors (Romei 2000: 6). A further dimension of this is the pretence of offering viewers the behind-the-scenes, hidden reality by calling attention to the 'constructedness' of much advertising and TV. Gow (1993) calls the latter production strategy 'pseudo-reflexivity' and it is designed to mask marketing intent. Cool hunters, therefore, must also be cool critics or, as Klein (2000) puts it, the Y Generation must be the why generation.

According to Gow (1993), media has become a positioning tool. This means that it sells products and personalities by 'creating, maintaining, or changing consumer perceptions of a product' (p. 319). Thus, it is not about the product so much as it is about the mind of the prospective consumer. Music videos are a good example of this. Impressions are created through the juxtaposition of aural, visual and narrative imagery which together become more than the sum of their individual parts. Together they create the persona/e of the performer or performers and manage the audience impressions of it/them by associating with desirable images and disassociating from undesirable ones. It is Gow's case that while sets, cast, lighting, camera angle and so forth can be used to create desirable associations, it is far more difficult to overcome the undesirable association between video music clips and commercialism.

Gow (1993: 320) cites Frith's contention that 'The belief in a continuing struggle between music and commerce is the core of rock ideology' (1981: 40–41). As Gow points out, commercialization has not harmed the careers of many pop stars, but then the market for pop music tends to be quite young. Youth, however, tend to want to express non-conformist or rebel identities (for young people's perspectives, see also Alvermann and Hagood 2000). Gow argues that in order to avoid giving the impression that they have sold out to consumer culture, many bands employ a pseudo-reflexive impression management strategy. By this he means the practice of employing: 'imagery that demystifies some, but not all, of the aspects of the video making process in order to draw audience attention away from the promotional motives underlying video production and enhance the anti-commercial stance typically adopted by hard rock musicians' (Gow 1993: 318). Rather than concealing the constructed nature of media products, this is deliberately foregrounded.

Authentic reflexivity in this instance involves shattering the 'illusion of reality' by making the codes of production transparent. It is potentially a subversive practice and, like much critical media education, invites a questioning of the ideological nature of the messages and of the social relationships they construct. By contrast, 'pseudo-reflexivity' is not deconstructive and, in fact, makes these things more difficult for the consumer to detect. The reflexivity or self-referentiality of commercials which parody themselves, for instance, 'is calculated to mystify rather than disenchant' (Stam 1992: 16). 'Videos structured along pseudo-reflexive lines', Gow argues, 'demystify one type of fiction, music video, in order to enhance the illusions surrounding another, sound recording' (1993: 322). In other words, viewers are encouraged to believe that 'the video makers – and, by virtue of the association principle, the band members themselves – are avoiding the usual practice of conjuring up a fantasy world in order to address their audience in an "honest" fashion' (Gow 1993: 322). However, only the production of the visual images is demystified, not the production of the music itself, and the reflexivity or interrogation of the one makes the other seem more authentic.

Examples of pseudo-reflexivity in video music clips include documentary style, behind-the-scenes glimpses of performers, production crew and hangers-on; juxtapositions of edited and 'raw' footage and of backstage and on-stage performances; and images involving audiences or fans. The hybridization of the reality and myth appears to invert convergences like the entertainment and advertising blend, because it foregrounds the difference between them. Its end, however, is identical, likewise intending to mask selling intent. What is particularly significant about Gow's research is that these production strategies are linked with the affective responses of the audience. They create a bond with the performers by inviting the members of the viewing audience 'backstage', by allowing them 'in' on the various technologies of production. They offer the consumer the pleasures of voyeurism. However, 'in the world of commercial entertainment such pleasures are often "bought only at the price of a corresponding blindness"' (Gow 1993: 325, quoting Altman 1987: 223). We wish to exploit and invert some of these pseudo-reflexive strategies in order to offer ways for young people to view and to consider their affective investment in consumer culture.

Students need a 'backstage pass' which offers them access to authentic reflexivity. By this we mean that students should be encouraged to look beyond the glamour and glitz of surface appearances and, by the same token, behind seemingly raw and spontaneous representations of consumer objects and identities. We propose that these not be confined to music. Backstage images of models preparing for the catwalk, for instance, offer an insider view merely to distract the viewer from the fact that the model's entire *raison d'être* is to sell fashion. Blockbuster movies are now sold to audiences using documentary-style promotions purporting to show the making of the movie. They condense a shoot of months into less than an hour, suppressing the tedious reality.

In making the backstage reality the object of investigation, it is not necessary to have access to supermodels, rock bands or sporting heroes, although print, TV and radio interviews and documentaries, biographies or autobiographies may offer insights. Far more accessible and far more useful are the experiences and impressions of sound technicians, make-up artists, photographers and camera crew, set designers, publicists, graphic designers and bit players in entertainment and advertising. Some of these may make themselves available to students for interviews. Others may be invited as guest speakers or as cultural intermediaries-in-residence. Other ways of accessing the backstage reality are industry publications as opposed to music, sport or fashion magazines which function as commercials targeting a youthful readership. Secondary materials, in particular social commentary aimed at a popular audience, are also sources of alternative perspectives. Kaz Cooke's *Real Gorgeous* (1994) reveals the reality behind the beauty myth in an engaging and humorous fashion.

However, as we have already indicated, there is another deeper and darker reality which exists behind the scenes: the 'night-time of the commodity'. In the following section, we look at how kids might become critical observers of the social and economic forces which drive, and are driven by, consumer–media culture.

◯ The youthful *cyberflâneur* as global citizen

The capacity 'To recognize yet disregard the invisible boundaries of the cityscape – this is the desire of the child and the regret of the adult' (Gilloch 1996: 85). For Benjamin, transgression is very much linked to the crossing of physical and spatial boundaries. It is linked with the pleasures of losing oneself in the streets of the metropolis. These are the pleasures of the *flâneur*, the male stroller or street reader. The pleasures of the *flâneur* have been described as those of 'just looking' (see Bowlby 1985). According to Nixon (1997: 334), 'the flâneur [is] an allegorical representation of the new relationship between the display of commodities and consumers' and, thus, of 'a new spectatorial consumer subjectivity'. In this regard, it refers not merely to the pleasures of window-shopping, but those of looking at oneself in the midst of this spectacle. Bowlby (1985) and Nixon (1997) have each considered the *flâneur* in relation to gender identity. Representations of gender identity in consumer culture act as a mirror to, and a model for, the production of gender identity. Although they contest the highly gendered nature of this figure and its association with the male gaze and, thus, visual mastery over women, these readings do not entirely reflect the *flâneur* – or the possibility of the *flâneuse* – as originally conceived.

Wilson (1992a: 93), identifying references to the *flâneur* as early as 1806, describes him as a 'key figure in the literature of modernity and

urbanization'. He is originally figured as 'a solitary onlooker' who 'stands
wholly outside production' (Wilson 1992a: 95). As initially interpreted
by Benjamin, he is a cultural critic and literary producer whose 'object
of inquiry is modernity itself' (Buck-Morss 1991: 304). Admittedly
always an ambivalent figure, his existence seemingly inconsequential,
his engagement with the city apparently superficial, the 'blend of excitement, tedium and horror' the urban world evokes for him points to the
ambivalence of urban life itself. He recognizes 'the enormous unfulfilled
promise of the urban spectacle, the consumption, the lure of pleasure
and joy which somehow seemed destined to be disappointed, or else are
undermined by the obvious poverty and exploitation of so many who
toil to bring pleasure to so few' (Wilson 1992a: 108).

Ultimately, the *flâneur* comes to epitomize these very things. Benjamin's
flâneur falls under the spell of 'the dreaming collective created by consumer capitalism' (Buck-Morss 1991: 312). He sells out. He becomes the
'prototype of a new form of salaried employee who produces news/
literature/advertisements for the purpose of information/entertainment/
persuasion' (Buck-Morss 1991: 306). In charting these changes, McLaren
and Hammer conclude that 'The postmodern *flâneurs* of today are corporate individuals cunningly managing and shaping the world of mass-
produced images, superannuated servants of the state whose forms of
knowledge production are mediated by and fastened securely to the
logic of consumption' (1995: 175). Finally, the *flâneur* 'advertise[s] not
simply commodities but ideological propaganda' (McLaren and Hammer
1995: 174).

We wish to redeem the concept of the *flâneur*, to rescue it from its
gendered connotations (if not the actual linguistic constraints of the
French language in this regard) and to reconstitute the relationship
between the pleasures of looking and cultural criticism. Further, we
wish to relocate the *flâneur* from the embodied and lustrous streets of
the metropolis to the disembodied nooks and crannies of the 'virtual
Rialto', the Internet, described here by Nunberg (1995):

It's urban, close, interior. Forget about cyberspace; this is cyberville,
cyberstadt, cyber-ciudad. You want a good metaphor for the Internet,
go to Venice in February. You thread your way down foggy streets
and over bridges till you lose all sense of compass direction, and
then all of a sudden you break into some glorious piazza. The rusty
gate on the alley over there might open into a lush garden, and
behind that might be a palazzo with long enfilades of rooms and
galleries, but you can't see anything from the street. It's a place you
get to know as an accumulation of paths and hidden passages, the
way a woodsman knows the forest . . . That's perfect for the Internet:
the virtual Rialto. Except that Venice is too permanent – you come

back after 50 years and everything's right where it was when you left. Whereas on the Internet addresses and connections change daily. Maybe we want to think of it as the Venice that Italo Calvino might have invented as one of his imaginary cities, a fantastic place where houses move over night from one quarter to another, where bridges disappear and canals reroute themselves with no warning . . . Or maybe the model isn't an old-world city at all, but one of those shantytowns that spring up overnight on the outskirts of Latin American cities – the barriadas of Lima, the favelas of Rio.

Ultimately, we want the youthful *cyberflâneur* to come to see that the threads of online networks that constitute the virtual Rialto are intermingled with those of what Klein (2000: 357) calls the 'branded web'. With its 'fiber optic cables and shared corporate cultural references', the branded web has 'provided a basis for meaningful global communication' and laid 'the foundations for the first truly international people's movement' (Klein 2000: 357). Through its networks, the connections between the theatrical spectacle of the virtual Rialto or marketplace and the sweatshops and shantytowns not only of Latin America, but Indonesia, China, Vietnam, the Philippines and other free trade zones, are revealed.

The Internet has become a common theme of much discussion of anti-corporate activism. Klein (2000: 356–7) points to the irony of this when she says:

> Now that the corporations have spun their own global rainbow of logos and labels, the infrastructure for genuine international solidarity is there for everyone to see and use. The logo network may have been designed to maximize consumption and minimize production costs, but regular people can now turn themselves into 'spiders' . . . and travel across its web as easily as the corporations that spun it . . . It's like the Internet in general: it may have been built by the Pentagon, but it quickly becomes the playground of activists and hackers.

Klein (2000: 357) goes on to explain that the branded web connects people who in one way or another are associated with a commodity. For instance,

> McDonald's workers around the world are able to swap stories on the Internet about working under the arches; club kids in London, Berlin, and Tel Aviv can commiserate about the corporate co-optation of the rave scene; and North American journalists can talk with poor rural factory workers in Indonesia about how much Michael Jordon gets paid to do Nike commercials.

There are strong synergies between the branded web and the Internet. In Turkle's (1995: 243) view, 'The Internet carries a political message about the importance of direct, immediate action and interest-group mobilization. It is the symbol and tool of a postmodern politics.' In addition to talking about resignification, as discussed above, we are talking here about networking, political organization and advocacy for just causes – global citizenship, if you like.

We have coined the term *cyberflâneur* to refer to the child who transgresses the spatial, physical and temporal boundaries of the corporate world through technology. The child 'is an apprentice in this "art of straying", in the still self-conscious crossing of the spatial limits of his or her class' (Gilloch 1996: 85). Our youthful *cyberflâneurs* are not limited by geography in making their connections on the web to the 'branded web'; as investigative activists, they stray where they may. They 'lose' themselves online in their search for information about corporate behaviour and for corporate activist sites and communities that they might learn from and belong to. They are spectators at the corporate bazaar, both real and virtual, but they are spectators of the 'watchdog' variety – they look back, not in wonder but with a sceptical and quizzical eye. Their object of inquiry is consumer–media culture. In short, the *cyberflâneur* is an excellent metaphor to deploy to point to the possibilities of youthful online activism on the 'branded web'.

Being a *cyberflâneur* is likely to be attractive to young people for several reasons. First, as noted, for postmodern youth, play and pleasure are often associated with adult-free zones and with the technologies that kids have seemed to 'master' much more adroitly than many of their parents. The conventional hierarchical adult/child politics of kids' everyday school lives are directly challenged in cyberspace. It has no government and in many ways is ungovernable. The key slogan of 'netiquette' is 'Information wants to be free'. Indeed, among many youthful users, there is an antipathy to any form of authority, be it governmental or commercial. Cyberspace offers webs and networks with multiple and shifting centres of power and authors of meaning. Fluidity, seamlessness, heterogeneity, interactivity, interconnectedness, reciprocity, community and freedom typify the medium and, as we have seen, its young consumers.

A second reason why being a *cyberflâneur* is likely to appeal to kids is because of the potential it provides to further build peer–peer communities. As we have shown, commodities and brands have provided a means by which kids have already forged bonds with each other. Kids like to connect with other kids and build on shared interests. Building online activist communities is simply an extension of this rapidly growing trend. But the point about kids' online communities does not stop there. Agre (1997) argues that, as the collective life of the Internet community has unfolds, communities are being rebuilt and the rules of social life are being renegotiated: 'Concepts of identity, civility, and community [have been] suddenly transformed beyond recognition' (1997: 13), Agre says. Rebuilding community and renegotiating the rules of social life are likely to be attractive propositions for young people, particularly for those who have been alienated and disadvantaged by the maxim that the commodity rules – OK! Turkle (1995: 239) draws on her studies of Net participation to argue that downwardly mobile young middle-class people in the USA are using MUDS (Multiple User Dungeons – text-based virtual reality) as 'a vehicle of virtual social mobility'. Feeling that 'they have no political voice, they look to cyberspace to help them find one' (p. 241).

The youthful *cyberflâneur* will note that there are many Net activists who argue that the easy replication and distribution of digitalized information provides a powerful resource for political activism. Klein (2000: 396) quotes environmentalist Tony Juniper who describes it as 'the most potent weapon in the toolbox of resistance'. This technology is seen as providing unprecedented opportunities for distributing subversive information, for resistance and for the development of alliances across differences. There are numerous examples of political activism online and, as Klein shows, many anti-corporate activists, ranging from reclaim the streets party organizers to human, worker and environmental rights groups, employ the Internet as a tool for awareness raising, information sharing, organization and strategy. Information sharing involves distributing facts, figures and real-life anecdotes. A prominent example of such sites is www.mcspotlight.org which exposes not only corporate practices of McDonald's, but retailers like Tesco and K-Mart, and corporations like Coca-Cola, Nike and the Body Shop.

McSpotlight is an information network run by volunteers from 16 countries. Begun in 1996, the site originally gave coverage of the notorious McLibel trial. McDonald's sued two members of a small activist group for defamation over a pamphlet which, according to Klein (2000: 388) 'used a single brand name to connect all the dots on the social agenda'. These included environmental issues, Third World poverty, nutrition, the exploitation of child consumers and youth employees, waste and animal cruelty. Like many such sites, McSpotlight offers links to other activist sites as well as to corporate homepages. For instance, the NikeWatch Campaign link connects to the Community Aid Abroad Australia site which contains reports, educational resources, lists of organizations campaigning for workers' rights and other campaign websites including United Students Against Sweatshops (USA), the Alberta Nike Campaign site and Adbusters (Canada). Adbusters, for example, in turn provides links to Global Exchange with its 'reality tours', and the youthful and less earnest Urban75 with its parodic Boycott Top Five:

NEW ENTRY! In with a bullet at Number Four is BP Amoco for their continued sponsorship of government death squads in Columbia as long as they help to keep the environmentalists off their back.

The fastest new climbers are Pepsi Co for their continuing business relationship with Burma, in defiance of an international boycott. The Burmese Government has an appalling human rights record. Extra points were scored for their sponsorship of Latin American Cockfighting . . . and for their sponsorship of bullfighting in Mexico, with their dodgy banners festooned all around bullrings.

Other corporate entries in the Boycott Top 5 – and contenders for a spot in the chart – are distinguished by their records in relation to the environment, human rights, testing on animals, child and sweatshop labour and so forth.

Sites like these offer opportunities for our *cyberflâneurs* to make the workings of the 'branded web', and its connections to youthful consumer–media culture, the object of their gaze. They reveal the reality behind many of the consumer goods and services we take for granted. How many children – and their parents and teachers – know that toys given away in McDonald's Happy Meals are made by children working in Chinese sweatshops, who earn $5.25 a day, work seven days a week and sleep 15 to a room on wooden bunks with no mattresses (*Sydney Morning Herald* 2000)? How many consider the possibility that a much-coveted object, a Nike soccer ball for instance, might have been made by a child as young as 6 for as little as 6 cents an hour? Certainly not many of the press reporting on the S11 protest at the World Economic Forum held in Melbourne in September 2000. Little front page coverage reflected on what Bigelow (1997: 114) describes as 'the glib premise, which underlies so much economic discussion, that foreign investment in poor countries is automatically a good thing'. This is what Bigelow asked of his students when he trialled a global studies curriculum.

Among the classroom strategies he used was what he called the Transnational Capital Auction. Students, divided into seven different 'countries', 'submitted bids for minimum wage, child labor laws, environmental regulations, conditions for worker organizing, and corporate tax rates' (Bigelow 1997: 114). In this corporate 'Game of Survival', economic and ethical imperatives were pitched against one another. Bigelow reports that 'in the frenzied competition of the auction', the students 'created some pretty nasty conditions because the game rewarded those who lost sight of the human and environmental consequences of their actions' (1997: 114). The students were subsequently invited to reflect on the impact on their 'country' of not having corporate taxes or child labour, minimum wage or environmental laws. What Bigelow did not do, but on later reflection realized he should have, was to bring the students back together and conduct the auction again. He believes that had the students done so, they

> could have practiced organizing *with* one another instead of competing *against* one another. They could have tested the potential for building solidarity across borders. At very least, replaying the auction would have suggested that people in Third World countries aren't purely victims; there are possible routes for action, albeit enormously difficult ones.
>
> (Bigelow 1997: 115)

In the final section of this chapter we explore the potential of the Internet and multimedia technologies as mechanisms for political activity and building solidarity within and between school and youth communities. Using them, though not constrained by them, the *cyberflâneur* becomes not merely a critical observer of culture, but a producer. Culture work is understood as political play.

◯ Teens, zines and culture jamming

'The mouse is more powerful than the remote control' (Weston 1994) and as such it offers new possible orientations to consumer–media culture. Students can readily recognize the different qualities of interactivity between the Internet and other media forms such as video on demand or video games. Given half a chance, they can also understand and benefit from the fact that 'Information is no longer constrained by the traditional mass media' (Storm 1995) with its highly stylized gender and racial modalities that we have discussed. The pleasures of 'just looking' can be accompanied by the pleasures of joining others who are doing life politics online, exposing corporate greed and calling on corporations to be good global citizens and to conduct their affairs ethically.

Online, students can self-publish and, in so doing, capitalize on the very different relationship between the author and the reader that the Internet offers. They can thus develop a strong sense of agency as producers of culture. This also allows them to move beyond a reliance on the few centralized corporations and to capitalize on this 'from many to many' paradigm of communication. Clearly, then, the Internet is not only a source of information and games for students. It offers children and youth a means to 'distribute' their voices and views in ways that they enjoy. It also offers them the opportunity to blend the playful and earnest. In this final section, we look at the ways that kids might capitalize on the distributed self-publishing opportunities now available to them.

In saying this, we are well aware that many schools now have their own websites where they publish student newspapers as well as provide links to galleries and libraries of student projects. We are also aware that by 2000, nearly 12,000 high schools in 72 countries used HighWired.com to publish their student newspapers and school news on the Internet. The content of these newspapers is entirely student-generated and varies in terms of its local and international significance. Claims about the number of hits registered at various sites and top ten lists under various categories are indicative of some of the personal pay-offs for participants. Participation comes at no cost to schools. Online publishing is a considerably cheaper alternative to print media and HighWired's costs are underwritten by sponsorship. Arguably involved in the commodification of schools, HighWired clearly engages students – or is that teachers?

If HighWired has regenerated the concept of the school newspaper by adapting it to the new technologies, the result seems otherwise conventional, if not old-fashioned. The standardized format clearly makes it easy for the schools to publish but it also makes it difficult for schools to give any initial impression of their particular student culture. We argue that much cyberpublishing originating in schools continues to reflect the centrality of print in education culture. It also reproduces other elements of the traditional school. While HighWired offers the opportunity for students to publish information relating to all aspects of school life and the curriculum, there is no sense that these newspapers address themselves to many tribes of young consumers or to youth subcultural style. The target audience, like the format, is homogenized. Further, although we have found some insightful articles on social justice issues and exposés of corporate practices, they were often earnest in tone and conventionally journalistic in style.

This raises two important questions. First, do these student journalists write with a view to informing and engaging a peer audience or do they anticipate the judging prerogative of adults, given that teachers are their ultimate editors/censors? Second, do such newspapers offer students an opportunity to produce their own culture and their own cultural criticism in their own 'voice', or do links with traditional English, media and journalism curricula lead them to recreate the degraded version of the *flâneur* who, as we saw above, merely 'produces news/literature/advertisements for the purpose of information/entertainment/persuasion' (Buck-Morss 1991: 306)? The fact that we did not find much that was feisty, subversive, politicized, alternative, celebratory, impassioned, fun or youthful suggests that the latter is the case in both instances.

There are, of course, a burgeoning number of youth interest/rights/activist websites and e-zines. Oblivionnine ('conglomerating youth angst through corporate buyouts and media mergers since 1995' at www.oblivion.net) and BRAT ('because your school newspaper sucks' at www.brat.org) are examples of the way e-zines promote young people's virtual communities around such shared interests such as film, games, music and politics. However, drawing on Kenway and Langmead (2000), we take the new generation of feminists who seek 'girl power' or more accurately 'Grrrl power' in and through new technology as an alternative model for online publishing for schools. These groups include such suitably insurgent titles as 'riot grrrls', 'guerrilla girls' and 'bad grrrls'. Grrrl power is an offspring of consumer/techno culture which venerates speed and change, the new, the novel, virtuality, simulation. The relevant sites online offer a wide range of cultural and sexual representations and interventions which take various forms and foci. They showcase prominent 'cybergrrrls' and act as 'guides to the wired world' with regard to such things as 'zines and comics, cyberpunk and gothic looks (nanofash)'. Their diversity is indicated by sites like chickclick.com with its network of links to 'girl sites that don't fake it'. These sites include the Riotgrrrl and Riotgrrl websites; Wired Woman ('explores how technology affects women's lives'); Smarty-Pants ('mixes style with substance'); Bohos (a comic about four teenagers and 'what it means to be cool in a world gone mad'); as well as Lawgirl, Teengrrl, Disgruntled Housewife, Breakup Girl, Hissyfit, GrrlGamer and DjDazy. These sites are quirky, smart and slick, fun and pop. They offer feisty articles and chic images which glorify new technologies, technological savvy and linguistic Net-speak panache. They are youth-orientated and aim for wide popular appeal.

These publications are part of a broader subcultural movement which combines politics with style through appropriation and subversion of the forms and genres of popular mass media and culture. Exploiting the new 'democratized technologies' to produce 'hybrid political texts such as zines' (Garrison 2000: 144), they subvert practices like cool hunting which we defined above. As Garrison (2000: 163) explains:

Like the major recording labels who 'plunder' music subcultures and 'indies' (independent bands and labels) for 'talents and trends', subcultures 'plunder' mainstream media, but their purposes are different: one is geared to profit margins and sustaining markets; the other to finding constructive meaning in a time of crisis and uncertainty. At a time when the mainstream mass media scripts politics as bumper stickers, soundbites, and tabloid sensationalism, it seems especially important to look for and foster (sub)cultural spaces that insist on political content and intent in members' activities and in the objects they create. These include the tactical subjectivities employed to counter and subvert the depoliticized politics of conspicuous consumption.

The website for *Bitch*, a magazine offering a feminist response to popular culture, puts it this way when it says its mission is about forging connections between the sociocultural messages we get and the commercial agendas of who's behind them. It's about asking ourselves and each other questions: where are the girl-friendly places in the mass media? Where are the things we can see and read and hear that don't insult our intelligence? How can we get more of them?

We can make them.

Taking Riot Grrrl as typical of the youth or 'third wave' feminist movement, Garrison (2000: 142–3) explains that it is 'an alternative subculture built around the opposition to presuppositions that young (usually white) US girls and women are too preoccupied with themselves and boys to be interested in being political, creative, and loud'. It is 'The tensions between this expectation and the political desires of members', she argues, that 'offers a powerful opportunity to learn different ways of resisting in a consumer-oriented culture' (Garrison 2000: 143). Indeed, as Garrison (2000: 143) goes on to add,

> For more and more subcultures (youth or otherwise), the ability to intertwine politics and style is a risky and necessary tactic in a cultural–historical period marked by 'the logic of late capitalism' in which the commodification of resistance is a hegemonic strategy. The hybrid political texts and distribution networks produced by feminists like Riot Grrrls are . . . both 'popular' and subcultural, they provide spaces for youth-controlled conversations, and they can operate as an interface between different Third Wave cohorts.

We believe that this emphasis on style is crucial if students are to invest in the production and politicization of elements of their own learning culture and to take pleasure in it.

As the Grrrl power story suggests, this need not mean an insistence on particular versions of citizenship. Grrrl power celebrates multiple ways of being female and disparate feminine cultures, sexualities, styles and pleasures. As Williams (n.d.) says, 'net chicks come in all varieties', they celebrate a 'feisty individuality' and even assert 'a girl's right to be feminine'. According to the Riot Grrrl Europe Manifesto (Riot Grrrl Europe n.d.), 'Amongst us are now grrrls and bois, ages fourteen or twenty seven, geeks and cheerleaders, dykes, punks. Try to call us all by name, you can't, cause we are everywhere. In every thinkable shape and form'.

While passionate, angry and aggressive tirades against Net-nerds and cowboys are in evidence, old-style rational and 'serious' feminist critiques are largely off the agenda. Racist, sexist, homophobic, classist and other derogatory material are also off the agenda if the code of conduct laid down by the Riot Grrrl ring mistress at the http://skapunx.net/ ~SallyTampon/grrrl/riotring website is any indication. She accepts 'personal pages, band pages, distro pages, zine pages, grrrl-friendly product pages, anything as long as you are a grrrl at heart and yr page shows creativity and insight'. It says to grrrls, 'Do it yourselves (DIY) and Do what you like'.

As the Riot Grrrl Europe Manifesto indicates, riot grrrls take a critical stance towards the world around them 'and not only in a feminist way'. The civic sphere for such groups is culture particularly and their tools of citizenship are often humour, irony, mimicry, parody, burlesque and transgression. They do not necessarily seek to unsettle gender and sexual binaries so much as to play with or mock, exaggerate and distort them. The 'Feed the Model' found at adiosbarbie.com offers an arcade-style interactive game. A more sophisticated version called 'Feed the Super-model' at the official riotgrrl.com website allows visitors to plump up photographic images of real models and actors 'by feeding them more than Carr's water cracker and a bottle of Evian'. When we visited, the featured 'superskinny model' was Jennifer Love Hewitt.

The ironical, iconoclastic and critical sensibilities of these grrrls have much in common with those of the anti-corporate activity known as 'culture jamming'. Klein (2000: 280) defines this consumer activist strat-egy – a kind of 'semiotic Robin Hoodism' – as 'the practice of parodying advertisements and hijacking billboards to drastically alter their mes-sages'. More broadly, it refers to anything 'that mixes art, media, parody and the outsider stance' (Klein 2000: 283). The object of culture jamming is to reclaim public space (including schools) which has been colonized by corporate messages. Klein says that 'The most sophisticated culture jams are not stand-alone ad parodies but interceptions – counter-messages that hack into a corporation's own method of communication to send a message starkly at odds with the one that was intended' (2000: 281).

The term culture jamming was coined in the 1980s by the techno-yippie band, Negativland, with 'jamming' referring to CB radio slang for the illegal electronic disruption of radio or TV transmissions. Today, culture jamming involves graffiti, vandalism, spamming (junk e-mail) and computer hacking. Some culture jamming practices are not merely subversive, they are blatantly illegal. Nevertheless, the principles behind them offer the opportunity for some pedagogical lateral thinking in relation to consumer–media education. Like e-zines, culture jamming offers a paradigm for kids to make their own media, using the same tools and techniques as the media. The 'newly accessible technologies that have made both the creation of and the circulation of ad parodies immeasurably easier' (Klein 2000: 285) are one means of translating culture jamming strategies to the classroom – with the irony that these technologies may have been made available to schools through corpor-ate sponsorship. Original versions of advertisements can be downloaded and reworked on the desktop. The 'Photoshop' program offers the facility to match colours and fonts. There is the potential to create parodies as flashy, fun and visually arresting as the media created for them.

According to Juliet Beck, ad parodies are an effective way of subverting the hold of corporate consumer culture over people's fantasies and desires, precisely because the corporations are so dependent on advertising and brand image (Straus 2000). They are especially effective, moreover, because as the popularity of satires like *The Simpsons* with its ample use of parody indicates, parody is pleasurable. As Dery (Dery n.d.) puts it, 'culture jammers are Groucho Marxists, ever mindful of the fun to be had in the joyful demolition of oppressive ideologies'. At the same time, because parody manipulates and mocks elements of genre, form, language, image and structure, it also demands a consideration of the function of each of these in the parodic target, thus revealing 'the deeper truth hiding beneath the layers of advertising euphemisms' of the original corporate strategy (Klein 2000: 282).

If the technologicalization of the classroom means that students will soon be able to create their own computer-generated parodies, they need not be limited by this. Fake ads can be created using time-honoured techniques like collage and juxtaposed or combined with counter-images of environmental destruction or child labour. As ad spoofs like 'Absolut Nonsense Vodka' suggest, a simple word pun can be effective enough. Parodies of media genres like award ceremonies, game shows, magazine quizzes, news reports, soaps etc. can also be co-opted for the classroom. Moreover, we suggest that the notion of culture jamming be extended to the imagining of an alternative culture which 'jams' the stranglehold of consumer–media culture, not only over kids' fantasies and desires, play and pleasure, but over the needs and wants of cash-strapped schools. To this end, education and activist websites offer a rich range of activities which can be adapted to the school domain. Examples of pleasurable strategies designed to promote a critical awareness of consumer culture and perhaps even to raise funds for school communities include 'recycle fashion' parades, swap party and barter auctions, boycotts, kid-coordinated fairs or carnivals in which amusements and products are made by and for the kids, and variations on Buy Nothing Day and No TV Day.

◯ Conclusion

We began this book with a discussion of the generalized sense of unease that parents and teachers often feel about young people today. We mentioned that many fear that childhood itself is ending, that children themselves are developing out of order, that adults have lost control of children to the media. It can be inferred from such concerns that some adults feel that it is possible to reverse-engineer children, to change them back to the way children are *meant* to be, and that if school education is retraditionalized, proper adult/child authority relations can be restored. In response to this way of thinking we have offered an alternative, suggesting that such concerns and such nostalgia have arisen because of the destabilizing effects of wide-scale social and cultural change.

We made the case that the 'overdeveloped' countries of the West are going through another historical period in the invention of the child. We argued that current versions of western childhood are very much the product of what we called consumer–media culture, and that this culture is underpinned in part by the sweated work of the 'othered' children of the so-called Third World. We explained how, with the aid of various media, the commodity form has increasingly become central to the life of the young of the West, constructing their identities and relationships, their emotional and social worlds. In so doing, we showed how adults and schools have been negatively positioned in this matrix to the extent that youthful power and pleasure are construed as that which happens elsewhere – away from adults and schools and mainly with the aid of commodities. In telling this story, we also told its parallel, the story of the changing face of capital as it redesigns institutions and people for profit. We showed how old institutional and cultural distinctions have given way to new uneven fusions between entertainment, advertising and education. Here we pointed to the seepage of the market form into more and more aspects of children's lives, even to the extent that schools are no longer understood as commercial-free zones run along market-free lines. Indeed, we showed how adults hope that the marketed school run according to traditional authority patterns will return children to their proper place – under adults' control. But as we indicated, it is far too late for that. Many kids have consigned schools to the periphery of their identities and concerns.

The scenario we have sketched clearly challenges many current notions of policy, curriculum and pedagogy, and notions of students and teachers. We hope that it will provoke people to ask, 'What new notions of schools, teachers, pedagogy and curriculum do these changes necessitate?' We have begun to answer part of this question by laying out some grounds for a pedagogy for young people who have grown up in 'the age of desire'. We have offered this example because we think these times require educators to look at schools and kids very differently, to ask new questions, to work in new ways and with different ideas but also to keep the notion of educating to the fore.

It is the responsibility of adults – teachers, parents, policy makers – to ensure that school education is not absorbed into the 'vortex of the commodity' (Sharp 1985) and that it makes powerful connections with the young people of today who, in many ways, have 'no choice' about their image- and commodity-drenched surroundings. At the very least, school could teach them to understand the differences between data, information, knowledge, education, entertainment and advertising. But can the marketized school tell the difference? Schools can play a role in alerting the young to matters of life politics in addition to matters of lifestyle. But if kids are to listen, we also need to re-enchant the school.

Bibliography

Adams, P. (2000) Secret parents' business, *The Weekend Australian*, 15–16 July.

Advertising Age (1997a) School computers run ads on screensavers in Canada, *Advertising Age, International Daily*, 30 April. http://adage.com (accessed 1 March 2000).

Advertising Age (1997b) Peer group more influential than ads in brand decisions, *Advertising Age, International Daily*, 25 September. http://adage.com (accessed 1 March 2000).

Advertising Age (2000) AOL Europe invests $75 million in German schools program, *Advertising Age, International Daily*, 23 February. http://adage.com (accessed 1 March 2000).

Agre, P.E. (1997) Computing as a social practice, in P.E. Agre and D. Schuler (eds) *Reinventing Technology, Rediscovering Community: Critical Explorations of Computing as a Social Practice*. Greenwich, CT: Ablex Publishing.

Alloway, N. and Gilbert, P. (1998) Video game culture: playing with masculinity, violence and pleasure, in S. Howard (ed.) *Wired-Up: Young People and the Electronic Media*. London: UCL Press.

Altman, R. (1987) *The American Film Musical*. Bloomington, IN: Indiana University Press.

Alvarado, M. and Thompson, J.O. (eds) (1990) *The Media Reader*. London: British Film Institute.

Alvermann, D.E. and Hagood, M.C. (2000) Fandom and critical media literacy. *Journal of Adolescent & Adult Literacy*, 43(5): 436–46.

Appadurai, A. (1986) Introduction: commodities and the politics of value, in A. Appadurai (ed.) *The Social Life of Things*. New York: Cambridge University Press.

Apple Computer Inc. (1994) (advertisement), *The Sunday Age*, 15 October.

Apple Computer Inc. (2000) (advertisement), *The Age*, 27 May.

Ariès, P. (1973) *Centuries of Childhood*, trans. R. Baldick, first published 1962. Harmondsworth: Penguin.

Aronowitz, S. and Giroux, H.A. (1985) *Education Under Siege: The Conservative, Liberal and Radical Debate Over Schooling*. Westport, MA: Bergin & Garvey Publishers Inc.

Ashdown, S. (1998) African-American kidvids: from niche distribution paths to head-to-head retail. *Kidscreen*, October. www.kidscreen.com/articles/ks23155.asp (accessed 26 July 2000).

Austin, M.J. and Reed, M.L. (1999) Targeting children online: Internet advertising ethics issues. *Journal of Consumer Marketing*, 16(6): 590–602.

Bagnall, D. (2000) Born to be wired, *The Bulletin*, 15 August.

Baker, K.G. (1999) The ethnic majority? *Kidscreen*, February. www.kidscreen.com/articles/ks24324.asp (accessed 28 February 2000).

Bakhtin, M. (1968) *Rabelais and His World*, trans. H. Iswolsky. Cambridge, MA: MIT Press.

Barker, K. (1999) Girls' games are in the pink. *Kidscreen*, August. www.kidscreen.com/articles/ks26270.asp (accessed 6 March 2000).

Barlow, M. and Robertson, H.J. (1994) *Class Warfare: The Assault on Canada's Schools*. Toronto: Key Porter Books.

Barthes, R. (1975) *The Pleasure of the Text*, trans. R. Miller. New York: Hill & Wang.

Barthes, R. (1983) *The Fashion System*, trans. M. Ward and R. Howard. New York: Hill & Wang.

Battaglio, S. (1987) Marketers see future in kids. *Adweek's Marketing Week*, 28(17): 1, 6.

Baudrillard, J. (1975) *The Mirror of Production*, trans. M. Poster. St Louis, MO: Telos Press.

Baudrillard, J. (1981) *For a Critique of the Political Economy of the Sign*, trans. C. Levin. St Louis, MO: Telos Press.

Baudrillard, J. (1983a) *Simulations*, trans. P. Foss, P. Patton and P. Beitchman. New York: Semiotext(e).

Baudrillard, J. (1983b) *In the Shadow of the Silent Majorities*, trans. P. Foss. New York: Semiotext(e).

Baudrillard, J. (1988) *Selected Writings*, ed. M. Poster. Cambridge: Polity Press.

Bazalgette, C. and Buckingham, D. (eds) (1995a) *In Front of the Children: Screen Entertainment and Young Audiences*. London: British Film Institute.

Bazalgette, C. and Buckingham, D. (1995b) The invisible audience, in C. Bazalgette and D. Buckingham (eds) *In Front of the Children: Screen Entertainment and Young Audiences*. London: British Film Institute.

Bel Geddes, J. (1997) *Childhood and Children*. Phoenix, AZ: Oryx Press.

Bell, E., Haas, L. and Sells, L. (eds) (1995) *From Mouse to Mermaid: The Politics of Film, Gender, and Culture*. Bloomington and Indianapolis, IN: Indiana University Press.

Bendick, J. (1954) *The First Book of Supermarkets*. New York: Franklin Watts.

Benjamin, W. (1982) *Das Passagen-Werk*, in R. Tiedemann and H. Schweppenhäuser (eds) *Gesammelte Schriften*. Frankfurt am Main: Suhrkamp Verlag.

Bennett, R. and Gabriel, H. (1999) Headteacher characteristics, management style and attitudes towards the acceptance of commercial sponsorship by state-funded schools. *Marketing Intelligence & Planning*, 17(1): 41–52.

Berger, J. (1972) *Ways of Seeing*. London: BBC/Penguin.

Bhabha, H. (1994) *The Location of Culture*. London: Routledge.

Bigelow, B. (1997) The human lives behind the labels: the global sweatshop, Nike, and the race to the bottom. *Phi Delta Kappa*, 79(2): 112–19.

Bigum, C. and Kenway, J. (1998) New information technologies and the ambiguous future of schooling: some possible scenarios, in A. Hargreaves, A. Leiberman, M. Fullan and D. Hopkins (eds) *International Handbook of Educational Change*. Boston, MA: Kluwer Academic Publishers.

Bigum, C., Fitzclarence, L., Kenway, J. with Croker, C. and Collier, J. (1993) That's edu-tainment: restructuring universities and the Open Learning initiative. *The Australian Universities Review: Special Issue on Marketing Education in the 1990s*, 36(2): 21–8.

Block, A.A. (1997) Reading children's magazines: kinderculture and popular culture, in S.R. Steinberg and J.L. Kincheloe (eds) *Kinder-Culture: The Corporate Construction of Childhood*. Boulder, CO: Westview Press.

Bourdieu, P. (1984) *Distinction: A Social Critique of the Judgement of Taste*, trans. R. Nice. London: Routledge & Kegan Paul.

Bowlby, R. (1985) *Just Looking: Consumer Culture in Dreiser, Gissing and Zola*. London: Methuen.

Brady, J. (1997) Multiculturalism and the American dream, in S.R. Steinberg and J.L. Kincheloe (eds) *Kinder-Culture: The Corporate Construction of Childhood*. Boulder, CO: Westview Press.

Braidotti, R. (1998) Cyberfeminism with a difference. www.let.ruu.nl/womens_studies/rosi/cyberfem.htm (accessed July 1999).

Brown, S. (1995) *Postmodern Marketing*. London: Routledge.

Brown, S., Steves, L. and Maclaran, P. (1999) I can't believe it's not Bakhtin!: literary theory, postmodern advertising, and the gender agenda. *Journal of Advertising*, 28(1). http://web6.infotrac.galegroup.com, Article A55438255.

Browne, B.A. (1998) Gender stereotypes in advertising on children's television in the 1990s: a cross-national analysis. *Journal of Advertising*, 27(1). http://web.4.infotrac.galegroup.com'itw/infomark/824/913, Article A21046802.

Buck-Morss, S. (1991) *The Dialectics of Seeing: Walter Benjamin and the Arcades Project*, first published 1989. Cambridge, MA: MIT Press.

Buckingham, D. (1995) The commercialisation of childhood?: the place of the market in children's media culture. *Changing English*, 2(2): 17–40.

Buckingham, D. (1998a) Media education in the UK: moving beyond protectionism. *Journal of Communication*, 48(1): 33–43.

Buckingham, D. (ed.) (1998b) *Teaching Popular Culture: Beyond Radical Pedagogy*. London: UCL Press.

Buckingham, D. (1998c) Pedagogy, parody and political correctness, in D. Buckingham (ed.) *Teaching Popular Culture: Beyond Radical Pedagogy*. London: UCL Press.

Buckingham, D. (2000) *After the Death of Childhood: Growing up in the Age of Electronic Media*. Cambridge: Polity Press.

Butler, J. (1990) *Gender Trouble: Feminism and the Subversion of Identity*. New York: Routledge.

Calver, G. (1999) When Postman Pat has a greater influence over kids than mother. *Kids Marketing Report*, 24 February. www.mad.co.uk/KMR/print/stories/1999/02/24/0029.asp (accessed 1 February 2000).

Calvert, J. and Kuehn, L. (1993) *Pandora's Box: Corporate Power, Free Trade and Canadian Education*. Toronto: Our Schools/Our Selves Education Foundation.

Carroll, T. (1996) *The Role of Social Marketing Campaigns Within Australia's National Drug Strategy*. Canberra: Commonwealth Department of Health and Family Services.

Cervini, E. (2000) Spin doctors take schools to market, *The Age*, 1 March.

Chambers, L. (1998) How customer-friendly is your school? *Educational Leadership*, 56(2): 33–5.

Christensen, J. (1999) Black History Month edges into the mainstream, *CNN Interactive*. www.cnn.com/SPECIALS/1999/blackhistory/overview (accessed 31 July 2000).

Christian-Smith, L.K. and Erdman, J.I. (1997) 'Mom, it's not real!': children constructing childhood through reading horror fiction, in S.R. Steinberg and J.L. Kincheloe (eds) *Kinder-Culture: The Corporate Construction of Childhood*. Boulder, CO: Westview Press.

Clegg, A. (1996) Colour blind, *Marketing Week*, 21 June. www.mad.co.uk/stories/1996/06/21/mw/0051.asp (accessed 28 February 2000).

Cohen, P. (1998) On teaching arts and 'race' in the classroom, in D. Buckingham (ed.) *Teaching Popular Culture: Beyond Radical Pedagogy*. London: UCL Press.

Collier, J., Kenway, J., Tregenza, K. with Bigum, C. and Fitzclarence, L. (1994) Schools as commercial free zones? in J. Kenway (ed.) *Schooling What Future? Balancing the Education Agenda*. Geelong, Victoria: Deakin Centre for Education and Change, Deakin University.

Collins, C., Kenway, J. and McLeod, J. (2000) *Factors Influencing the Educational Performance of Males and Females in School and their Initial Destinations after Leaving School*. Canberra: Commonwealth Department of Education and Training.

Collins, M. (1993) Global corporate philanthropy: marketing beyond the call of duty? *European Journal of Marketing*, 27(2): 46–58.

Computer Curriculum Corporation (1993) (advertisement). *Educational Leadership*, 51(1): 1.

Consumers (1994) Untitled. *Consumers*, December: 8.

Consumers Union Education Services (1990) *Selling America's Kids: Commercial Pressures on Kids of the 90s*. Yonkers, New York: Consumers Union Education Services.

Consumers Union Education Services (1995) *Captive Kids: A Report on Commercial Pressures on Kids at School*. Yonkers, New York: Consumers Union Education Services. www.consumersunion.org/other/captivekids/index.htm.

Cooke, K. (1994) *Real Gorgeous: The Truth about Body and Beauty*. St Leonards, NSW: Allen & Unwin.

Corporate Watch (1998) Race and classroom: the corporate connection (interview with Libero Della Piana), *Corporate Watch*. www.igc.org/trac/feature/education/race (accessed 23 May 2000).

Coupland, D. (1994) *Generation X*, first published 1991. London: Abacus.

Creighton, M.R. (1994) 'Edutaining' children: consumer and gender socialization in Japanese marketing. *Ethnology*, 33(1). http://web4.infotrac.galegroup.com, Article A14995874.

Cullingford, C. (1984) *Children and Television*. Aldershot: Gower.

Cunningham, H. (1995a) *Children & Childhood in Western Society Since 1500*. Harlow: Longman.

Cunningham, H. (1995b) Moral kombat and computer game girls, in C. Bazalgette and D. Buckingham (eds) *In Front of the Children: Screen Entertainment and Young Audiences*. London: British Film Institute.

Curran, C.M. (1999) Misplaced marketing. *Journal of Consumer Marketing*, 16(6): 534–5.

Curti, M. (1967) The changing concept of human nature in the literature of American advertising. *Business History Review*, 41: 335–57.

David, M., West, A. and Ribbens, J. (1994) *Mother's Intuition?: Choosing Secondary Schools*. London: Falmer Press.

Davies, J. (1996) *Educating Students in a Media-Saturated Culture*. Lancaster, PA: Technomic Publishing Co.

de Certeau, M. (1984) *The Practice of Everday Life*, trans. S. Rendall. Berkeley, CA: University of California Press.

de Mause, L. (ed.) (1974) *The History of Childhood*. New York: The Psychohistory Press.

Deem, R., Brehony, K. and Heath, S. (1995) *Active Citizenship and the Governing of Schools*. Buckingham: Open University Press.

Dell Clark, C. (1999) Youth, advertising, and symbolic meaning, in M.C. Macklin and L. Carlson (eds) *Advertising to Children: Concepts and Controversies*. Thousand Oaks, CA: Sage Publications.

Dery, M. (n.d.) Culture jamming: hacking, slashing and sniping in the empire of signs. http://gopher.well.sf.ca.us:70/0/cyberpunk/cultjam.txt (accessed 27 September 2000).

Deveny, K. (1990) Consumer-products firms hit the books: trying to teach brand loyalty in school, *Wall Street Journal*, 17 July.

Douglas, M. and Isherwood, B. (1979) *The World of Goods: Towards an Anthropology of Consumption*. London: Allen Lane.

Driscoll, C. (1999) Girl culture, revenge and global capitalism: cybergirls, riot girls, Spice Girls. *Australian Feminist Studies*, 14(29): 173–93.

Ducille, A. (1994) Dyes and dolls: multicultural Barbie and the merchandising of difference. *Differences*, 6(1): 46–68.

Duff, R. (1999) Children are discerning customers, *Kids Marketing Report*, 30 June. www.mad.co.uk.KMR/print/stories/1999/06/30/0029.asp (accessed 1 February 2000).

Eastwood, N. (1999) Possible ban on kids' TV ads forces marketers to consider alternatives, *Kids Marketing Report*, 28 October. www.mad.co.uk/KMR/print/stories/1999/10/28/0040.asp (accessed 1 February 2000).

Evans, C. and Thornton, M. (1989) *Women and Fashion: A New Look*. London: Quartet.

Ewen, S. (1976) *Captains of Consciousness: Advertising and the Social Roots of the Consumer Culture*. New York: McGraw-Hill.

Ewen, S. (1988) *All Consuming Images: The Politics of Style in Contemporary Culture*. New York: Basic Books.

Fairchilds, C.C. (1976) *Poverty and Charity in Aix-en-Provence 1640–1789*. Baltimore, MD: Johns Hopkins University Press.

Featherstone, M. (1992) *Consumer Culture and Postmodernism*, first published 1991. London: Sage Publications.

Fewster, S. (2000) Schools turn to 'creative' funding, *The Advertiser*, 20 May.

Fiske, J. (1989) *Understanding Popular Culture*. London: Unwin Hyman.

Fiske, J. (1994) *Television Culture*. London: Routledge.

Fiske, J. (1996) *Media Matters: Everyday Culture and Political Change*. Minneapolis, MN: University of Minnesota Press.

Fitzclarence, L. (1999) *A Final Report of the Developments in the Scitech Eisteddfod in the Rock Eisteddfod*. Geelong, Victoria: Deakin Centre for Education and Change, Deakin University.

Fitzclarence, L. (under review) Teachers' talk: descriptions of the generation divide in schools.

Fitzclarence, L. and Kenway, J. (1998) Marketing education, in T. Townsend (ed.) *Issues for the Primary School in the Age of Restructuring*. London: Routledge.

Fitzclarence, L., Bigum, C., Green, B. and Kenway, J. (1995) *The Rock Eisteddfod: Media Culture as a De Facto National Curriculum?* Geelong, Victoria: Deakin Centre for Education and Change, Deakin University.

Frith, S. (1981) *Sound Effects: Youth, Leisure, and the Politics of Rock 'n' Roll*. New York: Pantheon Books.

Fuery, P. (1995) *Theories of Desire*. Carlton, Victoria: Melbourne University Press.

Furnham, A., Abramsky, S. and Gunter, B. (1997) A cross-cultural content analysis of children's television advertisements. *Sex Roles*, 37(1/2): 91–9.

Gabriel, J. (1994) *Racism, Culture, Markets*. London: Routledge.

Gagg, M.E. (1958) *Shopping with Mother*. Loughborough: Wills & Hepworth.

Game, A. and Pringle, R. (1984) *Gender at Work*. London: Pluto Press.

Garrison, E.K. (2000) US feminism – grrrl style! Youth (sub)cultures and the technologics of the third wave. *Feminist Studies*, 26(1): 141–70.

Gerbner, G. (1973) Teacher image in mass culture: symbolic functions of the hidden curriculum, in G. Gerbner, L.P. Gross and W.H. Melody (eds) *Communications Technology and Social Policy*. New York: John Wiley & Sons.

Gewirtz, S., Ball, S.J. and Bowe, R. (1995) *Markets, Choice and Equity in Education*. Buckingham: Open University Press.

Giddens, A. (1991) *Modernity and Self-Identity: Self and Society in the Late Modern Age*. Cambridge: Polity Press.

Gilloch, G. (1996) *Myth and Metropolis: Walter Benjamin and the City*. Cambridge: Polity Press.

Gilroy, P. (1987) *There Ain't No Black in the Union Jack*. London: Unwin Hyman.

Giroux, H.A. (1992) *Border Crossings: Cultural Workers and the Politics of Education*. New York: Routledge.

Giroux, H.A. (1994) *Disturbing Pleasure: Learning Popular Culture*. New York: Routledge.

Giroux, H.A. (1997) Are Disney movies good for your kids? in S.R. Steinberg and J.L. Kincheloe (eds) *Kinder-Culture: The Corporate Construction of Childhood*. Boulder, CO: Westview Press.

Giroux, H.A. (1999a) *The Mouse That Roared: Disney and the End of Innocence*. Lanham, MD: Rowman & Littlefield Publishers.

Giroux, H.A. (1999b) Public intellectuals and the challenge of children's culture: youth and the politics of innocence. *The Review of Education, Pedagogy and Cultural Studies*, 21(3): 193–226.

Gittens, D. (1998) *The Child in Question*. Basingstoke: Macmillan.

Gow, J. (1993) Music video as persuasive form: the case of the pseudo-reflexive strategy. *Communication Quarterly*, 41(3): 318–27.

Grace, D.J. and Tobin, J. (1997) Carnival in the classroom: elementary students making videos, in J. Tobin (ed.) *Making a Place for Pleasure in Early Childhood Education*. New Haven, CT: Yale University Press.

Grant, M. (1997) Dressing up a self: fashion and Kristeva's 'subject in process'. *Melbourne Journal of Politics*, 24 (1). http://web2.infotrac.galegroup.com, Article A54495224.

Green, B., Reid, J.A. and Bigum, C. (1998) Teaching the Nintendo generation?: children, computer culture and popular technologies, in S. Howard (ed.) *Wired-Up: Young People and the Electronic Media*. London: UCL Press.

Greer, G. (1999) *The Whole Woman*. London: Doubleday.

Guber, S. and Berry, J. (1993) *Marketing To and Through Kids*. New York: McGraw-Hill.

Hall, S. (1988) Brave new world, *Marxism Today*, October.

Handel, K. (1999) The Lineker effect: using icons to reach the tween generation, *Kids Marketing Report*, 2 May. www.mad.co.uk/KMR/print/stories/1999/05/02/0041.asp (accessed 1 February 2000).

Hardman, J. (1998) Advertising to children. *Admap*: May. www.warc.com/print/5823p.stm (accessed 25 January 2000).

Harty, S. (1979) *Hucksters in the Classroom: A Review of Industry Propaganda in Schools*. Washington, DC: Center for Study of Responsive Law.

Harvey, D. (2000) *Spaces of Hope*. Edinburgh: Edinburgh University Press.

Harwood, V. (2000) 'Truth, power, and the self: a Foucaultian analysis of the truth of Conduct Disorder and the construction of young people's mentally disordered subjectivity', unpublished PhD thesis. University of South Australia.

Haug, W.F. (1986) *Critique of Commodity Aesthetics: Appearance, Sexuality and Advertising in Capitalist Society*. Cambridge: Polity Press.

Hawk, B. (n.d.) Simulation, *Baudrillard and Simulation*. www.uta.edu/english/hawk/semiotics/baud/htm (accessed 3 May 2000).

Heaney, C. (1994) A McFuture disaster, says professor, *Herald-Sun*, 12 February.

Hebdige, D. (1988) *Hiding in the Light: On Images and Things*. London: Routledge-Comedia.

Hendrick (1997) Constructions and reconstructions of British childhood: an interpretative survey, 1800 to the present, in A. James and A. Prout (eds) *Constructing and Reconstructing Childhood: Contemporary Issues in the Sociological Study of Childhood*. London: Falmer Press.

Hobson, J. (1999) Tapping into a child's visual world reveals way forward for packaging, *Kids Marketing Report*, 27 January. www.mad.co.uk/KMR/print/stories/1999/01/27/0034.asp (accessed 1 February 2000).

Holland, P. (1996) 'I've just seen a hole in the reality barrier!': children, childishness and the media in the ruins of the twentieth century, in J. Pilcher and S. Wagg (eds) *Thatcher's Children? Politics, Childhood and Society in the 1980s and 1990s*. London: Falmer Press.

Holmes, S. (n.d.) 'The emerging corporate culture in schools', unpublished paper. Ormiston College, Brisbane.

Hood, D. (1998) Sweden pledges Euro-ban on advertising to kids. *Kidscreen*, December. www.kidscreen.com/articles/ks23811.asp (accessed 1 February 2000).

Horkheimer, M. and Adorno, T.W. (1972) *Dialectic of Enlightenment*, trans. J. Cumming. New York: Herder & Herder.

Hornery (2000) Weet-bix kids fall prey to big brands, *Sydney Morning Herald,* 3 February.

Howard, S. (ed.) (1998) *Wired-Up: Young People and the Electronic Media.* London: UCL Press.

Humphery, K. (1998) *Shelf Life: Supermarkets and the Changing Cultures of Consumption.* Melbourne: Cambridge University Press.

IBM Australia Ltd (2000) (advertisement), *The Age,* 26 February.

Jackson Lears, T. (1983) From salvation to self-realization: advertising and the therapeutic roots of the consumer culture 1880–1930, in R. Fox and T.J. Lears (eds) *The Culture of Consumption.* New York: Pantheon.

Jacobson, M.F. and Mazur, L.A. (1995) *Marketing Madness: A Survival Guide for a Consumer Society.* Boulder, CO: Westview Press.

Jakubowicz, A., Goodall, H., Martin, J., Mitchell, T., Randall, L. and Seneviratne, K. (1994) *Racism, Ethnicity and the Media.* St Leonards, NSW: Allen & Unwin.

James, A. and Prout, A. (1997) *Constructing and Reconstructing Childhood: Contemporary Issues in the Sociological Study of Childhood,* 2nd edn. London: Falmer Press.

James, C. (1997) From *Rugrats* to *Spice Girls*: the role of characters and personalities in lateral marketing to child and youth markets, *European Society for Opinion and Marketing Research.* www.warc.com/print/9270p.stm (accessed 25 January 2000).

Jameson, F. (1979) Reification and utopia in mass culture. *Social Text,* 1(1): 130–48.

Jameson, F. (1984) Postmodernism and the consumer society, in H. Foster (ed.) *Postmodern Culture.* London: Pluto Press.

Jameson, F. (1991) *Postmodernism, or the Cultural Logic of Late Capitalism.* London: Verso.

Jhally, S. (1990) *The Codes of Advertising: Fetishism and the Political Economy of Meaning in Consumer Society.* New York: Routledge.

Johnson, B. (1999) Microsoft schools viewers on its values: new spots soft-sell advantages of using technology, *Advertising Age,* 8 March.

Kellner, D. (1989) *Jean Baudrillard: From Marxism to Postmodernism and Beyond.* Cambridge: Polity Press.

Kellner, D. (1997) *Beavis and Butt-head*: no future for postmodern youth, in S.R. Steinberg and J.L. Kincheloe (eds) *Kinder-Culture: The Corporate Construction of Childhood.* Boulder, CO: Westview Press.

Kennedy, M. (2000) Class struggle: the 'tug of war' surrounding school facilities and education-equity. *American School & University,* 72(8): 16–20.

Kenway, J. (1991) Conspicuous consumption: class, gender and private schooling, in D. Dawkins (ed.) *Education, Power and Politics in Australia.* London: Falmer Press.

Kenway, J. (ed.) (1994) *Economising Education: The Post-Fordist Directions.* Geelong, Vic.: Deakin University Press.

Kenway, J. (ed.) (1995) *Marketing Education: Some Critical Issues.* Geelong, Vic.: Deakin University Press.

Kenway, J. (1998) Pulp fictions? Education, markets and the education super-highway, in M.W. Apple and D. Carlson (eds) *Power/Knowledge/Pedagogy: The Meaning of Democratic Education in Unsettling Times.* Boulder, CO: Westview Press.

Kenway, J. and Epstein, D. (1996a) *Discourse Special Issue: Feminist Perspectives on the Marketisation of Education*, 17(3).

Kenway, J. and Epstein, D. (1996b) Introduction: the marketisation of school education – feminist studies and perspectives. *Discourse Special Issue: Feminist Perspectives on the Marketisation of Education*, 17(3): 301–15.

Kenway, J. and Fitzclarence, L. (1998a) Institutions with designs: consumer culture, consuming kids. *Journal of Education Policy*, 13(6): 661–77.

Kenway, J. and Fitzclarence, L. (1998b) Consuming children? in A. Reid (ed.) *Going Public: Education Policy and Public Education in Australia*. Deakin West, Vic.: Australian Curriculum Studies in Association with the Centre for Public Education, University of South Australia.

Kenway, J. and Fitzclarence, L. (2000) Designing generations and hybridising education, entertainment and advertising. *Australian Journal of Education: Special Issue on Educational Marketing* edited by Simon Marginson, 43(3): 300–17.

Kenway, J. and Langmead, D. (2000) Cyberfeminism and citizenship? Challenging the political imaginary, in M. Arnot and J. Dillabough (eds) *Challenging Democracy: International Perspectives on Gender, Education and Citizenship*. London: Routledge.

Kenway, J., Bigum, C., Fitzclarence, L. and Collier, J. (1993a) Marketing education in the 1990s: an introductory essay. *The Australian Universities' Review: Special Issue on Educational Marketing*, 36(2): 2–6.

Kenway, J. with Bigum, C. and Fitzclarence, L. (1993b) Marketing education in the post-modern age. *Journal of Education Policy*, 8(2): 105–23.

Kenway, J. with Bigum, C., Fitzclarence, L. and Croker, C. (1993c) To market to make it? the sorry tale of Australian education in the 1990s, in A. Reid and B. Johnson (eds) *Critical Issues in Australian Education in the 1990s*. Adelaide, SA: Painters Print.

Kenway, J., Bigum, C., Fitzclarence, L. and Collier, J. (1995a) *Educationally and Socially Responsible Marketing*. Geelong, Vic.: Deakin Centre for Education and Change, Deakin University.

Kenway, J., Bigum, C., Fitzclarence, L. with Collier, J. and Tregenza, K. (1995b) New education in new times. *Journal of Education Policy*, 9(4): 317–33.

Kenway, J., Blackmore, J. and Willis, S. (1996) The emotional dimensions of feminist pedagogy, in P. Murphy (ed.) *Effective Pedagogies? Educating Girls and Boys*. London: Falmer Press.

Kenway, J. with Fitzclarence, L., Collier, J. and Bigum, C. (1997) Consumer contexts, culture and kids, in B. Green, L. Fitzclarence and J. Kenway (eds) *Changing Education: New Times, New Kids*. Geelong, Vic.: Deakin University Press.

Kids Marketing Report (1999) Newspapers back schools, Kids Marketing Report, 30 September. www.mad.co.uk/KMR/print/stories/1999/09/30/0017.asp (accessed 28 February 2000).

Kidscreen (1996) Special report: NATPE – girls' shows a new attraction, but boys still set the trends. *Kidscreen*, January. www.kidscreen.com/articles/ks16837.asp (accessed 5 June 2000).

Kidscreen (2000) The *Kidscreen* strategy challenge. *Kidscreen*, January. www.kidscreen.com/articles/ks27665.asp (accessed 1 February 2000).

Kincheloe, J.L. (1997a) Home Alone and 'bad to the bone': the advent of a post-modern childhood, in S.R. Steinberg and J.L. Kincheloe (eds) *Kinder-Culture: The Corporate Construction of Childhood*. Boulder, CO: Westview Press.

Kincheloe, J.L. (1997b) McDonald's, power, and children: Ronald McDonald (aka Ray Kroc) does it all for you, in S.R. Steinberg and J.L. Kincheloe (eds) *Kinder-Culture: The Corporate Construction of Childhood*. Boulder, CO: Westview Press.

Kinder, M. (1991) *Playing with Power in Movies, Television and Video Games: From Muppet Babies to Teenage Mutant Ninja Turtles*. Berkeley, CA: University of California Press.

Kinder, M. (1995) Home Alone in the 90s: generational war and transgenerational address in American movies, television and presidential politics, in C. Bazalgette and D. Buckingham (eds) *In Front of the Children: Screen Entertainment and Young Audiences*. London: British Film Institute.

King, N. (1979) Play: the kindergartners' perspective. *Elementary School Journal*, 80: 81–7.

Klein, N. (1994) Only Pepsi to be sold in schools, *The Globe and Mail*, 15 January.

Klein, N. (2000) *No Logo*. London: Flamingo.

Kline, S. (1993) *Out of the Garden: Toys, TV and Children's Culture in the Age of Marketing*. London: Verso.

Kozol, J. (1992) Making McMinds: the corporate raid on education, *Broadside Weekly*, 7 October.

Kristeva, J. (1982) *Powers of Horror*, trans. L.S. Roudiez. New York: Columbia University Press.

Kuehn, L. (1996) Market mechanisms + education systems = inequality. *Canadian Dimension*, 30(5): 21–3.

Lacan, J. (1992) *The Ethics of Psychoanalysis 1959–1960*, trans. D. Porter. London: Routledge.

Lasch, C. (1979) *The Culture of Narcissism*. New York: Warner Books.

Lash, S. and Urry, J. (1994) *Economies of Signs and Space*. London: Sage Publications.

Lechte, J. (1990) *Julia Kristeva*. London: Routledge.

Lee, M.J. (1993) *Consumer Culture Reborn: The Cultural Politics of Consumption*. London: Routledge.

Lee, M.J. (ed.) (2000) *The Consumer Society Reader*. Malden, MA: Blackwell.

Leiss, W., Kline, S. and Jhally, S. (2000) The bonding of media and advertising, in M.J. Lee (ed.) *The Consumer Society Reader*. Malden, MA: Blackwell.

Lukàcs, G. ([1923] 1971) *History and Class Consciousness*, trans. R. Livingstone. London: Merlin Press.

Lum, M., Carroll, T. and Taylor, J. (1998) *Drug Offensive Research Report: Evaluation of the 1997 National Rock Eisteddfod Challenge TV Special and the Regional TV Specials Sponsored by the National Drug Offensive*. Darlinghurst, NSW: Commonwealth Department of Health and Family Services.

Lumby, C. (1997) The computer learning pickle, *The Age*, 6 October.

Lury, C. (1996) *Consumer Culture*. Cambridge: Polity Press.

Lyotard, J.F. (1984) *The Postmodern Condition: A Report on Knowledge*, trans. G. Bennington and B. Massumi. Minneapolis, MN: University of Minnesota Press.

McCann, A. (1997) The ethics of abjection: Patrick White's *Rider in the Chariot*. *Australian Literary Studies*, 18(2): 145–55.

McDonnell, K. (1994) *Kid Culture: Children & Adults & Popular Culture*. Toronto: Second Story Press.

McGuigan, J. (2000) Sovereign consumption, in M.J. Lee (ed.) *The Consumer Society Reader*. Malden, MA: Blackwell.

McIntosh, T. (1993) Software helps lift literacy, *The Australian*, 20 April.

Mackay, H. (1993) *Reinventing Australia: The Mind and Mood of Australia in the 90s*. Sydney: Angus & Robertson.

Mackay, H. (1997) *Generations: Baby Boomers, Their Parents and Their Children*. Sydney: Pan Macmillan.

McKenzie, A. (2000) Ads behaving badly, *The Weekend Australian*, 25–6 March.

Macklin, M.C. and Carlson, L. (eds) (1999) *Advertising to Children: Concepts and Controversies*. Thousand Oaks, CA: Sage Publications.

McLaren, P. and Hammer, R. (1995) Media knowledges, warrior citizenry, and postmodern literacies, in P. McLaren, R. Hammer, D. Sholle and S. Reilly (eds) *Rethinking Media Literacy: A Critical Pedagogy of Representation*. New York: Peter Lang.

McLaren, P. and Morris, J. (1997) *Mighty Morphin Power Rangers*: the aesthetics of phallo-militaristic justice, in S.R. Steinberg and J.L. Kincheloe (eds) *Kinder-Culture: The Corporate Construction of Childhood*. Boulder, CO: Westview Press.

Maclean's (1999) How teens got the power: Gen Y has the cash, the cool – and a burgeoning consumer culture, *Maclean's*, 22 March. www.web4.infotrac.galegroup.com, Article A54833728.

McLester, S. (1996) Revisiting edutainment. *Technology & Learning*, May/June: 42–54.

McNamee, S. (1998) Youth, gender and video games: power and control in the home, in T. Skelton and G. Valentine (eds) *Cool Places: Geographies of Youth Culture*. London: Routledge.

Marsh, J. (2000) Teletubby tales: popular culture in the early years language and literacy curriculum. *Contemporary Issues in Early Childhood*, 1(2): 119–33.

Martin, E. (1997) Young entrepreneurs: making the dream a reality, *Small Business Information*. http://sbi.../aa083197.htm (accessed 3 October 2000).

Marx, K. ([1867] 1976) *Capital: A Critique of Political Economy*, trans. B. Fowkes. Harmondsworth: Penguin.

Mercer, K. (1994) *Welcome to the Jungle: New Positions in Black Cultural Studies*. New York: Routledge.

Meredyth, D. and Tyler, D. (eds) (1993) *Child and Citizen: Genealogies of Schooling and Subjectivity*. Nathan, Qld: Institute for Cultural Policy Studies, Faculty of Humanities, Griffith University.

Messina, A. (1995) Belmont gets down to serious business, *The Age*, 5 September.

Meyrowitz, J. (1985) *No Sense of Place: The Impact of Electronic Media on Social Behavior*. New York: Oxford University Press.

Mitter, S. and Rowbotham, S. (eds) (1995) *Women Encounter Technology: Changing Patterns of Employment in the Third World*. London: Routledge.

Molnar, A. (1996) *Giving Kids the Business: The Commericalization of America's Schools*. Boulder, CO: Westview Press.

Molnar, A. (2000) The commercial transformation America's schools. Paper presented at the Association for Supervision and Curriculum Development

Conference, New Orleans, 26 March. www.uwm.edu/Dept/CACE/documents/cace-00-01.htm (accessed 23 May 2000).

Mormon, T. (1997) Hittin' the books: an interview with the founder of Cover Concepts, *Stay Free!*, Spring #13. http://metalab.unc.edu.stayfree/13/coverconcepts_text.html (accessed 23 February 2000).

Morrissey, G. (1996) *Sex in the Time of Generation X*. Sydney: Pan Macmillan.

Murphy, P. (ed.) (1996) *Effective Pedagogies? Educating Girls and Boys*. London: Falmer Press.

Nixon, S. (1997) Exhibiting masculinity, in S. Hall (ed.) *Representation: Cultural Representations and Signifying Practices*. London: Sage Publications.

Nucifora, A. (2000) Advertising age: Generation Y bears watching in marketing mix, *Houston Business Journal*, 30(44). http://web4.infotrac.galegroup.com/itw/infomark/566/946/ (accessed 27 June 2000).

Nunberg, G. (1995) Virtual Rialto, *Fresh Air* (national public radio programme).

O'Brien, T. (1990) *The Screening of America: Movies and Values from Rocky to Rainman*. New York: Frederick Ungar.

O'Leary, N. (1998) The boom boom tube, *Adweek*, 18 May. 45–52, www.adweek.com (accessed 27 June).

O'Regan, M. (2000) Children's programs on TV, *The Media Report*, 3 August. www.abc.net.au/rn/talks/8.30/mediarpt/stories/s159007.htm (accessed 15 September 2000).

Oates, J.C. (1994) Reflections on the grotesque, *Haunted: Tales of the Grotesque*. http://storm.usfca. edu/~southerr/grotesque.html (accessed 2 August 2000).

Oppenheim, C. and Lister, R. (1996) The politics of child poverty 1979–1995, in J. Pilcher and S. Wagg (eds) *Thatcher's Children? Politics, Childhood and Society in the 1980s and 1990s*. London: Falmer Press.

Owen, R. (1997) *Gen X TV: The Brady Bunch to Melrose Place*. New York: Syracuse University Press.

Painter, J. (1994) Lifeline to struggling school, *The Age*, 19 May.

Papert, S. (1993) *The Children's Machine: Rethinking School in the Age of the Computer*. New York: Basic Books.

Parker, C. (1999) Forget pester power: kids use more subtle techniques to get their way, *Kids Marketing Report*, 30 September. www.mad.co.uk/print/stories/1999/09/30/KMR/0043.asp (accessed 6 March 2000).

Parker, K. (1991) Sponsorship: the research contribution. *European Journal of Marketing*, 25(11): 22–30.

Pilcher, J. and Wagg, S. (eds) (1996) *Thatcher's Children? Politics, Childhood and Society in the 1980s and 1990s*. London: Falmer Press.

Postman, N. (1994) *The Disappearance of Childhood*. New York: Vintage Books.

Postman, N. (1999) *Building a Bridge to the 18th Century: How the Past Can Improve Our Future*. New York: Alfred A. Knopf.

Precision Marketing (1996) Every kind of people, *Precision Marketing*, 22 January. www.mad.co.uk/stories/1996/01/22/pm/0049.asp (accessed 28 February 2000).

Probert, B. (1993) Restructuring and globalization: what do they mean? *Arena Magazine*, 18 April–22 May.

Radner, H. (1995) *Shopping Around: Feminine Culture and the Pursuit of Pleasure*. New York: Routledge.

Rai, A. (1994) An American raj in filmistan: images of Elvis in Indian films. *Screen*, 35(1): 51–77.

Richards, C. (1995) Room to dance: girls' play and *The Little Mermaid*, in C. Bazalgette and D. Buckingham (eds) *In Front of the Children: Screen Entertainment and Young Audiences*. London: British Film Institute.

Riot Grrrl Europe (n.d.) Riot Grrrl Europe Manifesto. www.chickpages.com/rants/riotgrrrleurope/manifesto.html (accessed 4 September 2000).

Ritchie, T. (2000) The future of music, *Background Briefing*, 9 July. www.abc.net.au/rn/talks.bbing/specials/music/script.htm (accessed 25 August 2000).

Robertson, H.-J. (1995) Hyenas at the oasis: corporate marketing to captive students. www/resau-medias.ca/eng/med/class/edissue/hyenas.htm (accessed 23 May 2000).

Robertson, V. (1998a) Girls gaining in the kids programming playground. *Kidscreen*, August. www.kidscreen.com/articles/ks22429.aps (accessed 5 June 2000).

Robertson, V. (1998b) Fox separates the girlz from the boyz. *Kidscreen*, December. www.kidscreen.com/articles.ks23818.asp (accessed 5 June 2000).

Robertson, V. (1999) Wild hybrids for *Jumanji 2. Kidscreen*, August. www.kidscreen.com/articles/ks26272.asp (accessed 4 September 2000).

Robins, K. (1996) *Into the Image: Culture and Politics in the Field of Vision*. London: Routledge.

Rodrik, D. (1997) *Has Globalization Gone Too Far?*. Washington, DC: Institute for International Economics.

Roedder John, D. (1999) Through the eyes of a child: children's knowledge and understanding of advertising, in M.C. Macklin and L. Carlson (eds) *Advertising to Children: Concepts and Controversies*. Thousand Oaks, CA: Sage Publications.

Romei, S. (2000) Who wants to be a voyeur? *The Weekend Australian*, 1–2 July.

Romero, M. (1989) Work and play in the nursery school. *Educational Policy*, 3(4): 410–19.

Ross, A. (1989) *No Respect: Intellectuals and Popular Culture*. New York: Routledge.

Rossiter, W. (1999) Ethical stance towards marketing in schools is key to effective schemes, *Kids Marketing Report*, 24 March. www.mad.co.uk/KMR/print/stories/1999/03/24/0034.asp (accessed 1 February 2000).

Russo, M. (1986) Female grotesques: carnival and theory, in T. de Lauretis (ed.) *Feminist Studies/Critical Studies*. Bloomington, IN: Indiana University Press.

Sa, S. (1992) Another foundation goes to school: the Panasonic foundation's school restructuring program. *Teachers College Record*, 93(3): 463–71.

Sacks, P. (1996) *Generation X Goes to College: An Eye-Opening Account of Teaching in Postmodern America*. Chicago: Open Court.

Salkowski, J. (1997) We'll return to history class after these messages, *StarNet Dispatches*, 8 April. http://dispatches.azstarnet.com.features/ad.htm (accessed 23 February 2000).

Sassen, S. (1996) Toward a feminist analytics of the global economy. *Indiana Journal of Global Legal Studies*, 4(1): 7–25.

Schneiderman, I. (2000) Echo boomers: staggering spending power, *WWD*, 3 February. http://web4.infotrac.galegroup.com, Article A59221600 (accessed 27 June 2000).

Schroeder, R. (1994) Cyberculture, cyborg post-modernism and the sociology of virtual reality technologies: surfing the soul in the information age. *Futures*, 26(5): 519–28.

Schultze, Q.J., Ankar, R.M., Bratt, J.D., Romanowski, W.D., Worst, J.W. and Zuidervaart, L. (1991) *Dancing in the Dark: Youth, Popular Culture and the Electronic Media*. Grand Rapids, MI: Midwest Publications.

Sefton-Green, J. (ed.) (1998) *Digital Diversions: Youth Culture in the Age of Multimedia*. London: UCL Press.

Seiter, E. (1995) *Sold Separately: Children and Parents in Consumer Culture*. New Brunswick, NJ: Rutgers University Press.

Shahar, S. (1990) *Childhood in the Middle Ages*. London: Routledge.

Sharp, G. (1985) Constitutive abstraction and social practice. *Arena*, 80: 42–82.

Sholle, D. and Denski, S. (1995) Critical media literacy: reading, remapping, rewriting, in P. McLaren, R. Hammer, D. Sholle and S. Reilly (eds) *Rethinking Media Literacy: A Critical Pedagogy of Representation*. New York: Peter Lang.

Sibley, D. (1995) Families and domestic routines: constructing the boundaries of childhood, in S. Pile and N. Thrift (eds) *Mapping the Subject: Geographies of Cultural Transformation*. London: Routledge.

Simmel, G. (1971) Fashion, in D.N. Levine (ed.) *On Individuality and Social Forms: Selected Writings*. Chicago: University of Chicago Press.

Singer, P. (1993) *How Are We To Live? Ethics in the Age of Self-Interest*. Melbourne: The Text Publishing Co.

Skelton, T. and Valentine, G. (eds) (1998) *Cool Places: Geographies of Youth Cultures*. London: Routledge.

Skirrow, G. (1990) Hellivision: an analysis of video games, in M. Alverado and J.O. Thompson (eds) *The Media Reader*. London: British Film Institute.

Slater, D. (1997) *Consumer Culture and Modernity*. Cambridge: Polity Press.

Smith, G. (1997) How to advertise effectively to children and youth, *European Society for Opinion and Marketing Research*. www.warc.com/fulltext/esomar/9267.htm (accessed 25 January 2000).

Smith, Z. (2000) *White Teeth*. Ringwood, Vic.: Penguin.

Sommerville, C.J. (1982) *The Rise and Fall of Childhood*. Beverly Hills, CA: Sage Publications.

Spock, B. (1976) *Baby and Child Care*. New York: Pocket Books.

Stam, R. (1992) *Reflexivity in Film and Literature: From Don Quixote to Jean-Luc Goddard*. New York: Columbia University Press.

Steinberg, S.R. and Kincheloe, J.L. (1997) Introduction: no more secrets – kinderculture, information saturation, and the postmodern childhood, in S.R. Steinberg and J.L. Kincheloe (eds) *Kinder-Culture: The Corporate Construction of Childhood*. Boulder, CO: Westview Press.

Steward, J. (1998) Kids and advertising: kids clued up on the purpose of ads, *Kids Marketing Report*, December. www.mad.co.uk/KMR/print/stories/1998/12/01/0020.asp (accessed 1 February 2000).

Storm, A.K. (1995) The psychology of cyberspace. *The Chronicle of Higher Education*, 41(29): B1–B3.

Straus, T. (2000) Baby steps to a global revolution?: Barbara Ehrenreich and Juliette Beck discuss the new activism, *Alternet.org*, 27 April. www.alternet.org/print.html?StoryID=9069 (accessed 22 August 2000).

Sydney Morning Herald (2000) Sweatshops make McDonald's toys, *Sydney Morning Herald*, 28 August.

Symes, C. (1998) Education for sale: a semiotic analysis of school prospectuses and other forms of educational marketing. *Australian Journal of Education*, 42(2). http://web6.infotrac.galegroup.com, Article A55618813.

The Dallas Morning News (1998) Baby boomers' little echoes ring in a computer-savvy future, *The Dallas Morning News*, 15 March. http://elibrary.com/s/edumarkau/getdoc.cgi (accessed 27 June 2000).

The Seattle Times (1998) Coke pops schools' bubble with $6 million, *The Seattle Times*, 4 August. www.seattletimes.com/news/editorial/html98/cokeed_080498.html (accessed 7 February 2000).

The Sunday Age (2000a) Promoting philanthropy: building a relationship with long-term donors, *The Sunday Age*, 20 February.

The Sunday Age (2000b) Starting young: students learn how to support those in need, *The Sunday Age*, 20 February.

Tobin, J. (1997) Introduction: the missing discourse of pleasure and desire, in J. Tobin (ed.) *Making a Place for Pleasure in Early Childhood Education*. New Haven, CT: Yale University Press.

Townsend, T. (1998) Third world or third millennium?: the impact of the economy on schools and families in Australia. Paper presented at the Ninth Conference of the International Roundtable on 'School, Family and Community Partnerships', San Diego, CA, 13 April. http:edx1.educ.monash.edu.au/peninsula/publications/townsend/APRIL98.htm (accessed 27 July 2000).

Traiman, S. (1998) Kids' 'edutainment' multimedia titles multiply, *Billboard*, 14 November. http://web4.infotrac.galegroup.com, Article A53214315.

Turkle, S. (1995) *Life on the Screen: Identity in the Age of the Internet*. New York: Simon & Schuster.

Turnbull, S. (1998) Dealing with feeling: why girl number twenty still doesn't answer, in D. Buckingham (ed.) *Teaching Popular Culture: Beyond Radical Pedagogy*. London: UCL Press.

Urban 75 (2000) Boycott Top 5, *Urban 75*. www.urban75.com/Action/boycott.html (accessed 4 July 2000).

Valentine, G., Skelton, T. and Chambers, D. (1998) Cool places: an introduction to youth and youth cultures, in T. Skelton and G. Valentine (eds) *Cool Places: Geographies of Youth Cultures*. London: Routledge.

Veblen, T. ([1899] 1970) *The Theory of the Leisure Class: An Economic Study of Institutions*. London: Allen & Unwin.

Wagg, S. (1996) 'Don't try to understand them': politics, childhood and the new education market, in J. Pilcher and S. Wagg (eds) *Thatcher's Children? Politics, Childhood and Society in the 1980s and 1990s*. London: Falmer Press.

Walkerdine, V. (1991) *Schoolgirl Fictions*. London: Verso.

Walkerdine, V. (1999) Violent boys and precocious girls: regulating childhood at the end of the millennium. *Contemporary Issues in Early Childhood*, 1(1): 3–23.

Webb, J. (1999) Avoid stereotypes when trying to appeal to today's youth, *Brand Strategy*, 19 March. www.mad.co.uk/stories/1999/03/19/bs/0006.asp (accessed 28 February 2000).

Wernick, A. (1991) *Promotional Culture*. London: Sage Publications.

Weston, J. (1994) Old freedoms and new technologies: the evolution of community networking. Paper presented at the 'Free Speech and Privacy in the Information Age' symposium, 26 December, University of Waterloo, Canada.

Wexler, P. (1987) *Social Analysis of Education: After the New Sociology*. London: Routledge & Kegan Paul.

Whittaker, M. (1998) Advertiser offers £5,000 a year for corridor space, *The Times Educational Supplement*, 27 February. www.tes.co.uk (accessed 9 May 2000).

Whitworth, D. (1999) How can companies ethically market to children via classrooms? *Kids Marketing Report*, 24 February. www.mad.co.uk/print/stories/1999/02/24/KMR/oo31.asp (accessed 28 February 2000).

Williams, M.E. (n.d.) happymutantnetchick, *geekgirl*, 4. www.geekgirl.com.au/geekgirl/004maid/mutant.html (accessed July 1999).

Williams, R. (1982) *The Sociology of Culture*. New York: Schlocken Books.

Williams, R. (1980) Advertising: the magic system, in R. Williams (ed.) *Problems in Materialism and Culture: Selected Essays*. London: Verso.

Wilson, E. (1992a) The invisible flâneur. *New Left Review*, 191 (January/February): 90–110.

Wilson, H. (1992b) Marketing the canon. *Discourse*, 12(2): 116–26.

Wood, J. (1999) Reaching the inner adolescent – of all ages, *Admap*. www.warc.com/print/9736p.stm (accessed 25 January 2000).

Young, B.M. (1990) *Television Advertising and Children*. Oxford: Clarendon Press.

Zukin, S. (1991) *Landscapes of Power: From Detroit to Disney World*. Berkeley, CA: University of California Press.

Index